FINANCIAL TIMES
MANAGEMENT

Knowledge   Skills   Understanding

Financial Times Management is a new business created to deliver the knowledge, skills and understanding that will enable students, managers and organisations to achieve their ambitions, whatever their needs, wherever they are.

Financial Times Pitman Publishing, part of Financial Times Management, is the leading publisher of books for practitioners and students in business and finance, bringing cutting-edge thinking and best practice to a global market.

To find out more about Financial Times Management and Financial Times Pitman Publishing, visit our website at:

www.ftmanagement.com

'Ambitious in intent, meticulous in detail and penetrating in analysis, Sir James Ball's absorbing book tackles, head on, some of the toughest economic questions of our time.'

SIR BRIAN PITMAN
Chairman, Lloyds TSB Group plc

'Ball on Britain is a mature man on a mature economy. Anyone trotting out their favourite monocausal explanation for the shortcomings, past and present, of the United Kingdom as a productive unit will have to consult this volume. Invariably they will find themselves refuted. This is as irritating as it is necessary.'

PROFESSOR PETER HENNESSY
Professor of Contemporary History
Queen Mary and Westfield College

'In contrast with the soundbite style of so much contemporary comment on economic policy and performance in the UK, this study is rigorously objective and thorough. Jim Ball's surgical dissection of new conventional wisdoms and of the good as well as the bad experiences of the last 20 years is meticulous. No-one who reads it will do so without having some nostrum tested and challenged – and perhaps even exploded – on issues as significant and diverse as the underlying state of health of the British economy, the development of the European Union and the responsibilities of boards of directors. This book is a compelling read for anyone involved in forming opinion and policy in this country over the next few years.'

SIR DAVID WALKER
Chairman, Morgan Stanley Group (Europe) Plc

'This forensic analysis of the economic events of the last half century, and the economic prospects for the decades ahead, will make uncomfortable reading for policy makers and pundits of all political parties – and they should read it for that reason alone. The demolition job on the host of myths, misconceptions, and misleading propaganda that surround Britain's economic policy and performance is thorough, persuasive, and a necessary precursor to understanding the problems that we now face. The central focus of the book is sharply defined, but the range is wide. Be it the fragility of the post-Keynesian commitment to free markets, or the "missed boat" theses of European policy; be it the common weaknesses of old paternalism and the new collectivism, or the key issues of labour markets and investment levels, the analysis is always insightful, informative and incisive. All of these analyses are harnessed to answer the fundamental question – which path should Britain take at this crossroads in its history?'

THE RT HON MR DAVID DAVIS MP

THE
BRITISH ECONOMY
AT THE
CROSSROADS

✳

Sir James Ball

Professor of Economics
London Business School

FINANCIAL TIMES
PITMAN PUBLISHING

LONDON · HONG KONG · JOHANNESBURG
MELBOURNE · SINGAPORE · WASHINGTON DC

FINANCIAL TIMES MANAGEMENT
128 Long Acre, London WC2E 9AN
Tel: +44 (0)171 447 2000
Fax: +44 (0)171 240 5771
Website: www.ftmanagement.com

A Division of
Financial Times Professional Limited

First published in Great Britain 1998

© Financial Times Professional Limited 1998

The right of Sir James Ball to be identified as author of this work
has been asserted by him in accordance with the Copyright,
Designs, and Patents Act 1988.

ISBN 0 273 63702 9

British Library Cataloguing in Publication Data
A CIP catalogue record for this book can be obtained from
the British Library.

1 3 5 7 9 10 8 6 4 2

Typeset by Northern Phototypesetting Co Ltd, Bolton.
Printed and bound in Great Britain by
Biddles Ltd, Guildford and King's Lynn.

*The Publishers' policy is to use paper manufactured
from sustainable forests.*

FOR SIR JAMES BENJAMIN BALL,
M.Inst.C.E.
(1865–1919)

In memory of my late Grandfather,
whom I never knew but whose image has been
before me all my life.

CONTENTS

....

List of Tables	ix
List of Figures	xi
Preface	xiii
Introduction	xv

1 THE BRITISH ECONOMY SINCE 1945 — 1

Introduction	3
Post-war recovery	5
The years of prosperity 1950–73	8
Britain in the golden age	16
The years of turbulence 1973–79	18
Britain in the years of turbulence	22
The eighties 1979–89	24
Britain in the eighties	28
The recession in the nineties	33
Britain's economic performance 1960–95	34

2 ECONOMIC GROWTH — 37

Introduction	39
The economics of growth	41
The role of public expenditure	45
Investment and the financial system	52
Social capability and human capital	62
Macroeconomic policy	67
Conclusions	71

3 MANUFACTURING INDUSTRY, TRADE AND COMPETITIVENESS — 75

Introduction	77
Economic growth and manufacturing industry	78
Manufacturing output and employment	82
The balance of payments as a constraint on growth	87
The balance of payments in the post-war period	91

Growth, trade and competitiveness 97
The performance of manufacturing industry 105

4 UNEMPLOYMENT AND INFLATION 113

Introduction 115
Keynesianism 117
Monetarism 119
The re-emergence of unemployment 123
Unemployment policies 131
The labour market and unemployment in Britain 136
Inflation 145

5 PUBLIC FINANCE AND THE ROLE OF THE STATE 151

Introduction 153
The state and the economy 157
The role of markets 161
The principles of public expenditure and fiscal policy 166
Privatisation and regulation 171
Public expenditure in the United Kingdom 176

6 BRITAIN IN THE WORLD 183

Introduction 185
The Atlantic alliance 188
The Treaty of Rome and after 190
The Single Market concept 192
The Treaty of Maastricht 197
Monetary union 200
Is the Union working? 205
Britain in Europe 208

7 BRITAIN AT THE CROSSROADS 213

Introduction 215
Public finance and the conduct of policy 220
The behaviour of markets 226
The market economy and the future of capitalism 233
Epilogue 240

References 243
Index 249

LIST OF TABLES

....

1.1 Growth rates in the OECD   11
1.2 Gross domestic product per capita: changes relative to the UK   13
1.3 Growth of output and trade, annual average growth rates   14
1.4 Growth of consumer prices in the G7, annual average
     growth rates   14
2.1 Shares of investment and total outlays of government in GDP
     and annual rates of growth, 1960–1995   47
2.2 UK government expenditure and PSBR as a percentage of GDP   50
2.3 Investment ratios and % growth performance (excluding
     residential construction)   55
2.4 Effect on growth of a 1% change in the investment ratio   56
2.5 Business sector investment as a percentage of GDP
     at 1990 prices   57
2.6 Vocational qualifications of the manufacturing workforce
     in UK and Germany, 1987   66
2.7 Highest qualifications held by the UK working age population   67
2.8 Growth rates of GDP, 1981–89, %   71
3.1 Distribution of total output   84
3.2 Distribution of total employment   85
3.3 The current account of the balance of payments   95
3.4 Exports of goods and services as % of GDP   98
3.5 World trade in manufactures   103
3.6 Definitions of the 'North' and the 'South'   104
3.7 Exports of the North and South by destination   105
3.8 Growth of output per hour in manufacturing, %, 12 countries,
     selected periods   108
3.9 Imports of manufactured goods (% total visible imports
     by value)   112
4.1 Unemployment and inflation rates   116
4.2 Male unemployment rates % by qualification   129
4.3 Length of time in present employment   141
4.4 Changes in the industrial structure of employment in Britain   143
4.5 Changes in the occupational structure of employment   144

4.6 The highest qualifications held by the working age population   145
5.1 Government outlays as a percentage of GDP   154
5.2 Government outlays as a percentage of GDP   154
5.3 Gross public debt as % of nominal GDP   155
5.4 UK public expenditure since 1979   181
5.5 Public expenditure ratios in 1995   182
6.1 European Union intra-trade and share of world trade   197
7.1 Gross domestic product per capita, % rates of growth   218

LIST OF FIGURES

....

1.1 GDP – % deviations from trend in UK and OECD   4
1.2 Inflation – % deviations from trend in UK and OECD   4
1.3 OECD production and real money supply   20
1.4 World inflation – OECD consumer prices   20
1.5 Employment: EU, USA, UK and Japan   21
1.6 US competitiveness – % deviation from purchasing power
     parity   26
1.7 Manufacturing output relative to trend   29
1.8 UK competitiveness – % deviation from purchasing power
     parity   30
1.9 UK interest rates, money supply growth and PSBR   32
2.1 GDP growth and public expenditure   48
2.2 GDP growth and investment   54
2.3 Business sector profitability (UK, Germany, France,
     Japan and USA)   61
2.4 UK and European economic growth (annual % change in GDP)   70
3.1 The current account (% of nominal GDP)   93
3.2 Index of production: manufacturing (1990=100)   106
3.3 UK share of world trade in manufactures   110
7.1 Extrapolation of trend rate of growth of UK GDP   219

PREFACE

....

The aims of this book are described in the Introduction. It is intended for
those who are concerned with the important issues that relate to the
British economy, from the perspective of their businesses, their organisations, whether in the public or the private sector, or their roles in national
politics. It is written primarily from my point of view as an economist, and I
hope that it will be of some interest to my fellow economists.

While I write from my perspective as an economist, I should record that I
have spent many years in business, on the boards of public companies, both
here and abroad, and on the board of a nationalised industry. This does not
add any credibility to the analysis set out in this book, but many of the views
expressed have been prompted by my experience rather than simply theoretical considerations.

I am grateful to many people, too numerous to mention, who have taught
me much and shaped my views on the issues dealt with in this book. Immediate thanks are due to Nicholas Crafts, Joe Palmer, Peter Riddell, Harold
Rose and Andrew Sentance for having taken the time to read an earlier draft
and to offer helpful criticism and guidance. I am particularly indebted to
John Hunt for a detailed review of the text and the ideas presented which
has proved invaluable. I hasten to add that the views expressed and the errors
and omissions that remain are entirely my responsibility.

I much appreciate the kindness of the London Business School for reliev-
ing me of teaching responsibilities in the Summer term of 1997 in order for
me to complete my work. I am grateful for help received from Jennifer
Greenslade and James Clarke from the Centre for Economic Forecasting,
Stella Horsin from the Economics subject area, and Stephen Hume from the
Information Services Department of the School.

This book would never have seen the light of day without the patience,
support and commitment of my secretary, Juliet Smith. Apart from the initial organisation of the typescript, she has prepared the text for publication
in camera ready form, which is in itself a Herculean task. Her contribution
has been indispensable and I have much appreciated it.

INTRODUCTION

....

At the end of the 1970s the UK economy appeared to be in chaos, unmanageable, and to some ungovernable. The early 1980s and after appeared to reflect a new beginning, with a major shift in macroeconomic policy and objectives, the advent of privatisation (partly by accident!) and an overt emphasis on the importance of market forces in determining the allocation of scarce resources. By the end of the decade, the optimism that in many quarters characterised these developments appeared to have sunk in a welter of inflation, rising unemployment and economic recession that persisted into the early 1990s.

The interpretation of these events is much disputed. While some saw the industrial developments during and after the recession of 1980–81 as a necessary part of the restructuring of UK industry in an increasingly competitive world, others saw it as a major diminution of the UK's industrial capability. The apparent reliance on market forces to generate desirable social outcomes was seen by many in the late 1980s and early 1990s to be synonymous with greed and a lack of caring in society. A wedge began to be driven in many minds between economic efficiency and social concern. Recent attitudes toward health care reforms in the United Kingdom epitomise the issue.

In 1989, I wrote an article on the conduct of economic policy. In it, amongst other things, I observed that:

> I suspect that in the 1990s British economic policy will swing back toward the postwar consensus, whichever political party is in power. Whatever the practice of the policies followed, the principles of the 1980s reflected a belief in the virtue of sound money as a fundamental basis for economic health, and a deep distrust of state intervention of an essentially corporatist nature. The acceptance of these principles by government resulted in high unemployment and the worst recession since the Second World War. Tactically, it was not well done. But it was necessary to restore some kind of economic discipline following the excesses of the 1970s. (1989, p. 28)

But there is little doubt that Margaret Thatcher failed to market these ideas successfully to a significant majority of the population. There is a serious doubt that the conduct of macroeconomic and industrial policy will have undergone a significant and permanent change:

> Such a change requires a major shift in the attitudes of people in general, and listening to what I hear, and reading what I read, one can only say that the jury is very much out on this one, and it will be some time before we know the verdict. The

belief that the pursuit of wealth is inconsistent with a caring and humane society seems to me to be very much with us. To the extent that it remains (returns?) the importance of the market place relative to government intervention will be much curtailed. (1989, pp. 28–9)

Meanwhile, the world outside is on the move. The ending of the Cold War in its historical form has raised new questions for the major economic players of the world. Technological developments have shrunk the element of distance in the world economy. The structure of world economic activity is changing as the share attributable to the G7 countries declines and that of all-Asia (including China and India) rises. The future of Europe as an economic and political entity poses new questions for its members.

As we stand at present there is much pessimism expressed with regard to the economy and its foreseeable future – all this despite its apparent health given the major macroeconomic statistics available at the end of 1997. This pessimism is underwritten by the view that nothing has basically changed since 1979 – except perhaps for the worse.

Selected almost at random the following quotations catch the mood of the previous paragraph. The highly successful book by Will Hutton records that:

... the British experience offers a salutary warning to others. While individual countries may have at least one horror story of radical marketisation similar to Britain's, only Britain has them all. The process has gone much further and faster from an already weakened condition, and the failure and shortcomings that followed bear close examination. (Hutton, 1995, p. 18)

In a sober, and often penetrating, analysis of present day Britain, the Commission on Social Justice argued that:

No one is satisfied with the state of the UK today – and with good reason. In economic and social terms the gap between this country and our foreign neighbours is shaming. (Report of the Commission on Social Justice, 1994, p. 52)

In a more recent pre-election publication, the MP for Cannock Chase, Tony Wright, asserted that:

The growing concern about our competitive position is entirely justified, but the tragedy is that it has taken so long to recognize the problem. While swathes of British industry were casually driven to the wall in the first Conservative recession of the early 1980s, the victims of a dogma that showed a reckless disregard for the needs of the real economy, while the economic mismanagement that produced the last Conservative recession in the early 1990s, is the indispensable context within which the current pre-election recovery has to be set. (Wright, 1997, p. 15)

With regard to history prior to these perceived years of disaster, Wright suggests that:

The world before 1979 was not a halcyon age of cakes and ale, although to many it will now be seen like a lost haven of security and stability. (Wright, 1997, p. 12)

Following the landslide victory of the Labour Party in the May 1997 election, the Prime Minister Tony Blair, on the occasion of the Queen's Speech, declared that:

We will not put right the damage of eighteen years in eighteen days, or even eighteen months.

This makes it official. A grim prospect indeed.

Against this background, this book has three main purposes. The first is to attempt to put these judgements into perspective when viewed against Britain's economic performance since the Second World War. The thesis here is that the story of Britain's 'inexorable decline' is at best grossly exaggerated and, at worst, in some significant details not true.

The second is the need to examine a number of myths and misconceptions about Britain, and the way in which the British economy works, on which judgements of the kind referred to above are often based. They begin with the myth that John Maynard Keynes 'solved' the problem of unemployment, and that the abandonment of Keynesian policies accounts for much of what is wrong with the British economy today. Such a view is still alive and well, and supported by a second misconception, namely that British economic policy for much of the post-war period was actually conducted according to Keynesian principles. But for a quarter of a century after the war, stabilisation policy in the United Kingdom was determined by the requirements of the Bretton Woods Agreement and the commitment to pegged exchange rates. The historic experience of those years also gave rise to another erroneous belief, that the economic growth of the United Kingdom was in some way constrained by the behaviour of the balance of payments, and in particular by the behaviour of the current account. To this is usually added the idea that the future of Britain is critically and uniquely tied to the performance of manufacturing industry. The failure to sustain a substantial historical surplus in manufacturing trade is seen as a palpable weakness, reflecting a terminal decline in competitiveness. Finally on the macroeconomic front, there are the myths that suggest that there have been significant policy failures as a result of elevating the objective of restraining inflation at the expense of stimulating employment.

On the supply side of the economy, the central myth that appeals to many is the idea that British economic performance has been hopelessly inadequate because of a lack of investment. The reason for this allegedly poor investment performance has been the British financial system which has deprived businesses of necessary finance by demanding excessive dividend payments and generated higher hurdle rates of return on investment relative to our competitors. On the supply side of the economy there are many other myths, including the belief that during the 1980s the benefits and opportunities provided by the coming of North Sea oil were shamefully wasted.

The third purpose of this book is to evaluate the economic policies that have been pursued, on both the demand and the supply side of the economy. Much of the discussion is implicit in the treatment of the two previous objectives. Historical analysis, which is relevant to the first objective, requires judgements about what kinds of policies worked and what did not. Similarly acceptable and unacceptable policies are implied by the discussion of what have been referred to as the many myths that surround the analysis of the current economic state of modern Britain.

All this must be set in the context of some vision of Britain in the world. At the heart of these issues lies Britain's future involvement in Europe, and its relationship with the United States. Decisions with regard to monetary union and the impact of future European Union legislation relating to product markets, labour markets and capital markets will be crucial in determining Britain's future. Much of the discussion spills over into wider questions of the behaviour of markets and the future development of Western capitalism. For many, so-called Rhine capitalism, as exemplified by Germany, has presented an attractive model for Britain to follow, in contrast to what is perceived as the capitalism of Anglo-Saxon society. The future of the domestic economy is critically tied up with developments in the economic and political world outside.

The bottom line of all this is that the British economy is not the basket case that many people wish to represent it as. Nor is it in some sort of economic crisis. Nor is it in inexorable decline.

As will be argued later, in relation to the peer group that is defined in the forthcoming chapters, Britain is in better shape than most to deal with many of the economic problems that are discussed subsequently. As a starting point at least, the glass is half full rather than half empty. However, the overwhelming defeat of the Conservative Party at the 1997 election symbolises the end of one era and the beginning of another. Britain has reached the crossroads. She may go forward, she may go back, or she may simply go sideways. The choice is to be made. What follows suggests some directions that should be taken, some steps backward that should be avoided, and some blind alleys that we should not go down. The principal danger is that we may have suffered much and learned little, and that expectations have been created that cannot be realised. Perceived failure in the future will be the real legacy of having failed to learn from the past.

CHAPTER 1

THE BRITISH ECONOMY SINCE 1945

INTRODUCTION

History is the stuff of which economic ideas and theories are made. The social scientist is rarely able to conduct controlled experiments to separate the contributing factors that explain a specific kind of behaviour. The interpretation of events as they occur in real time is the task of the economist. It is never easy. And while differences in value judgements are often the root cause of differences in viewpoint between economists, as we shall see in much of this book, differences in empirical assessment are equally divisive. A new economic perspective is often simply a reinterpretation of history – of what actually happened.

We begin, therefore, with a review of the history of the British economy since the end of the Second World War, as a setting for a more detailed examination of the ideas and economic policies with which we will be subsequently concerned. Apart from the point already made, that it is from that history that conclusions must flow, an historical perspective has other virtues. It puts in context the different issues that we seek to discuss. Among many jokes about economists there is the one that says that in economics the questions always remain the same, it is the answers that keep changing. Today's perennial problems have not emerged overnight. The fact that we do seem to ask the same questions often suggests that answering those questions is not an easy task. If it were we would have found the answers long ago. In many cases history suggests that since many questions appear to remain unresolved, a sensible approach is not simply to continue the search for the Holy Grail, but to ask how should we formulate and conduct policy when we do not know what the answers to our questions are. The focus is then on the robustness of policy actions that will reduce the sensitivity of the outcomes if our underlying beliefs turn out to be wrong.

Finally, we may remind ourselves, if that is necessary in this day and age, that all economies must be seen in an international context. The economic behaviour of economies has differed in many significant respects over the last fifty years, for many different reasons that are the subject of discussion in the next chapter. But from a cyclical or conjunctural viewpoint, major shifts in the world economic climate affect all. Figures 1.1 and 1.2 compare the deviations of output growth and the inflation rate for the United Kingdom from their average values, with similar statistics for the OECD as a whole. While the cor-

Figure 1.1
GDP – % deviations from trend in UK and OECD

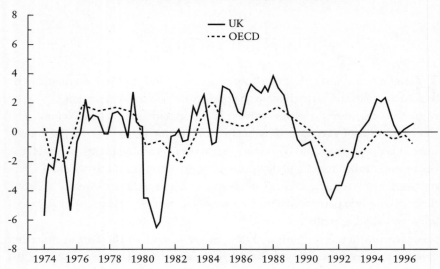

Source: Office for National Statistics, Statistics OECD Paris

Figure 1.2
Inflation – % deviations from trend in UK and OECD

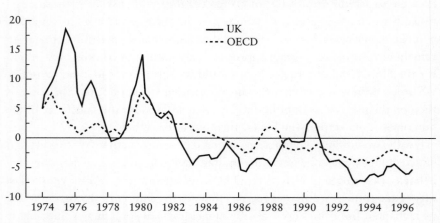

Source: Office for National Statistics, Statistics OECD Paris

relations are by no means perfect and the amplitudes differ (particularly with regard to inflation) the visual impression is clear. The world to a large extent rises and falls together. The stories of the major industrial economies of the world cannot be told in isolation. The international environment and its behaviour play a major role in the behaviour of each of them.

POST-WAR RECOVERY

The concerns of the Western world after the Second World War were focused, in economic terms, on the need to avoid the disasters of the 1930s, and in political terms, on the threat posed by the Soviet Union and its satellites.

To some degree, the economic and political considerations were intertwined as they always are. The fear of the spread of Communism, particularly into France and Italy after 1948, was certainly a factor that prompted US concern for the economic health of Europe, that culminated in the setting up of the Marshall Plan to assist European economic recovery in 1948. In addition, United States support for free trade, in part, was the outcome of American foreign and security policy. The United States, wisely at that time, saw that open economic relationships were part of a coherent set of political relationships which were necessary to bind the countries of the West together. As we shall see later, the political case for free trade in America has long since gone, and the concept is now having to struggle for its life.

The events of the 1930s were indelibly stamped on the minds of policy makers who gathered together toward the end of the war to prepare an economic world fit for the heroes to come home to. Unemployment and the disruption of international trade that followed the great American crash of 1929, and the subsequent depression, dominated their agendas. There had to be a world from which unemployment was banished and stable patterns of trade restored.

The financial and trade environment dominated the agenda, particularly of those who gathered together at Bretton Woods, New Hampshire in 1944 to put together a blueprint for the brave new world. On the financial side, there was seen to be a need for stability in exchange rates and interest rates which had fluctuated so much in the 1930s. Competitive depreciation of currencies gave rise to the idea of 'beggar-my-neighbour' policies, in an attempt to ward off the economic consequences of depression. On the trade side, there was a demand for openness and free trade, in contrast to the erection of tariff barriers and direct controls on imports that had characterised the years after 1929.

All this was taken on board by John Maynard Keynes for the United Kingdom and Harry Dexter White for the United States, the two principal negotiators of the Bretton Woods Agreement. On the financial side, exchange rate stability started from the agreement of the United States to fix the gold price of the dollar and to make the dollar fully convertible into gold. The remaining parties to the Agreement were then required to maintain parity with the dollar, within very narrow bands, by intervening, buying and selling currency in the market as was appropriate. On the institutional side, the International Monetary Fund was established as a source of short term credit which was designed to smooth out balance of payments problems over economic cycles, avoiding the necessity of deficit countries deflating their economies in order to adjust their balance of payments position. In addition, the IMF played a watchdog role over currency behaviour. Any devaluation of a currency greater than 7 per cent had to be referred to members of the Fund for ratification.

The United States pressed strongly for the liberalisation of trade, although the US Congress refused to agree to the setting up of the World Trade Organization in parallel to the IMF. Instead, the leading countries established the General Agreement on Tariffs and Trade (the GATT) as a means of conducting trade negotiations between its members. The initial concern of the United States was to secure the lifting of exchange controls on current account transactions in goods and services, the achievement of which was known as 'convertibility'. Exchange control and restrictions on imports, largely through licences, had been a feature of the economic apparatus constructed by Britain as part of her wartime economic programme, and there were considerable doubts as to the wisdom of dismantling such restrictions too rapidly in the face of expected post-war problems. In the event it was not until 1954 that the last vestiges of trade restrictions in this form were swept away together with rationing. Full convertibility was not however achieved until even later.

However, while there was some agreement that the abolition of exchange control over current transactions was desirable, it was felt that exchange control over capital movements should be maintained, leaving aside the specific difficulties of individual countries short of foreign exchange (meaning effectively US dollars). The principal reason for this stemmed from the belief that capital movements in the 1930s had been destabilising. So-called 'hot money' had migrated from one financial centre to another causing fluctuations in both interest rates and exchange rates. Thus it was felt, in the interests of world financial stability, that a tighter control should be maintained over the movement of capital by exercising exchange control. Leaving aside for the moment any general loss of economic welfare by distorting world capital markets, this decision placed excessive emphasis on the behaviour of the balance of payments on current account. The adherence to a pegged exchange rate that the Bretton Woods system required, when added to the inability of capital to respond to balance of payments disequilibrium, put all the pressure in times of crisis on foreign exchange reserves. In the United Kingdom this state of affairs was manifest in the belief that Britain suffered from a 'balance of payments' constraint on its rate of economic growth, an idea that is still alive in some quarters today. The current account was treated as an economic totem pole, and its behaviour as a symbol of national economic virility.

It is important to understand the economic significance of the Bretton Woods Agreement in terms of the constraints that were imposed upon its members. The economic dominance of the United States meant that a shortage of dollars became a major determining factor in the rest of the world's economic progress. More important still, however, was the fact that given the obligations on the participating members to peg their currency to the dollar, it meant that the world was to all intents and purposes on a dollar standard. It was no accident that, in Britain in those days, reference was made continually to the 'gold and dollar reserves'. Effectively, the dollar was as good as gold. However, more significantly, since monetary policy in the participating countries was aimed at maintaining the peg, it could not be used for anything else. American monetary policy became world monetary policy. And as we shall see later it was the changed status of the dollar and the conduct of American monetary policy that eventually led to the demise of the Bretton Woods system.

Whatever the merits of this brave new world on paper, reality was a hard taskmaster. The central issue that dominated the early post-war scene was simply the overwhelming economic power of the United States *vis-à-vis* the rest of the world. This was a problem recognised by many in Britain, but she was in no position to impose her views. The Allies in Continental Europe had suffered destruction and disorganisation. Germany was once again on its knees together with Japan. The imbalance between the economic power of the United States and the rest of the world was, if anything, greater than after the First World War. Such an overall imbalance could not have been cured by the rest of the world depreciating its currencies against the dollar as it would have been unable to supply the requisite goods and services. The problem of adjustment between America and the outside world stood in the way of European reconstruction, creating again a potential recycling problem (analogous to the oil problems of the 1970s) if recovery in Europe were to be completed and full employment achieved. In addition, the United States had become alarmed by the sound of the drums from the East which made it more difficult for her to retreat into the isolationist stance that she adopted after the First World War.

In the event, the giving of aid and the financial arrangements that had already been made at the end of the war sufficed to assist the process of economic recovery in Europe without creating a lasting burden of deadweight debt in the rest of the world. Britain benefited from the writing off of her residual obligations under the Lend Lease agreement, that had sustained her during the war itself. Europe, in general, benefited from the Marshall Plan. In the 1950s the occupying Americans encouraged protectionism in Japan and laid the foundations for a Japanese economic upsurge which reached its peak in the 1960s.

Perhaps the most important and impressive event of the 1950s was the economic recovery of what had become West Germany. It was the decade of the German 'economic miracle'; the 'Wirtschaftswunder'. From 1949 to 1963 the Federal Republic was led by Konrad Adenauer as Chancellor. In broad terms, Adenauer may be regarded as the founder of post-war Germany, matching the achievement of his illustrious nineteenth-century predecessor, Bismarck. Adenauer's principal interest was in external affairs, and he saw it as his personal task to keep the Federal Republic in the West, and to this end forged strong links with the United States. At a later stage, he played a key role in the establishment of what was then the EEC. The conduct of economic affairs and the implementation of the 'economic miracle' were largely in the hands of Ludwig Erhardt. Erhardt promoted the interests of private enterprise, combined with a firm commitment to monetary stability. Between 1950 and 1960 gross domestic product per capita in the Republic grew at the rate of 6.5 per cent per annum, slowing to 3.7 per cent between 1960 and 1973. Having begun with a per capita level of gross domestic product in 1950 of some 60 per cent of the British standard, by 1973 Germany had achieved equality. Other European economies such as France and Italy made similar progress through the 1950s and 1960s as the process of European recovery was continued.

THE YEARS OF PROSPERITY 1950–73

While slicing up time retrospectively is always somewhat arbitrary and artificial, it is important, as will be argued subsequently, to distinguish between the different periods that make up the history since the Second World War. Conventionally, the years from 1960 to the present have tended to be divided up as set out in Table 1.1 for the so-called G7 countries. In large measure, the history of the G7 dominates much of the period, at least until the early 1980s. Here, and for the remainder of our historical discussion, the focus will be on the G7 countries in particular, and the OECD in general. Table 1.2 sets out changes in real gross domestic product per capita relative to the United Kingdom for selected countries between 1950 and 1989.

The years from 1950 to 1973 are often referred to as a 'golden age'. The period as a whole for the OECD countries experienced a remarkable, and not since repeated, rate of economic growth and a major expansion in world trade. By and large, most countries experienced what could be described as full employment, and compared with what was to come later in the 1970s, relatively low rates of inflation. True, such rates of growth in gross domestic product per capita were not shared by the United States or by the United Kingdom, an issue that will be discussed below. But leaving that on one side, there were clearly general economic forces at work that encouraged the overall rate of expansion of economic activity in the OECD countries.

Crafts (1994) argues that many reasons have been expressed to explain the phenomenon of the golden age. Some of the more specific ideas that relate to the nature of economic growth are discussed in the next chapter. A central issue throughout is the influence of 'catch up' and the nature of the process of convergence. The simplest starting point is the observation that, given equal access to technology and the availability of human and financial capital, it would seem reasonable to suppose that those who had started behind in economic terms had at least the *opportunity* to exploit the knowledge and best practice of those who had gone before. On this simple basis, convergence in terms of economic growth rates was to be expected.

However, such convergence may not occur for at least two reasons. The first is that some countries may lack what is sometimes described as the 'social capability' to take advantage of the opportunities available. This may come about for social or cultural reasons. There might be no entrepreneurial class, for example, no motivating forces that push one to exploit economic opportunity. Such explanations on the face of it seem more plausible if applied to the so-called developing or emerging economies and contribute to the explanation of why some developing economies never seem to get off the ground. They remain permanently poor.

The second reason why convergence may not take place stems from the idea of the importance of human capital in the growth process coupled with the additional proposition that ultimately investment in 'broad' capital (physical and human) will not necessarily exhibit diminishing returns to scale. The implication of this for the back markers is that they may not have the human resources capable of catching up the front runners effectively. The implication for the front runners is that they might be capable of continuing to outrun the pack and create a serious permanent advantage; always one step ahead. (A corporate analogy was the dominant position of IBM Corporation over twenty years ago. It would never be caught.)

From Tables 1.1 and 1.2 it can be seen that the performance of countries outside the United Kingdom and the United States resulted in significant 'catch up' with both these countries by 1973. From the point of view of 'social capability' it is puzzling to see why one would have expected anything else. It is difficult to believe retrospectively that over a twenty year time span anyone could have doubted Germany's 'catch up', given its educational investment and industrial tradition. Had Britain grown at the same rate as Germany and France, the absolute gap in the standard of living would have widened over the period to an extent that is simply not plausible. Whatever the precise nature of the convergence process, it can hardly be doubted that after over twenty years Germany and France would have caught up the United Kingdom and made great efforts to close the gap with the United States.

Similarly, there would also seem to be an inevitability of some relative decline in the United States *vis-à-vis* the rising countries of Europe. In many respects it can be argued that as a result of the momentum of the war, the United States started with such an economic advantage that she was more difficult to catch. The Japanese story came later in the piece, but by 1973 she had achieved 90 per cent of the level of per capita gross domestic product in the United Kingdom and 65 per cent of the American. There are of course other factors that must have played a significant role in encouraging overall economic performance to the benefit of all. Despite the threat that free trade is frequently under today, the liberalisation of trade played an important role in encouraging general economic growth. As seen in Table 1.3, growth in world trade consistently outstripped the growth of gross domestic product and the ratio of traded to non-traded goods rose throughout the period. However, some measure of the damage done by the collapse of trade in the 1930s is reflected in the fact that it was only in 1969, towards the end of the golden age, that the ratio of traded to non-traded goods achieved the level last seen in 1913.

Table 1.1
Growth rates in the OECD, %

	1960–73	1973–79	1979–89	1989–95	1960–95
USA					
Growth in GDP	4.0	2.6	2.4	1.9	2.9
Growth in GDP per capita	2.7	1.6	1.5	0.9	1.8
Growth in GDP per employee	2.0	0.2	0.7	–	–
Japan					
Growth in GDP	9.7	3.5	3.8	1.9	5.5
Growth in GDP per capita	8.4	2.4	3.1	1.6	4.6
Growth in GDP per employee	8.2	2.8	2.6	1.1	4.4
Germany					
Growth in GDP	4.3	2.4	2.0	2.0	2.9
Growth in GDP per capita	3.7	2.5	1.9	1.3	2.6
Growth in GDP per employee	4.1	2.7	1.5	–	–
France					
Growth in GDP	5.4	2.7	2.1	1.3	3.3
Growth in GDP per capita	4.4	2.2	1.6	0.8	2.6
Growth in GDP per employee	4.7	2.3	2.0	1.0	2.9
Italy					
Growth in GDP	5.3	3.5	2.4	1.3	3.4
Growth in GDP per capita	4.6	3.0	2.3	1.1	3.1
Growth in GDP per employee	5.8	2.6	2.0	–	–

Table 1.1 Growth rates in the OECD, % (continued)

	1960–73	1973–79	1979–89	1989–95	1960–95
UK					
Growth in GDP	3.1	1.5	2.4	1.0	2.3
Growth in GDP per capita	2.6	1.5	2.2	0.7	2.0
Growth in GDP per employee	2.8	1.3	1.9	1.5	2.1
Canada					
Growth in GDP	5.4	4.2	3.1	1.2	3.8
Growth in GDP per capita	3.6	2.9	1.8	−0.1	2.3
Growth in GDP per employee	2.6	–	1.1	0.7	–
G7					
Growth in GDP	4.8	2.8	2.6	1.7	3.3
Growth in GDP per capita	3.8	2.1	2.0	1.0	2.5
Growth in GDP per employee	3.7	1.5	1.5	0.7	2.1
EU(15)					
Growth in GDP	4.7	2.5	2.2	1.5	3.1
Growth in GDP per capita	4.0	2.1	2.0	1.1	2.6
Growth in GDP per employee	4.4	2.3	1.7	0.7	2.6
OECD					
Growth in GDP	4.9	2.8	2.6	1.8	3.4
Growth in GDP per capita	3.7	1.9	1.7	0.9	2.3
Growth in GDP per employee	3.8	1.7	1.4	0.9	2.3

Source: OECD Historical Statistics, 1960–95, Paris, 1997

Table 1.2

Gross domestic product per capita: changes relative to the United Kingdom

	1950	1950–73	1973	1973–89	1989	1950–89
Australia	105	−2%	103	−2%	101	−4%
Austria	50	+72%	86	+8%	93	+86%
Belgium	75	+25%	94	+2%	96	+28%
Canada	108	+9%	118	+10%	130	+20%
Denmark	92	+14%	105	−5%	100	+9%
France	73	+41%	103	0%	103	+41%
Germany	59	+70%	100	+4%	104	+76%
Italy	50	+70%	85	+13%	96	+92%
Japan	28	+229%	92	+22%	112	+300%
Netherlands	83	+23%	102	−7%	95	+14%
Sweden	94	+19%	112	0%	111	+18%
Switzerland	116	+13%	131	−13%	114	−2%
UK	100	–	100	–	100	–
USA	152	−8%	140	−3%	136	−11%

Source: Maddison, 1991, Dynamic Forces in Capitalist Development, Oxford University Press, Table 1.1, pp. 6–7

Table 1.3
Growth of output and trade, average annual growth rates, %

	1960–73	1973–79	1979–89	1989–95
EC				
Output	4.7	2.5	2.2	1.5
Exports	8.1	4.9	4.0	4.5
OECD				
Output	4.9	2.8	2.6	1.8
Exports	8.0	5.2	4.5	5.6

Source: OECD Historical Statistics, 1960–95, Paris, 1997

Moreover the 1950s and 1960s were exceptionally good years to be a manufacturer. The real price of energy fell every year from 1951 to 1969. The terms of trade between manufactured goods and raw materials favoured the manufacturer. The outbreak of the Korean War in 1950 had sent raw material prices skyrocketing as the United States, in particular, stockpiled in the shadow of a Third World War. After prices fell back in 1953, a long period of benign raw material costs encouraged profitability in industry.

Finally, the golden age was encouraged and protected by the stability of the international monetary environment, until it began to disintegrate in the late 1960s. Exchange rate stability and relatively low rates of inflation characterised the period, as the founding fathers had hoped. Until into the 1960s, dollar shortages and a conservative American monetary policy appeared to make it a fit keeper of the world inflation rate, and as can be seen from Table 1.4 over the early years of the 1960s the United States inflation rate was lower than that of Germany.

Table 1.4
Growth of consumer prices in the G7, annual average growth rates, %

	1958–67	1968–73	1974–78	1979–82	1983–87	1988–96
USA	1.6	5.0	7.2	10.0	3.3	3.6
Japan	4.9	7.1	8.3	5.1	1.3	1.5
Germany	2.4	4.6	4.2	5.7	1.2	3.1
France	3.8	6.1	10.0	12.9	4.8	2.5
Italy	3.3	5.8	16.0	19.1	7.6	5.2
UK	2.8	7.5	16.0	12.7	4.7	4.6
Canada	2.0	4.6	8.8	11.1	4.2	2.8

Source: International Financial Statistics, IMF, 1997

The remaining issue that has been of particular interest to British commentators is the extent to which the prosperity of the golden age was due to more enlightened economic policies, particularly those associated with the ideas of John Maynard Keynes. In Britain at least, the mythology still suggests that macroeconomic policy was largely conducted on Keynesian lines, the elements of which will be discussed in Chapter 4. Whatever the virtues of Keynesian thinking, it is clear that as a result of the Bretton Woods system, no country other than the United States could conduct an independent monetary policy, even in the presence of exchange control over capital movements. It is certainly true that successive British governments after the Second World War, and up and until the mid-1970s, engaged in Keynesian rhetoric when presenting their policies. But the system always defeated them. Under a pegged exchange rate regime, the major effects of monetary expansion resulted not immediately in an acceleration of the inflation rate, but a deterioration of the current account of the balance of payments as imports were sucked in from abroad.

The consequences of this for Britain during the years of prosperity were manifest. The emergence of unemployment, even on a modest scale, as in the early 1950s, the late 1950s and the early 1960s, was followed by inflation, tax cuts, and increased public spending which promoted excessive monetary expansion. In these episodes, some direct effects on price inflation were observed, but the major consequence was a deterioration in the current account balance which, if left to carry on, threatened the existing parity with the dollar. The result in each case was a retreat from the initial expansion, although finally following the expansion of 1963–64, it was no longer possible to hold the line, and the Wilson government devalued sterling in 1967. These episodes of so-called 'stop-go' simply made manifest the impossibility of fine tuning the economy along Keynesian lines, if the parity of the currency was to be maintained. As we shall see later, an attempt to be Keynesian, following the first oil price shock, had disastrous consequences and the experiment has not, at least to date, been repeated.

Intellectual obeisance to Keynesian ideas was paid not only in Britain but also in the Netherlands, the Scandinavian countries, and indeed in the groves of academe in the United States. However, little of a practical nature emerged from Keynes's ideas. As already recorded, the expansion of Germany was conducted on conservative economic lines, combined with a serious intent to free the hands of business rather than to promote growth through government spending and taxation policies. In the United States, the Eisenhower administration in the 1950s equally pursued conservative financial policies combined with a (much criticised) desire to balance the fiscal budget. With the coming of Kennedy in 1960, the climate changed. But the separation of powers under the American constitution, between the President, the Congress, and the Federal Reserve, conspired to make it difficult for fine tuning along Keynesian lines to take place. The final conclusion must be that the golden age of the OECD countries in the years of the 1950s and 1960s owed little to the successful application of new ideas with regard to economic policy making that had become popular since the war.

Eventually the Bretton Woods system collapsed. Its demise began in the early 1960s soon after President Kennedy entered the White House. The underlying reason was simple enough. The pessimists of the 1950s, who had predicted long term persistence of a dollar shortage, turned out to be wrong. The competitiveness of the rest of the world outside the United States improved dramatically as the golden age wore on. The position of the dollar progressively weakened, and the strength of the American balance of payments was undermined. President de Gaulle resented the fact that, under the Bretton Woods system, the United States in creating dollars had a licence to create gold – as long as no one took seriously the commitment of America to exchange dollars for gold on demand. But given the rise in American external dollar obligations this became an increasing fiction. Superimposed on this development came the Vietnam War, which in turn fuelled American monetary expansion and alarmed the Germans on the grounds that the United States was exporting inflation to the rest of the world, which called for a devaluation of the dollar and/or a revaluation of the mark. The Bretton Woods system limped on to be terminated formally, at least, by President Nixon when he suspended the convertibility of the dollar into gold in August 1971. It was the end of an era.

BRITAIN IN THE GOLDEN AGE

It has been observed by Bean and Crafts:

> It is obviously important to bear in mind that the UK had less scope for rapid catch-up or reconstruction based growth than most European countries in the early post-war period. Even so, it seems clear that Britain was less successful in exploiting what opportunities there were for catch-up and attention needs, therefore, to be directed at Abramovitz' emphasis on the role of 'social capability' in this context. Here particular importance attaches to industrial relations, competition policy and capital markets. In each of these the UK exhibited significant idiosyncrasies which had important effects on the environment in which British company management – perhaps the most common scapegoat of all – operated. (Bean and Crafts, 1996, p. 132)

These views are widely held. Bean and Crafts further comment:

It is a commonplace that the growth and productivity performance of the British economy has been disappointing in the post-war period, at least until the 1980s, which can be regarded as still controversial. (Bean and Crafts, 1996, p. 131)

This is certainly true. Concern with Britain's economic performance stems from the perception of the late 1950s that other European countries, notably Germany, were making considerable industrial progress. This resulted in the then Conservative government establishing the National Economic Development Office to consider obstacles to economic growth and to review alternative economic policies relating to the supply side of the economy that might improve Britain's relative economic position. This concern was echoed and reinforced by the incoming Labour government of Harold Wilson in 1964 which pursued a major new approach to economic policy in the medium term based on a more effective exploitation of technology and a National Economic Plan. From the early 1960s a significant pessimism was spawned about Britain's overall economic performance and the need felt for some radical change in economic policy; another Holy Grail that has been pursued by some governments of the left and the right ever since. (More detailed consideration of the issues here is left over for subsequent chapters.) The question to be asked here is, was it on an overall basis appropriate to be so concerned about British economic performance in the golden age?

The answer depends heavily on what economists describe in their jargon as the 'counterfactual' picture of what economic performance might have been. Critics have directed their attention to British performance in this period with regard to a lower rate of investment, a poorer educational base, and a system of industrial relations (of which more anon) that inhibited economic performance. Ironically, many look back to the 1950s and 1960s not only as a world golden age but also as a British golden age of full employment and low inflation. Yet the main concern with British economic performance, both then and subsequently, has focused on *relative* rather than *absolute* decline. From a British point of view, the 1950s and 1960s were regarded by many as an unmitigated disaster. Insofar as we compare ourselves reasonably with our leading European partners (Germany, France, the Netherlands) most of the decline in the British standard of living, relative to these countries, took place between 1950 and 1973.

If we focus on France and Germany as comparators, we can see that, whereas France and Germany began in 1950 with 70 per cent and 60 per cent respectively of the British standard, by 1960 the rapid growth of Germany (the 'economic miracle') resulted in gross domestic product per capita achieving parity by 1973 with France slightly ahead of that again. As we shall see later, many economists focus on other indices of performance, particularly those related to the behaviour of manufacturing industry. However, at the aggregate level, gross national product per head of population is the best we can do to assess overall performance. Clearly, one must be careful not to relate such a statistic to economic welfare in any global sense.

If one's principal concern focuses on the change in the British standard of living relative to our European colleagues, then the vast majority of that change since 1950 came in the golden age. To put this in perspective, consider the numbers in Table 1.1. If we take as a whole the sixteen year period from 1973 to 1989, we see that in terms of the rate of growth of gross domestic product per head of population, there has been little significant difference in the performance of the United Kingdom relative either to Germany or France. Over this period Japan has been the star turn, but even in 1973 Japan had only achieved 92 per cent of the British standard and was, therefore, 'entitled', as was Italy, to an overall faster rise in their standard of living since they were both still coming from behind.

Serious criticism of Britain's economic performance in the golden age requires a clear specification of the 'counterfactual' referred to earlier. Would Germany have maintained a British type relative superiority from 1950 had the position been reversed? We will never know. But if the change in the relative economic position of the United Kingdom since the Second World War is the key issue that concerns us, it is clear where we should start looking for it, namely in the period from 1945 to 1973.

THE YEARS OF TURBULENCE 1973–79

There was no sudden transition from the golden age to what we now describe as the 'years of turbulence', the 1970s. There were three significant events that were signposts along the road of transition: the Vietnam War, the suspension of the convertibility of the dollar into gold in August 1971, and the dramatic rise in the price of oil, OPEC I. From the peak of post-war recovery, which can probably be dated as around 1960, there were signs of change. The growing strength of the rest of the world *vis-à-vis* the United States was substantially responsible for the difficulties that were to come.

In 1971, the so-called Smithsonian agreement resulted in the first significant realignment of exchange rates for some years. In practice, the result was, initially, an uncomfortable half-way house between a system of pegged exchange rates on the one hand and fully floating rates on the other. The dollar, for a period at least, continued to be important as a reserve currency, although without the *de facto* guarantees from central bank behaviour that had ruled during the post-war period. For a short period, at least, the world continued to adapt to the dollar standard. But that situation was abruptly challenged by the dramatic increase in the world price of oil following the outbreak of the Arab–Israeli war in September 1973.

The macroeconomic response of the OECD countries to the ending of the Bretton Woods system was, in general, disastrous. Figure 1.3 shows the relationship between the real stock of money in the OECD world and the behaviour of industrial production during the 1960s and the 1970s. The abandonment of the dollar peg meant that individual countries regained control of their monetary policies in the sense that they could either choose to stabilise their exchange rates, as had been the case under Bretton Woods, or choose new targets for control of their inflation rates. Unfortunately, the universal choice that they made was to use their monetary and fiscal policies in an attempt to stimulate the growth of real output and reduce the unemployment rates that had been gently rising throughout the OECD countries from the late 1960s into the early 1970s. The result was a major expansion in the world's real money supply as shown in Figure 1.3. Output with a lag responded accordingly. Inflation accelerated. Between July 1972 and July 1973 commodity prices, whose behaviour as previously recorded had been benign since the end of the Korean War, rose by 50 per cent in a year. In September, the Arab-Israeli war began. By January of 1974 the price of oil had quadrupled. The world was subjected to the impact of OPEC I.

The economic importance of the rise in the oil prices, OPEC I, and a similar impact on the real output and inflation of the OECD countries caused by OPEC II (in 1978) can be segmented into a number of components. There was an impact effect on the price level, although the extent to which this was translated into a significant upturn in the inflation rate for a subsequent period depended on how monetary policy was conducted following the initial oil price increase. The behaviour of the inflation rate in the OECD after OPEC I and OPEC II is illustrated in Figure 1.4. The impact of the rise in the real price of oil has serious implications for the different sectors of the economy. The rise in the oil price imposed a burden on industrial sectors of the world's economies. A critical starting point was the extent to which the burden of real income adjustment fell on the private rather than the public sector.

Figure 1.3
OECD production and real money supply (% change)

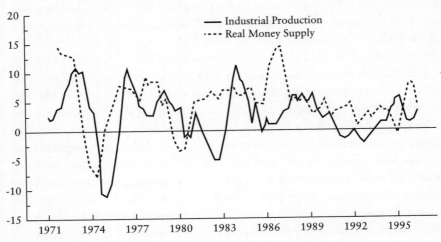

Source: OECD Main Economic Indicators

Figure 1.4
World inflation – OECD consumer prices (% change)

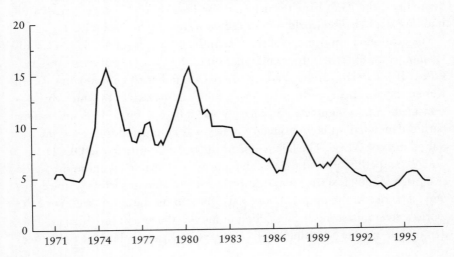

Source: OECD Statistics, Paris

If we analyse the effect in terms of the impact on the major European economies, Japan and the United States, the conclusions are very clear. In general, Europe (including the United Kingdom which was now a member of the EEC) opted to try to preserve the position of the public sector, and to maintain public spending at the expense of the private sector. Since most of the burden fell on the private sector in the European Community, the real rate of return on investment collapsed, unit labour costs in real terms continued to rise and the loss of competitiveness was exacerbated. The protection of the public sector meant that inevitably fiscal deficits in the European Community (as it then was) also rose substantially. The United States and Japan on all counts responded more flexibly to the change in the economic environment. The result in terms of corporate profitability, the behaviour of unit labour costs, and the control of inflation can be seen in the behaviour of employment in the United Kingdom and in the EEC compared with the United States and Japan in Figure 1.5. In Continental Europe the sharp increase in the ratio of public spending to gross domestic product was associated with the rise in unemployment as the generous welfare provisions established during the golden age cut in.

Figure 1.5
Employment: EU, USA, UK and Japan

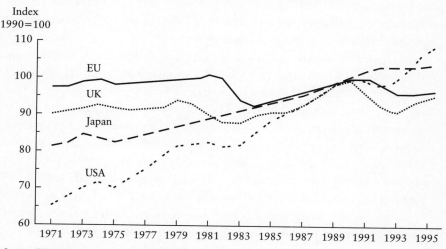

Source: OECD Statistics, Paris, ANALISTAS

As can be seen in Figure 1.3, the recession of 1974–75 that followed OPEC I was sharp and brief and recovery took place in 1976. But this was followed in 1978 by OPEC II, which was a somewhat more prolonged and double dip recession due to initial lax monetary policy in the United States followed by a sharp crackdown as the American inflation rate reached 12 per cent and Paul Volcker took over the chairmanship of the Federal Reserve. These events in the OECD were accompanied by the rise of indebtedness of Third World countries without oil, resulting at a later stage in the problem of sovereign debt that had a major effect on economic behaviour in the 1980s.

BRITAIN IN THE YEARS OF TURBULENCE

In the United Kingdom, the inflationary situation after the rise in the price of oil deteriorated rapidly. The oil price increase was superimposed on a major boom, the so-called Barber boom, created by the expansionist fiscal and monetary policies of the government. The upswing of the economy in 1972–73 had been accompanied by major monetary growth, due in part at least to the relaxation of the previous system of credit controls in 1971.

The collapse of the Heath government at the polls, in the face of his effective defeat by the coal miners, brought a second Harold Wilson administration to power, this time with Denis (now Lord) Healey as Chancellor of the Exchequer. Threatening noises were made in advance of Healey's intention to tax the rich until 'the pips squeaked', and the new government set off at a gallop down the path of 'tax and spend'.

It is arguable that the conduct of fiscal policy at this time constitutes the only serious, practical attempt to avoid a recession by applying what had come to be regarded as standard Keynesian policies (whether Keynes would have done so is another matter!). The public sector was protected at the expense of the private, not simply on ideological grounds but also as part of the process of sustaining the level of demand. Monetary expansion proceeded apace reaching a peak annual rate of 27 per cent in 1973 predictably followed two years later by an annual inflation rate of nearly 25%. The United Kingdom stockmarket collapsed in 1974–75, and as British monetary expansion exceeded that of other principal competitors such as the United States, Germany and Japan, by a huge margin, the pound sank like a stone with some company, at least, in the shape of the Italian lira and the Swedish krona.

So it was in 1976, for the second time since OPEC I, the government of the day turned to so-called 'incomes policies' to stem the inflationary tide, as a substitute for government expenditure cuts and a contraction of the public sector deficit, which had been fuelling monetary growth. The focus of attention became the 'social wage' rather than take home pay. Paradoxically, the form that the incomes policy took on the wage side, with a flat rate increase of £6 a week across the board, was itself inflationary since for many it was an increase they would not have secured at the negotiating table. The familiar pattern of dividend controls and restrictions on the salaries of the 'high paid' became the order of the day. However, these steps failed to secure the much needed control over public sector borrowing and monetary growth. The current account of the balance of payments had deteriorated in line with the government deficit and eventually it was deemed necessary to send for the brokers' men from the IMF. The United Kingdom found itself *pro tempore* in the international pawn shop.

The deflationary measures taken in the budget in November 1976 with severe cuts in public spending produced dramatic effects. Sterling had slumped to a low point of $1.57 in 1976. In the first three months of 1977 monetary growth was reduced virtually to zero. Confidence in the pound rose sharply and by the early weeks of the year it was clear that it was distinctly undervalued. But both government and industry were obsessed with the need for a competitive pound, rather than allowing it to appreciate and so contribute to the reduction in the inflation rate. By the time the pound was uncapped by the end of the year, money had poured into Britain from abroad and short term interest rates came tumbling down. On top of this inflammatory influx came tax cuts and increases in public spending again, accompanied externally by the second rise in the oil price, OPEC II. The ingredients of a further explosive mixture were in the bowl. The advantage gained in the Budget of 1976 was largely lost.

The result was a rapid rise in real consumer spending of nearly 10 per cent between the end of 1977 and 1979. The boom was on again. The upward pressure of domestic demand, coupled with the incoming inflationary pressure from OPEC II, laid the foundations for the total non-acceptability of the 5 per cent incomes policy introduced by the government in 1978. The arithmetic of the policy did not add up. With monetary growth at 12 per cent and an output growth expected of around 3 per cent, an inflation rate of at least 10 per cent looked to be on the cards. (In the event the consumer price increase was nearly 14 per cent.) Small wonder that organised labour jibbed at the 5 per cent limit. The uproar and unrest of the final quarter of 1979 cannot simply be interpreted, as it was by the overseas press, as the beginnings of a new class war, or alternatively, as a peasants' revolt. It can be seen as a predictable free market reaction to the government's stance on fiscal and monetary policy, coupled with the unwinding of anomalies between the public and the private sectors that the incomes policy had produced. The 'winter of discontent' of 1978–79 turned into a 'summer of joy' for the Conservative Party as it resumed power. The Thatcher era had begun.

The bottom line of all this, at the aggregate level of gross domestic product, can be seen in Table 1.1. Following OPEC I, the growth rates of all the G7 countries fell sharply. The fall was particularly dramatic in the case of Japan. The country that, on the face of it, was least affected was Canada, followed by Italy. It is difficult not to ascribe the relatively poorer performance of the United Kingdom, compared with Germany and France, to the misconduct of monetary and fiscal policy in the face of the oil price shocks. More effective macroeconomic policies carried out by governments after the ending of Bretton Woods and in the face of OPEC I and II should have led to a lower overall rate of inflation in this period and a greater degree of stability in terms of the behaviour of output and employment. Over this period, at least, there is a *prima facie* case for the attribution of relatively lower economic performance, overall, to a failure of stabilisation policy, rather than to deeper structural problems.

THE EIGHTIES 1979–89

The period from 1979 to 1989 spans two peaks in terms of the level of economic activity in Britain. It was the decade of Margaret Thatcher as the Prime Minister of the United Kingdom.

Following the inflationary impact of OPEC II, as in the case of OPEC I, a sharp reduction occurred in the growth rates of the OECD and European Union countries, that lasted over the period 1980–1982. As pointed out earlier, the pattern of the recession differed from that of OPEC I because of the different policy response of the United States in the face of the shock. The result was that gross domestic product in the United States declined only slightly in 1980 and recovered significantly in 1981. When this was accompanied by an acceleration in the inflation rate, a tightening of monetary policy occurred resulting in a sharp fall in US output in 1982. In Continental Europe, the recession was also more prolonged, particularly in Germany which on a net basis showed zero growth over the period. By contrast, Japan handled the situation far better than any of the other G7 countries and the members of the European Community. Over the recession period 1980–1982, Japan grew at an average rate of 3.3 per cent per annum. Japan had learned much from the experience of OPEC I with regard to the conduct of monetary policy. Whereas in 1974 the rate of consumer price inflation in Japan escalated to 21 per cent for the year as a whole, the average inflation rate over the period 1980–1982 was held to just under 5 per cent compared with American inflation of nearly 9 per cent and inflation in Britain of over 12 per cent.

Recovery in the United States began in 1983, and the economy grew rapidly throughout 1984. The recovery was accompanied by a significant deterioration in the American fiscal deficit. President Reagan had been persuaded that cutting tax rates, particularly at the higher levels, need not necessarily result in lower tax revenues, since the incentives created would result in higher levels of income, the extra revenue from which would offset the apparent loss due to lower rates. In addition, the President was anxious to spend more money on defence, particularly in support of the so-called Star Wars programme.

The resulting tax cuts and expenditure increases did not have the expected results. Instead, to some the fiscal expansion that took place looked in effect suspiciously like Keynesianism through the back door. The fiscal deficit expanded, but so subsequently did the current account deficit of the balance of payments. There were two significant factors at work. The first was the fiscally induced increase in output that resulted in more imports. The second was the dramatic appreciation of the US exchange rate as is seen in Figure 1.6. In order to finance the deficits, the United States had to borrow heavily from abroad, forcing up the level of interest rates to attract the necessary capital inflows. The inflow of capital in turn drove up the exchange rate as the influence of the movements in the capital account swamped the effect of basic factors affecting the current account.

At the same time general concern had been mounting with regard to the debt position of Third World countries that had arisen as a result of OPEC I and OPEC II. The situation following OPEC I left the oil producers with large surpluses of funds and the poorer countries of the world without. Such imbalance could not be solved by exchange rate movements, any more than could the imbalance between the United States and the result of the world after the Second World War. The oil producers' ability to consume their surpluses was limited. The producers, therefore, needed to lend their money and the oil consumers needed to borrow it.

Following OPEC I, in 1973 the principal source of intermediation was through the world's private banking system. Despite calls for centralised intervention, through the IMF for example, the private sector coped with the situation reasonably well, although the outcome was by no means ideal. The lenders wanted liquidity and there was little incentive for them to tie up their money on a long term basis. However, the borrowers had long term needs, resulting in the inevitable mismatch between assets and liabilities. Despite this, a crisis might have been avoided had it not been for OPEC II in 1978. The result of this was the creation of sovereign debt on a much larger scale, reinforced by optimism about the economic future of some of the borrowers, particularly in Latin America.

Figure 1.6
US competitiveness – % deviation from purchasing power parity

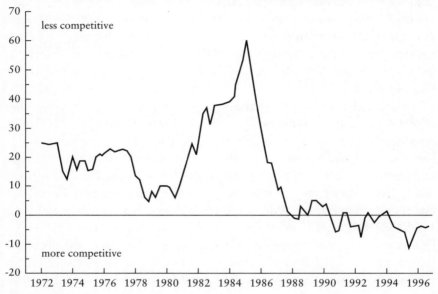

Source: IMF International Financial Statistics

All this raised concerns with what had become known as the 'twin deficit' problem of the United States, and its potential impact on the Third World sovereign debt problem. There were two issues. The first was concern about the level of world interest rates as a result of the United States' absorption of a substantial proportion of the world's savings. The second was whether the resolution of the 'twin-deficit' problem (on the assumption that America could not continue, indefinitely, to accumulate external liabilities) necessitated a recession in the United States that would affect the rest of the world. Interest rates would be too high, and the Third World countries would be unable, in a recessionary world, to earn enough export income to pay the interest on their debt, let alone repay the capital. For some Armageddon loomed; the arrival of a major world recession coupled with massive default on the part of the issuers of sovereign debt.

During and after the recession of 1980–1982, inflation rates fell everywhere. From the mid-1980s onward, Europe began to expand more rapidly. Both these developments were reinforced by the fall in oil prices in 1986, OPEC III. In 1987, the world's equity markets grew rapidly, while bond yields began to rise, prompted, in part at least, by fears of the ultimate consequences of the 'twin deficit' adjustment. Finally, in October 1987, the gap between equity and bond yields became too great and the elastic snapped. Wall Street and the European markets went into free fall. At this stage only Tokyo was immune.

The dramatic fall in the world's stockmarkets set the alarm bells ringing. Those with an historical perspective realised that the real problem of the depression of the 1930s stemmed, not from the downturn of 1929 and the great fall in Wall Street, but from the aftermath of the collapse of 1930. This conclusion was convincingly argued by Milton Friedman and Anna Schwartz (1963); it was the policy pursued by the Federal Reserve that converted a pause in the growth of economic activity in the United States into an economic rout.

When banking crises occur, the key question is always whether the crisis is the result of insolvency or simply a problem of liquidity. In the latter case it is appropriate for the lender of last resort to supply liquidity to the system. In the former it pays to take 50 cents on the dollar and run. In 1930, the United States Federal Reserve Bank took the view incorrectly that the banking system was insolvent. It, therefore, failed to exercise its function as the lender of last resort. It cut support to the banking system so precipitating a domino effect that resulted in the American banking system collapsing like a house of cards. In the crisis of 1987 and before there had been the threat of another domino collapse as the result of the exposure of the OECD banks to sovereign debt. The issue was the same, liquidity and insolvency. The central bankers and finance ministers of the OECD decided wisely that they faced a problem of liquidity. For some of the players, such as the commercial banks, losses were inevitable. However, a compromise was reached – some debts were written off, and the ship was left afloat. At the time of the stockmarket collapse of 1987, central bankers and finance ministers, such as Alan Greenspan in the United States, had read their history. There was an apparent danger that with 1987 looking like 1929, 1988 would turn out to be like 1930. The central bankers and finance ministers opted wisely for a strategy of reducing interest rates and supplying liquidity to financial markets. It was a sensible insurance policy.

At the time it was commonly supposed that economic growth in the world as a whole was relatively weak. The stimulus to the expansion of world output resulting from the fall in the oil price in 1986, OPEC III, did not, by the middle of 1987 at least, appear to have materialised. But unfortunately for the policy makers, a head of steam was building up in the world economy, which in the event was hardly affected by the stockmarket fall. Those who predicted that after it recession would follow, like night follows day, were totally wrong. Indeed by early 1988 it became apparent that economic activity was expanding more rapidly in the OECD countries than had been the case since 1984. In Europe, 1988 was a faster year of expansion than any since the recovery year of 1976. The problem that now faced policy makers was not recession but renewed inflation.

In Japan, growth accelerated dramatically in 1988, along with the rest of the OECD. But inflation, in terms of the price of goods and services, remained non-existent. Indeed, in 1988, Japanese consumer prices actually fell. But the monetary stimulus to the world in general was reflected in Japan in a major boom in asset prices both in land and in the stockmarket. In Germany, inflation also remained moderate, but the reunification of West and East Germany soon began to create strains on German monetary policy as it sought to compensate for the expanding fiscal deficit that resulted from the costs of unification. By 1991, with the exception of Japan and Germany, the OECD was in recession. By 1993 the aftermath of the collapse of the Japanese financial system, and the secondary consequences of German reunification, meant that Japan and Germany had joined their European colleagues. At that time the Anglo-Saxon world led by the United States started off on a road to recovery.

BRITAIN IN THE EIGHTIES

As can be seen in Table 1.1, Britain's aggregate economic performance in the 1980s showed a significant improvement over the 1970s, but was below that of the 1960s if looked at in growth terms. Gross domestic product per person employed in the United Kingdom grew significantly faster than the average for the G7. For the first time it exceeded both the average for the enlarged European Union (with fifteen countries) and the average for the OECD as a whole. The significance of the performance is debated in the next section. Here we focus on the narrative.

The first eighteen months of the new Thatcher administration turned out to be disastrous. Inflation and interest rates rose sharply, sterling appreciated strongly, and a million people lost their jobs. Output and employment in manufacturing industry collapsed. The behaviour of manufacturing output since 1970 and the impact of the recession are illustrated in Figure 1.7. The trend line indicates the absolute decline in manufacturing output during the 1970s.

In large measure the depth of the recession in output was self-inflicted. Inflation, on top of the impact of OPEC II, was given a further impetus as a result of the implementation of the commitments entered into in the Conservative Party's election manifesto. Large increases in pay recommended by the Clegg Commission had been promised to public servants and teachers. Value added tax was increased and there were also sharp increases in the prices of the nationalised industries. Government spending, as a proportion of the gross domestic product, rose, rather than fell, out of line with the incoming government's intentions. The appreciation of sterling (see Figure 1.8) stemmed, in part, from people's expectations created by the coming on stream of North Sea oil, but also as a result of the rise in interest rates emanating from Thatcher's loose fiscal policy. The incoming government inherited from its predecessors a tiger on an economic rampage, but, over the initial period of office, it singularly failed to bring the animal to heel.

Figure 1.7
Manufacturing output relative to trend

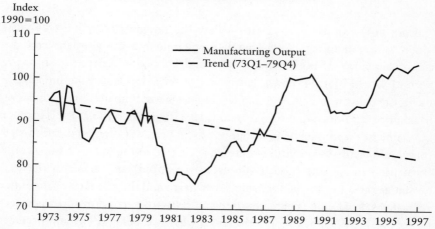

Source: Economic Trends, Office for National Statistics, July 1997

The turning point for both the government and the economy came in 1981. The Budget for that year sought, seriously, to bring both the money supply and public finances under control. A so-called new medium-term financial strategy (the MTFS) was put in place. Coherence in the medium term was to be established between government spending plans, taxation and the growth of the money supply (however measured).

Figure 1.8
UK competitiveness – % deviation from purchasing power parity

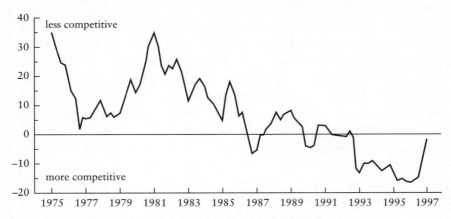

Source: Centre for Economic Forecasting, London Business School, July 1997

From a macroeconomic point of view the Budget of 1981 marks what might be described as the real Thatcher experiment. It was a retreat from the consensus views of both Conservative and Labour governments since the Second World War. Hitherto, in the face of recession and rising unemployment, the conventional Keynesian wisdom suggested the need for reductions in taxation and the expansion of public spending. In contrast, the Thatcher government's approach was to tighten fiscal policy in the expectation that this would justify lower interest rates, a reduction in the inflation rate (as the fiscal pressure on the money supply was reduced) and a fall in the real exchange rate. The Budget brought forth wrath and the condemnation of the economics profession. Three hundred and sixty-four economists signed a letter to *The Times*, attacking the theory of what was being done, and predicting that the economy would never recover if policies like this were implemented. Almost immediately the economy began to recover and between 1982 and 1989 delivered the fastest overall rate of growth of gross domestic product that had been seen in the United Kingdom since 1959 to 1966.

In the context of the development of ideas about fiscal and monetary policy (which will be discussed in Chapter 4) it is important to distinguish between the ideas and principles that underlay the formulation of policy and the practical consequences of implementation. The economic policies pursued by the government at the time have been described as 'monetarist', a term which in recent years has been interpreted as one of abuse. The single underlying principle of what was attempted, was indeed to substitute *nominal* for *real* economic targets; the growth of nominal income rather than the real rate of economic growth which was to move in the longer run roughly in line with the growth of the economy's productive potential.

But perhaps even more significant was the fact that, contrary to the beliefs that characterised the conduct of such policies since the Second World War, the overall level of employment was regarded by the government as a microeconomic rather than a macroeconomic problem. Jobs were seen to depend essentially on the profitability of employing people, except in the non-marketed sector of the economy. Employees could price themselves out of work by demanding excessively high wages. With extreme rigidities in the process of adjusting the real price of labour, simply pumping money into the economy resulted not in the permanent creation of more jobs but ultimately in more inflation. The government's view was that a reduction in the inflation rate was not simply necessary for its own sake, but was an essential part of the story of economic recovery and the restoration of jobs.

It is fair to say at the outset that the government pursued a particularly crude form of monetarism, believing that simply controlling the broad measure of the money supply, sterling M_3, was sufficient to keep nominal demand on course within the framework of the MTFS. This proved difficult, given the abandonment of exchange controls and a further deregulation of the financial system, analogous to some degree to the ending of the controls on credit expansion in 1971. Moreover, there were strong feedback effects from the level of interest rates on the demand for money itself. The target for sterling M_3 had to be persistently increased, which brought the procedure into disrepute.

In these early days of Thatcher's rule, the attitude to the exchange rate was that it was simply another price, and that having determined the stance of fiscal and monetary policy, the exchange rate should go where it will. Over time, this attitude to the nominal exchange rate shifted, as indeed it did in the United States after the severe appreciation of the dollar during this period. The exchange rate and other measures, such as the narrow measure of the supply of money M_0 (notes and coins in circulation), came to be looked at as indicative of the monetary stance. Thus, while underlying principles were clear, to keep the aircraft flying at a sensible level, which were the relevant dials on the instrument panel to look at was a matter of debate. The short run management of nominal expenditure flows presents technical difficulties which in implementation are always likely to require the exercise of considerable judgement.

In broad terms, following a bad start the Conservative government made progress toward achieving at least its macro-financial goals. Figure 1.9 shows the reduction in the rate of growth of the narrow measure of the supply of money M_0 and the decline in the ratio of the public sector borrowing requirement to gross domestic product between the financial years 1974–80 and 1988–89. Figure 1.9 also shows the course of short term interest rates over this period. Between 1979 and 1987, the inflation rate in Britain fell from nearly 14 per cent in 1979 to 3.5 per cent in 1987.

Figure 1.9
UK interest rates, money supply growth and PSBR (%)

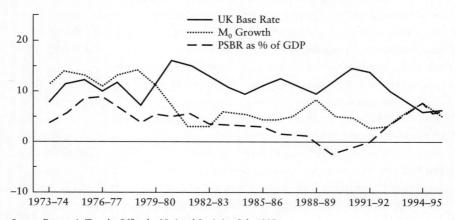

Source: Economic Trends, Office for National Statistics, July 1997

In terms of the real economy, it has already been recorded that, following the 1981 Budget, the United Kingdom economy grew faster than at any time since the early 1960s. In many quarters this performance was dismissed as insignificant because of the benefits that were received over this period from the coming on stream of North Sea oil. However, between 1983 and 1987, as North Sea oil production approached its peak, gross domestic product excluding oil rose marginally faster than the total.

The economic effects of North Sea oil have been much misunderstood. There have been frequent allegations that the benefits of North Sea oil were in some sense wasted. Many believed that its existence provided some sort of new resource base for special capital investment in British industry and a dramatic improvement in economic productivity and efficiency. Such beliefs were part of a mirage, engendered by a failure to distinguish between nominal money and real resources, and a reappearance of the familiar and incorrect argument referred to earlier, that the current account of the British balance of payments has exercised a constraint on British economic growth. This argument was based on the proposition that an improvement in the current account of the balance of payments would enable overall demand to grow faster without difficulty. Such a thesis ignored the impact of North Sea oil flows on the exchange rate.

From an economic point of view, the coming on stream of North Sea oil could be likened to the discovery of gold. The effect on the employment of resources such as labour was specialised and minimal. The major immediate effect was the saving of the foreign exchange needed to finance the previous import bill. But insofar as the economy was relatively fully employed, the only way in which the real income value of the oil could be enjoyed was through overseas expenditure, either on goods or services or on overseas assets. If the economy was deemed not to be at full employment as a result of demand deficiency that could be remedied in familiar ways without any need for North Sea oil. If the economic benefit was secured by additional overseas spending on goods and assets, balance of payments equilibrium would have been maintained at the same level of traded goods (substantially manufactures). However, to the extent that that was not so, and the benefit was accrued in the form of a payments surplus, the real exchange rate had to rise, squeezing out the supply of traded goods that were no longer needed to keep the current account of the balance of payments in equilibrium. If this turned out to be the case, employment could only be maintained by shifting resources out of the trading and into the non-trading sector (basically into domestic services). Over the period 1979–89 the coming of North Sea oil resulted in a clear benefit to the United Kingdom's standard of living. The suggestion that it was in some sense 'wasted' does not stand up to serious scrutiny.

THE RECESSION IN THE NINETIES

After 1988, the growth of the economy slowed sharply as interest rates rose. Ironically, while the economics profession had angrily criticised the Conservative government in 1981 for excessively tight fiscal and monetary policies, the three years, 1986, 1987 and finally 1988, showed an average growth rate of 4.7 per cent, way above anyone's serious estimate of the long term growth capability of the British economy. Indeed, measured in growth terms, it was the fastest three year growth period since the Second World War and quite likely for all time. Interest rates were falling, and the fall in the price of oil brought inflation in Britain down to a level not experienced since 1967. The relaxation of liquidity and interest rates after the stockmarket crash of 1987, coupled with an expansionary budget in 1988, fuelled a dramatic increase in house prices and an acceleration in the inflation rate. Interest rates rose accordingly and by 1990 reached levels not seen since 1980. The housing market collapsed and the United Kingdom economy was again in recession. Once again, too rapid expansion led to the familiar consequences of a significant deterioration in the current account of the balance of payments, the public sector borrowing requirement and the inflation rate.

In the eyes of many, the situation was aggravated by the Conservative government's decision to join the Exchange Rate Mechanism of the European monetary system. For some, the decision to join was wrong in principle, reducing the ability for British monetary policy to be flexible in the face of rising inflation and incipient recession. For others, the argument was simply that the exchange rate of sterling *vis-à-vis* the German mark was too high at the outset, requiring British (and indeed French and Italian) interest rates to reach levels that were fundamentally inconsistent with domestic considerations. There was little doubt that the decision with regard to German reunification was a major shock to the European system, for which the British government could hardly be blamed, other than for failing to foresee the levels at which real interest rates in Germany would have to remain to counterbalance the rise in the Federal deficit as the costs of reunification came home. When the exit of Britain from the system came in 1992, it resulted not only from the level of real interest rates in Germany, but also as a result of the weakness of the dollar. Unlike Germany, the United Kingdom depended to a much greater extent on trade with the United States. It could not stand a major revaluation of the pound against the dollar.

Following the departure from the ERM, the United Kingdom economy began to recover, stimulated by export performance as the nominal exchange rate fell. Interest rates also fell from the peak to levels not seen since the 1960s in 1996. In 1993 unemployment began to fall. Contrary to the prognostications of many, inflation did not rise on the back of a sharp fall in the nominal exchange rate.

BRITAIN'S ECONOMIC PERFORMANCE 1960–95

A recent symposium on Britain's economic performance since 1960 began with the following paragraph:

In 1890, Britain was the largest and most powerful economy in the world. Now a century later, it is not. If you start from the top, there is only one way that you can go: down. Britain's relative decline over the last century is, however, more than a question of mean reversion or of the 'convergence' of growth rates. This has become particularly apparent since 1960 when several similar European economies (most notably Germany and France) have not only caught up with Britain but overtaken her: they have been able to sustain substantially higher growth rates over the post-war period. Further afield Japan and others have also thrived in this period. (Dixon, 1996, p. 170)

A health warning has already been given with regard to the welfare implications of aggregate statistical data. All data are subject to some degree of scepticism, but it is on relatively aggregate measures that most of the criticism of Britain's economic performance rests. Subject to all the qualifications (which also apply in many other areas, including the distribution of income) the gross domestic product per capita is the simplest measure of economic performance we have. Productivity or output per person employed is not necessarily a superior measure of performance since, in theory, improvement could simply be associated with a rise in unemployment which might be viewed negatively. The growth of gross domestic product in itself needs to be treated with care, since its relationship to population growth must be taken into account if some minimal welfare conclusions are to be reached. The level and growth of gross domestic product in China can only be put in perspective by recognising the existence of one billion Chinese people, and growing.

Table 1.1 summarises data with reference to gross domestic product per capita for the G7 countries between 1950 and 1989. The subsequent period to date has been materially affected by the recession of the 1990s. We consider matters at this stage from the point of view of a mythical Man from Mars who appears in 1989 and reviews the history of these economies in those terms since 1950.

Over the period 1950–1989 real income per head in the United Kingdom grew by 250 per cent. In absolute terms, the Man from Mars might have thought this was a satisfactory performance. But from a relative point of view such a performance has been regarded as profoundly disappointing. From the quotation earlier we learn that this is more than a question of 'mean reversion or the convergence of growth rates'. But how much more, might the question now be asked? Since no one has sought to establish par for the course, how can the round be judged? This is not to say that British economic performance over the period might not have been improved, or reasonably expected to be better, issues that come later. But it is to start with some commonsense observations as a prelude to the discussion.

Table 1.2 makes it crystal clear that the significant changes in the relative position of the United Kingdom to the countries listed all took place by 1973. The continued relative decline with regard to Japan was shared by all countries from 1973. It was not confined to the United Kingdom. Arithmetically and not surprisingly therefore, as the data show, only Japan in the G7 countries, and Italy, still only 85 per cent of the British level of gross domestic product in 1973, grew at faster rates. The first point, therefore, is that the major relative decline had taken place before 1973. The second is that the growth of gross domestic product per capita compares unfavourably with most other OECD countries in the period 1973–79. The third is that over the period 1979–89 the United Kingdom outperformed all the G7 countries with the exception of Japan. On the figures the Man from Mars would find it difficult to be so dismissive of the catch-up theory as a significant explanation of Britain's economic performance during the period.

At worst, the Man from Mars might wonder what the furore was about. Clearly, on the numbers in Table 1.2, the USA, Canada, Japan and Switzerland appear by 1989 to enjoy a significantly higher standard of living than the United Kingdom. On the other hand, the United Kingdom standard of living so measured is only marginally below that of Germany and France, and equal or better than Italy, Holland, Austria, Belgium, Denmark and Australia. The interpretation of such a situation as some kind of national economic disaster reflects a mindset of a bygone era, rather than an appreciation of today's economic reality. The bottom line is that as far as the mature economies of the European Union are concerned, standards of living in an aggregate sense are not particularly different. Differences in welfare are however another matter that cannot be settled by aggregate economic data.

The overall conclusion is that from an historical point of view, it is important to draw clear distinctions between the different periods of time, 1960–1973, which has been called the golden age, the 1970s which may be described as the 'years of turbulence', and the 1980s which clearly represent the years of recovery. Each period has specific characteristics that help to explain the behaviour of the aggregate economy. As we shall see in Chapter 2, it is difficult to find any overarching explanation of the change in Britain's relative economic position in the world since 1945.

CHAPTER 2

ECONOMIC GROWTH

INTRODUCTION

The history of the United Kingdom economy in terms of the behaviour of gross domestic product per capita shows clearly that its relative position changed significantly between 1950 and 1989. The major part of the decline occurred between 1950 and 1973 and the annual growth rate, after this period, is not materially different from that experienced by its European neighbours. However, such an aggregate measure of economic performance leaves something to be desired as an indicator of changes in the welfare of the economy over this period.

The history also suggests that a large part of the so-called decline between 1950 and 1973 was inevitable. Peer group countries such as Germany and France had major opportunities for 'catch up'. While there are well known arguments about the extent to which technology is a public good, it is difficult to see *a priori* why it should have been reasonable to expect the United Kingdom to have maintained its relative advantage in the 1950s and 1960s. The period of the 1970s and the 1980s is another matter which will be discussed below.

To take the matter further requires us to consider in more detail the factors that may have affected the performance of the United Kingdom economy over the period 1950–1989. For the moment at least the recession of the early 1990s and subsequent effects are left on one side. At the back of one's mind it is important to be clear about the nature of the questions that one is examining. Moreover, it should be clear that in this chapter we continue, as in our historical review, to focus on the performance of Britain relative to its OECD peers of which the G7 countries are an important sub-set. As discussed in Chapter 3, it is arguable that there are many different issues that arise in comparing the performance of the mature economies of the world with developments in South East Asia and the so-called Emerging Markets. It is reasonable to start with the presumption that, in the case of the mature economies at least, there is considerable homogeneity in many respects with regard to economic resources and their potential use. This is not to say of course that there may not be some significant differences between them. Indeed, that is what we propose to examine.

The discussion of the economic performance of the United Kingdom since 1950 invariably starts from the assumption that it has been poor and needs explaining. In so doing it is important and difficult to distinguish between the proximate and the ultimate drivers of such performance. Clearly in the period 1950–1973, from an arithmetic point of view, relative decline was accompanied by much lower growth in overall productivity. At the next stage one asks why this was the case. Emphasis on 'catch up' relies on the fact that such differences reflect different distances from the technological frontier of economic activity. A common presumption, as we shall see, is that relative productivity growth was slow because of inadequate investment. If so, why was investment inadequate? The search for the ultimate drivers of the growth of aggregate productivity is driven back yet another step.

It is also important to distinguish between trying to determine the causes of perceived relative decline and the question of whether, had policy or circumstances been different, actual performance would have been improved. While in the 1980s the overall, relative performance of the British economy improved significantly compared with the 1950s and 1960s, this was due to a fall in peer growth rates, rather than any absolute improvement in Britain. However, there is a *prima facie* argument that the conduct of macroeconomic policy after the two oil price shocks, and in the latter part of the 1980s could, with hindsight at least, have been substantially improved, moderating the loss of output that resulted from the subsequent recessions. A less critical view of Britain's relative economic performance between 1950 and 1973 than is generally taken, still leaves significant scope for what might have improved it.

In this chapter (bearing in mind the focus on mature economies, the OECD peer group), we consider, first, the current state of thinking among economists that tries to explain why rates of growth are what they are. We follow this up with a more detailed consideration of a number of specific ideas that have been used to explain Britain's relative economic performance and to suggest ways of improving it. These include the impact of taxation and public expenditure on growth, the role of investment, the character of the financial system, industrial relations, and the effects of fiscal and monetary policy on economic fluctuations. Attention is deferred until the next chapter to what many regard as the heart of such weaknesses that the British economy may have, namely the performance of its manufacturing industry which has been linked to the consequences of weaknesses in the current account of the balance of payments. And finally we look at some of the issues raised by the development of human capital and the role of education and training.

THE ECONOMICS OF GROWTH

The simplest starting point for an analysis of the process of economic growth is the observation that output, or the growth of outputs, is related to the level of inputs or the rate of growth of inputs, or factors of production to use the jargon. The relationship between output and factors of production is defined as the production function, or the aggregate production function if we are looking at the economy as a whole. Typically, in describing the growth of modern industrial economies, land is ignored as a factor of production. The key factors of production are taken at the outset to be physical capital and the input of labour.

An early approach to understanding the growth process took the form of what was known as 'growth accounting'. If it were possible to measure the behaviour of output over sufficiently long periods of time, together with the time path of the factors of production, it was possible to try to allocate the increases in output to the various factors. This kind of analysis in the United States reached its peak with the work of Denison (1962).

The interesting thing about Denison's analysis of the behaviour of output in the United States over long periods of time was that a relatively small proportion (less than half) of the increase in output could be attributed to increases in the volume of factors of production. The remainder or the 'residual', as it was known, that was left behind reflected an increase in the productivity of the factors of production – taking capital and labour together, an increase in total factor productivity. This increase in total factor productivity, or the efficient use of productive resources, came to be regarded as something called 'technical progress'. Various studies attempted to explain this 'residual' or 'technical progress' relating it to such factors as education, research and development, and patent data. As recorded by Nicholas Stern:

> We seem to have too many theories claiming property rights in the unexplained residual, and have no reassurance that any of them separately or together really capture what is going on. Just as worrying is that they omit many issues which are probably crucial to growth in the medium term including economic organization and the social and physical infrastructure. (Stern, 1991, p. 131)

This aggregate production function that we have described was incorporated into what became known as the neo-classical theory of economic growth, best exemplified by the seminal work of Robert Solow (Solow, 1956, for which he received a Nobel Prize). To the supply side of the economic system, as represented by the production function, Solow added two things, a given rate of saving out of income, which in equilibrium determined the investment ratio, together with a given rate of population growth, which added to (or subtracted from) the supply of labour. Technical progress or the rate of increase of total factor productivity was assumed to be given, or in the jargon, exogenous. Full employment was assumed to hold and the result of the model was to define an equilibrium growth path to which the economy would tend at the aggregate level, which was a perfectly competitive equilibrium.

Despite its simplicity, this model of the growth process for a given economy generates a number of very specific predictions about economic behaviour. It predicts that, irrespective of the starting point (the so-called initial conditions), given its rate of saving, the rate of technical progress, and the rate of population growth (which are all parameters in the model), the economy will converge to a steady rate of growth of per capita income. The higher the rate of saving, the higher the steady state level of income, and the higher the rate of population growth, the converse. The steady state rate of growth of income per person depends only on the rate of technical progress. It does not depend on the rate of saving or population growth. In the steady state the rate of return on capital will remain roughly constant while the real wage of labour will rise at the rate of technical progress as the average rate of labour productivity also rises.

At a first pass fairly simple empiricism might suggest that this model has some relevance to our understanding of the growth process. Suppose that we focus on a set of countries for whom population growth is relatively low, or at least differences between the countries are not that great, and while there may be differences in savings ratios, those differences are not dramatic. If the production functions that face those countries are also similar, then it would be reasonable to conclude that whatever the starting points of the individual countries they would eventually tend to converge. On the face of it, as we have seen this has tended to be a pattern in the way in which growth rates in the European peer group have behaved since 1950. For the G7 countries (including of course the United Kingdom) as we have seen growth rates have been converging from the end of the 1960s onwards.

This raises the important question of what we mean by 'convergence'. It should be noted that the model we are discussing does not, in general, predict convergence in growth rates. Taking a wide sample of countries in the world at large does not suggest strong convergence. Poor countries for example do not generally grow faster than rich countries, although some of them have, with the result that they are no longer poor. The model implies convergence only when the parameters for the different countries are such as to imply similar steady state growth behaviour. The model itself implies what is described as conditional convergence with the particular country steady state depending on its own parameters. Nevertheless, as discussed in the last chapter and briefly above, there is substantial *prima facie* evidence that a process similar to that implied by the neo-classical model broadly fits the behaviour of the United Kingdom peer group since 1950, although the question as to what constitutes a good fit may continue to be contentious (see the excellent discussion in Crafts, 1993, and Crafts, 1995).

Be that as it may, there are two major issues that in different ways make people uncomfortable with the model described as a description of the growth process. They have one thing in common, namely a feeling of unhappiness with the somewhat stark policy conclusions that the neo-classical model suggests. First, as remarked by Robert Lucas (Lucas, 1988), given that such a major role is assigned to 'technical progress', there is little room for any other explanations of growth over time, and growth between countries which emphasise other factors. The conclusion it suggests (which is not necessarily wrong) is that 'The growth rate of an entire economy is not an easy thing to move around.' (Lucas, 1988, p. 13.)

There is no link established between economic policy and the rate of 'technical progress'. Secondly, there is no role in the description of the process for cultural, social and organisational issues, which may be summed up in Abramovitz's expression (Abramovitz, 1986) as 'social capability'. Again, this may be a matter that turns out to be more important in dealing with countries with wider growth and cultural diversity than exist between the United Kingdom and the OECD peer group.

Recent economic theory has tried to deal with the first of these issues by focusing on explaining the generation of 'technical progress' as the result of rational economic decision making. As described by Nicholas Crafts, the new so-called theory of 'endogenous growth':

> … emphasises the role of profit-motivated investments in discovering new products and/or processes. This has involved the development of growth models of an aggregate economy in which at the micro-level production takes place under conditions of imperfect competition which allows the appropriation of profits to cover the fixed costs of research and development. The key feature of these models is that growth depends on the incentives to invest in improving technology. (Crafts, 1995, p. 2)

Once it is postulated that 'technical progress' can itself be created by investment, on the face of it this opens up possibilities for policy intervention in the growth process such as policies to encourage innovation which did not exist before. A leading exponent of 'endogenous' growth theory, the American economist Paul Romer, has gone so far as to suggest that it is this possibility that has generated criticism of endogenous growth theory:

I am frequently warned that the models I use and the results I describe could be used to justify bad government policies. (Romer, 1995, p. 315)

There is an analogy here with the issue of comparative advantage which we shall discuss in Chapter 3. As noted by Crafts, however, the empirical support for this new model remains weak. Moreover:

The policy implications of endogenous growth models include support for subsidising various forms of capital accumulation because social returns will exceed private returns for pursuing infant industry policies and for intervening to combat market failure. All these could, of course, be seen as hallmarks of British industrial policy during the 'picking winners' years of the 1960s and 1970s when relative economic decline was at its most virulent. (Crafts, 1993, p. 38)

The second issue focuses on both the social and institutional framework that has been summed up in the phrase 'social capability'. Both these issues may be linked. A particular criticism of the neo-classical growth model emanating from Romer (Romer, 1995) is that it assumes that technology is a public good in that it is shared by all. As presented by Gregory Mankiw (Mankiw, 1995) this simply means that a given group of countries is faced with the same production function. For Mankiw:

To say that different countries have the same production function is merely to say that if they had the same inputs they would produce the same output. Different countries with different levels of inputs need not rely on exactly the same processes for producing goods and services. (Mankiw, 1995, p. 281)

The reason for this is fairly obvious, namely while in principle technology and production capability in a knowledge sense may be shared, cultural and institutional factors may impede its exploitation. In this context, it is interesting to observe the conclusion drawn by Crafts as a result of a close review of the European experience:

This scrutiny of recent historical research strongly suggests that policy choices and institutional arrangements were central to the Golden Age ... Economists need to take the 'social capability' aspects of growth more seriously. (Crafts, 1995, p. 2)

The introduction of social, cultural and organisational factors into the analysis of the growth process leads, among other things, to a consideration of the institutional framework, which is not captured by the economic models of the kind we have described. The quality of management and the nature of industrial relations in Britain have been frequently cited as partial explanations of the perceived lack of economic performance. This has led, in many cases, to the advocacy of institutional change, for example, in the legal framework of industrial relations. It also leads in some cases to a demand for sweeping changes in the institutions of the financial system and/or changes in the role of the civil service in decision making.

The bottom line of all this is that, from economic and institutional analysis of the growth process, there does not emerge any widely agreed model of that process or agreement about the economic policies that seek to improve growth performance. It is small wonder therefore that there is a continuous search for the Holy Grail that will reveal all – more specifically there is a search for the OBE of growth, the One Big Explanation, that will cut through the Gordian knot of economic explanations. Before returning to an evaluation of growth performance in Britain since 1950, we shall review the most important of these *seriatim*.

THE ROLE OF PUBLIC EXPENDITURE

Attempts have been made periodically to discriminate between the growth performance of individual countries by reference to comparative levels of public expenditure. After coming to power in 1979, Margaret Thatcher's government issued a White Paper on public spending that attributed slow growth in Britain to an excessively large share of gross domestic product attributable to government spending. The election of Ronald Reagan to the presidency in the United States prompted the idea that by cutting taxes and public spending more control over spending would be returned to private hands. In Britain, the idea that the size of the public sector was inimical to growth was promoted in the well known book by Bacon and Eltis (Bacon and Eltis, 1977), *Too Few Producers*.

In Chapter 5 we will review more generally the issues of public expenditure, and the relationship between the private and public sectors. Here we are concerned with the more focused issue of the size of the public sector and its relationship to the growth process. To begin with we must define what we mean by public expenditure.

In terms of the measurement of the national accounts, government expenditure reflects the direct claims of government for productive resources and for goods and services. Such claims can be divided between public consumption and public investment. Comparative data for peer group countries in total are difficult to interpret since differences in public investment also reflect differences in the ownership of assets, both between countries and for individual countries over time – the impact of privatisation for example.

A second measure of public expenditure takes into account what the statisticians define as transfers between one group of the population and another, for example old age pensions, unemployment benefit, subsidies of one kind and another and interest payments on the national debt. These payments do not correspond to the production of any form of output. Increases in pensions, for example, paid out of an increase in taxes, take money out of some people's pockets and puts it into others. On the face of it, such a transfer does not affect the government's claim on real resources, although, as we shall see later, such transfers will not necessarily have neutral effects on the behaviour of real output and the rate of growth. When measured in this way of course, the size of public expenditure relative to the gross domestic product is generally substantially increased. It is this larger figure that has most relevance to the behaviour of government borrowing and to the tax policies that the government pursues.

The data set out in Table 2.1 include all three components of public expenditure, consumption, investment and transfers. There are three aspects of the size of the public sector that are relevant to the present discussion, the direct impact of government spending on real resources, the possible disincentive effects on growth caused by the required tax burden and the consequences of financing government expenditure other than by taxation. As far as the United Kingdom is concerned, the initial question is whether the behaviour of public spending over the period 1960–1995 has deprived the private sector of real resources. When put in these terms, the answer to this question is 'no'. This is not to be confused with the proposition that the overall public expenditure ratio, including transfer payments, may not have been excessive from time to time as defined and discussed later in Chapter 5 and again in Chapter 7.

In the first place, as a generalisation, across the peer group there is only weak evidence that 'high' or 'low' ratios of public expenditure to gross domestic product are associated with 'low' and 'high' rates of growth respectively. The data plotted in Figure 2.1 show only a weak correlation between the two. Secondly, the idea of 'too few producers' since the original Bacon and Eltis analysis does not appear to be supported by the behaviour of the data on employment. The suggestion that too much labour was employed in the supposedly 'unproductive' public sector rather than the 'productive' private one is impossible to reconcile with the rise in the unemployment rate since the late 1970s, and the fall in the ratio of public sector employment. Indeed, since then, employment in manufacturing industry has fallen by over 40 per cent. Moreover, while there was some increase in public sector employment in the 1970s, this was largely attributable to the increased employment of women.

Table 2.1
Shares of investment and total outlays of government in GDP and annual rates of growth, 1960–1995

Country	% Change in GDP	Investment as % of GDP	Total outlays of Government as % of GDP
USA	2.9	18.3	32.5
Japan	5.5	31.0	27.0
Germany	2.9	22.3	44.1
France	3.3	22.2	44.7
Italy	3.4	22.6	43.0
UK	2.3	17.9	41.4
Canada	3.8	21.9	39.7
Australia	3.8	24.1	31.7
Austria	3.3	23.8	45.3
Belgium	3.0	19.9	50.1
Denmark	2.8	20.6	48.0
Ireland	4.4	20.4	42.1
Netherlands	3.2	22.4	51.5
Spain	4.1	22.9	32.1
Sweden	2.5	20.7	52.8
Switzerland	2.3	25.5	26.9

Source: OECD Historical Statistics 1960–95, Paris, 1997

If the size of the public sector is primarily determined by the ability to raise revenue from taxation, in theory at least, high levels of taxation imposed on the private sector (and those employed in the public sector) might inhibit effort, enterprise and saving to the detriment of the growth rate.

With regard to taxation, hard empirical evidence is difficult to come by. Critics of the view that, over the period under discussion as a whole, growth was seriously reduced as the result of high taxes point to the fact that 'slow' growth in Britain as a phenomenon pre-dates the substantial increases in taxation of the Second World War and after. Moreover, while the 1950s and 1960s were a period of relative decline, in absolute terms it was also a period of the fastest rate of growth that the British economy has experienced. It is a fact, however, that clearly since that time the tax paying public has become much enlarged and that the payment of taxes is something that affects the behaviour of the community at large. On the face of it there is a popular view that taxation has been excessive, despite the beliefs that there are others who should pay more.

Figure 2.1
GDP growth and public expenditure

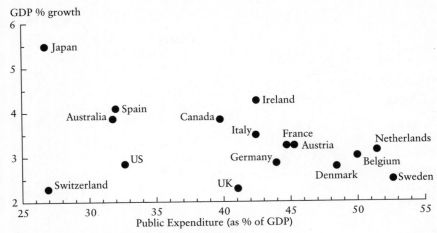

Source: OECD Historical Statistics 1960–95, Paris, 1997

In considering the effects of taxation, it is important to distinguish between the forms in which taxation is raised, the total burden of taxation and the relationship between the average and the marginal tax rates. By international standards, Britain prior to 1980 had raised a larger than average proportion of her taxation in the form of income taxation and it was arguable that greater incentives would result from a shift from direct to indirect taxation. Indeed, it is often argued that in an ideal world some form of expenditure tax is highly desirable. However, in terms of the total proportion of income taken in taxes, the United Kingdom is by no means at the top of the league. It is possible to argue that highly taxed countries such as Sweden and Denmark have shown relatively slow growth since 1973. But on balance it is difficult to conclude, categorically, or to quantify its effect, that the overall burden of taxation in the United Kingdom, relative to other countries, has been excessive.

Some critics have sought to dismiss the effects of tax cuts on incentives, particularly for the higher paid, on the grounds that there is no evidence of short run changes in behaviour. People at the top neither work harder nor do they work better. This is to ignore the key point, that the structure of taxation has in principle important long term effects on the allocation of resources between different kinds of occupation and attitudes to risk taking. It is a familiar complaint of British industry that many able people in the 1950s and the 1960s were not interested in industrial employment, but chose to seek rewards in what appeared to be more status giving jobs in the higher reaches of the public service and the professions. In addition, it is difficult not to believe that the high marginal rates of income tax before 1979 were a disincentive to enterprise, but it is clear that the precise nature of the impact remains highly speculative. Finally, the long term effects of a tax system that clearly discourages economic activity cannot be measured in terms of lost output alone. When the tax system begins to make rogues out of honest men, the specifics of the system must become suspect.

There is a saying that all government spending is paid for out of taxation, it is simply a matter of what form the taxation takes. Other than raising revenue in the form of conventional taxes, governments have the special privilege of creating money to meet their obligations or to borrow. When money is created, it is argued, governments appropriate resources by means of an inflation tax – the one tax it is often remarked that parliament does not vote for. If governments borrow excessively, interest rates tend to rise to the disadvantage of the private sector whose spending plans are 'crowded out'.

As we shall see in Chapter 4, the post-war legacy of Keynes was the belief that the economy could be tuned to produce full employment by the use of fiscal policy. Fiscalisation stood at the centre of stabilisation policy. As we saw in the last chapter, prior to 1973, the British economy was subjected to phases of 'stop-go', about every five years. Rising unemployment was countered by tax cuts and increases in public spending, mainly the latter. On each occasion, a deterioration in the current account of the balance of payments added to a commitment to maintain the sterling/dollar parity led to these expanding phases being put into reverse. While these 'stop-go' episodes hardly did anyone any good, the discipline effectively imposed by the Bretton Woods system prevented excess, and as can be seen in Table 2.2 the fiscal deficit of the United Kingdom prior to 1970 was kept in reasonably good order.

With the formal end to the Bretton Woods system in 1971, the discipline it had imposed ended. Governments generally launched into major monetary and fiscal expansion, world output grew rapidly and commodity price inflation took off. The United Kingdom led the charge. On top of this major expansion, the real price of oil rose dramatically. OPEC I had arrived. The expansion of public spending was combined with a floating exchange rate in the United Kingdom to deal with the side effects of a deteriorating current account of the balance of payments.

Table 2.2
UK government expenditure and PSBR as a percentage of GDP

	GGE(X)[a]	GGE[b]	PSBR
1965–66	36.5	37.75	2.75
1966–67	38	39.5	3
1967–68	41.5	43.25	5
1968–69	40	41.5	0.75
1969–70	39.25	41	−1.25
1970–71	39.5	41.25	1.5
1971–72	40	41.75	2.75
1972–73	39.75	41.5	3.75
1973–74	41.5	43.5	6
1974–75	46.75	48.75	9
1975–76	47.25	49.25	9.5
1976–77	44.75	46.75	6.5
1977–78	41.5	43	3.5
1978–79	42.25	44	5.5
1979–80	42.5	44	4.75
1980–81	44.75	46.5	5.25
1981–82	45.5	47	3.75
1982–83	45.5	47.25	3.25
1983–84	44.75	46.25	3.25
1984–85	45.25	46.25	3
1985–86	43.25	44.25	1.5
1986–87	42.25	42.75	1
1987–88	40.5	40.75	−0.75
1988–89	38	37.75	−3
1989–90	38.25	38.75	−1.5
1990–91	39	39.25	0
1991–92	41	40.75	2.25
1992–93	43.5	43	6
1993–94	43.5	43.25	7
1994–95	42.75	42.5	5.25
1995–96	42	42.5	4
1996–97	40.5	41	3

[a] general government expenditure excluding privatisation receipts
[b] general government expenditure
Note: figures have been rounded

Source: Financial Statement and Budget Report, 1996–97, 5 November

The impact of OPEC I pitched the peer group countries and the United Kingdom into recession. In Britain, the incoming Labour government in 1974 was still, as were the Conservatives, committed to the perceived principles of Keynes in developing policies. However, in addition the Labour government was effectively committed to underwrite the real level of expenditure in the public sector. The whole burden of adjustment in the early stages of OPEC I fell on the private sector, until the 1976 cuts in public spending described in the last chapter. As also recorded, many of the cuts were soon restored and the economy was off to the races before being hit on the head again by the second round of oil price increases, OPEC II.

In the sense that there was a commitment to maintaining the real level of public expenditure in the 1970s at the expense of the private sector, it could be regarded as excessive. Certainly, macroeconomic policy was highly destabilising throughout the 1970s, and the commitment to expanding and then maintaining the real levels of government spending was a significant contribution to the underperformance of the United Kingdom economy during this period.

The principal conclusion that emerges from this discussion is that there is little evidence that the public sector pre-empted the more effective employment of economic resources over the period as a whole. As far as the incidence of taxation is concerned, its impact is difficult to measure and one's judgement of by how much economic performance might have been improved remains justified only on *a priori* grounds. This is not to say that it may not have been significant, but simply to reassert that empirically based judgement is difficult.

However, there is a strong case for arguing that during the 1970s at least, if not during other periods, either before 1973 or after 1979, the commitment to maintaining real levels of public spending at the expense of the private sector resulted in a level of real government spending that could be described as excessive. Damage to the rate of economic growth occurs when the gap between the political markets that generate commitments to the public by political parties, and economic markets that must deliver reality rather than promises, becomes too wide. It is at such moments, as lucidly explained by Peter Jay some years ago (Jay, 1976), that matters go wrong. In most cases, the result of this disequilibrium is inflation as political parties are afraid to raise taxation and resort to more dubious ways to finance their promises such as the creation of money and excessive borrowing. The bottom line at this stage is that it is probably more important to worry about how government spending is to be financed than to focus on the particular significance of the level itself.

INVESTMENT AND THE FINANCIAL SYSTEM

There is no question, that to achieve sustained economic growth requires investment in physical and intangible assets (such as human capital) in such proportions as may be appropriate to the development of technology and ideas at the time. In the short run, improvements in productivity and so an increase in the observed rate of economic growth may come about simply as the result of a reorganisation of the way in which existing resources are used. Such reorganisational changes will not necessarily, as is often implied (e.g. Haskel and Kay, 1991), be of a one-off nature. They may lead to a sustained ability to generate productivity improvements. However, it is reasonable to suppose as a starting point that sustainable economic growth will require capital accumulation, although the nature of that accumulation must be carefully considered. Statements to the effect that economy A has had too low a rate of investment and needs to increase it are virtually meaningless without a great deal of clarification of the kind considered below. The character of the investment not simply its volume becomes important. This is particularly the case when investment is considered in the context of the new endogenous theories of growth which emphasise the importance of the growth of more intangible assets – particularly the development and transmission of knowledge.

Moreover, three other issues should be recognised at the outset of any discussion of the role of investment in the growth process. The first is simply that while capital accumulation is almost certainly a necessary condition for sustained economic growth, it is equally certainly not sufficient. Incentives for business to invest at a higher rate offer no guarantee that such investment will be made in productive and profitable activities, rather than leading to the subsidisation of low quality products and inefficient processes. In the kind of economic model of the growth process described earlier, there is little scope for formally incorporating entrepreneurial failure and managerial inefficiencies, although the new theories of endogenous growth emphasise the development of ideas and innovation. Statistics concerning simply the volume of investment and its effects on growth must be carefully examined if they are to tell us anything about reality.

This leads us to the second issue, namely that of the productivity of investment as contrasted with its volume. The volume of investment required to sustain a given rate of economic growth clearly depends on its quality, or productivity. As a matter of arithmetic, growth rates of two countries with identical ratios of investment to gross domestic product may differ very substantially as the result of differences in capital productivity. The interaction of quantity and quality is of major importance in assessing the impact of investment on the rate of economic growth.

Finally, a further difficulty in evaluating the role of investment in the growth process stems from the problem of causality. The rate of investment has specific effects on the behaviour of capacity and output, but is clearly also affected by the rate of growth of the economy itself. In a wider sense the question is to what extent we can regard the rate of capital accumulation as an independent variable of the economic system. Insofar as investment is simply the medium through which ideas about new goods and economic processes are translated into physical fact, the ultimate driver of the growth process lies elsewhere in the generation of such ideas. On this interpretation it is on this process, as suggested by endogenous growth theory, that attention should be focused rather than the volume of investment *per se*.

Taking these considerations into account, it is not very surprising that, beginning at the most aggregate level, the relationship between investment ratios and rates of economic growth for what we have called the United Kingdom OECD peer group is not that strong. Rates of growth and investment ratios for the selected countries are given in Table 2.1 and plotted in Figure 2.2. The investment ratio given here is simply the ratio of gross fixed capital formation to the gross domestic product. This is, in itself, a somewhat narrow definition of capital formation, if we are to take note of the considerations raised by the new theories of economic growth. Physical capital is only part of the growth story. There is no attempt to incorporate investment in human capital, while there is often a lack of consistency in the treatment of research and development expenditure, in some cases being capitalised and others written off as a current expense.

If (as in many other examples) we exclude Japan as a flier in the sample, the ability of these aggregate investment ratios to explain differences in economic growth rates is, *prima facie*, very limited. At this level, a crude measure of capital productivity at the margin is obtained by dividing the growth rate by the investment ratio. This demonstrates the considerable variation in the apparent quality of investment as so measured between the countries listed.

Returning to the specifics of the impact of the behaviour of investment in the United Kingdom and its consequences for economic growth, it is convenient to position the discussion in the context of a widely held thesis as to Britain's investment performance and its financing (examples are Hutton, 1995 and Caborn, 1996).

The starting point is the assertion that (at the time of writing) the United Kingdom is faced with a crisis, based on a failure to be 'competitive'. The economic standing of the nation is said to have plunged to a new low. Unless

Figure 2.2
GDP growth and investment

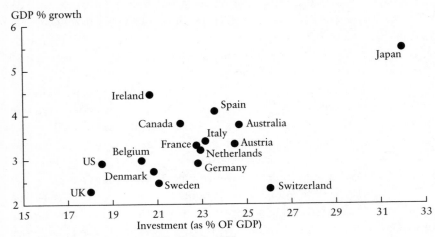

Source: OECD Historical Statistics, 1960–95, Paris, 1997

the structural and cultural weaknesses of the society are addressed, the situation will worsen.

This decline in competitiveness is attributed primarily to a relatively low rate of investment in the United Kingdom. This low rate of investment, in turn, is attributable to the performance of the British financial system. Three aspects of the financial system are then taken to task to explain why the system has failed the nation. The first is the idea that so-called bank financed systems such as Germany, in particular, and Japan have provided for the needs of industry better, so facilitating higher rates of investment and growth. The second idea is that a more equity based system has been dominated by the 'short termism' of both banks and fund managers in Britain who demand higher returns over shorter periods than their counterparts in their peer group (with the notable exception of the United States and the other Anglo-Saxon countries). The third idea is that this 'short termism' has been coupled with an excessive desire for dividend payments. To quote Richard Caborn, the main reason for this low rate of investment has been that:

> ... the availability of income dedicated for investment continues to be squeezed by the relentless pressure for higher and higher dividend growth. (Caborn, 1996)

The general question of competitiveness is taken up in the next chapter. Here we confine the discussion to the history of British investment behaviour

Table 2.3
Investment ratios and % growth performance (excluding residential construction)

	1960–1973		1973–79		1979–89		1960–95	
	Investment Ratio	Growth Rate	Investment Ratio	Growth Rate	Investment Ratio	Growth Rate	Investment Ratio	Growth Rate
Australia	20.2	5.2	18.0	2.8	19.1	3.3	18.8	3.8
Austria	19.3	4.9	19.3	3.0	17.3	2.1	18.6	3.3
Belgium	16.5	4.9	15.6	2.3	13.8	1.9	15.2	3.0
Canada	16.7	5.4	15.5	4.2	15.1	3.1	15.9	3.8
Denmark	16.5	4.3	15.3	1.9	13.5	1.8	14.9	2.8
France	16.3	5.4	15.6	2.7	14.6	2.1	15.5	3.3
Germany	17.3	4.3	14.4	2.4	14.3	2.0	15.7	2.9
Italy	16.6	5.3	17.0	3.5	15.3	2.4	15.8	3.4
Japan	26.5	9.7	24.2	3.5	23.4	3.8	25.0	5.5
Netherlands	19.8	4.8	15.7	2.6	14.6	1.9	16.8	3.2
Sweden	16.8	4.1	15.9	1.8	14.7	2.0	15.4	2.5
UK	14.6	3.1	15.3	1.5	13.8	2.4	14.2	2.3
USA	13.5	4.0	14.4	2.6	14.4	2.4	13.6	2.9

Source: OECD Historical Statistics, 1960–1995, Paris, 1997

and the alleged problem of its financing. As can be seen from Table 2.1 for the period as a whole, in percentage terms the ratio of total investment to gross domestic product was significantly lower than in other countries in the peer group, with the exception of the United States. Japan clearly stands out with an investment ratio for the period as a whole that no other country comes close to matching and it is reasonable for some purposes to look at behaviour excluding Japan from calculations.

The performance of the United Kingdom relative to other countries in the group, notably Germany, is affected significantly by the behaviour of investment in residential construction. As a first pass, it is reasonable to exclude residential construction on the grounds that to a large extent it reflects a rising standard of living resulting from, rather than contributing to, economic performance. The resulting numbers and the associated growth rates as set out in Table 2.3 reflect investment in business activities and government investment other than in residential construction.

Table 2.4
Effect on growth of a 1% change in the investment ratio*

Country	1960–73	1973–79	1979–89	1960–95
Australia	0.26	0.15	0.17	0.20
Austria	0.25	0.15	0.12	0.18
Belgium	0.29	0.15	0.14	0.20
Canada	0.32	0.27	0.20	0.24
Denmark	0.26	0.12	0.13	0.19
France	0.33	0.17	0.14	0.21
Germany	0.25	0.17	0.14	0.18
Italy	0.32	0.20	0.16	0.22
Japan	0.37	0.14	0.16	0.22
Netherlands	0.24	0.17	0.13	0.19
Sweden	0.24	0.11	0.14	0.16
UK	0.21	0.10	0.17	0.16
USA	0.29	0.18	0.17	0.21

* investment defined as gross fixed capital formation less residential construction

Source: OECD Historical Statistics 1960–95, Paris, 1997

When residential construction is excluded, and while the United Kingdom ratio for the period as a whole is second from bottom to the United States, the differences with the peer group are materially reduced. Moreover, with the notable exception of the United States, Australia and Japan, all countries between the golden age and the 1980s experienced significant falls in their investment ratios. In the 1980s, for example, the German ratio fell to 82 per cent of its golden age period compared with 95 per cent for the United Kingdom. As can be seen the convergence of growth rates in the peer groups has been accompanied by convergence in the investment ratios toward the United Kingdom and the United States.

The key distinction between the quality and the quantity of investment was drawn earlier. The productivity of physical capital assets is a critical factor in the growth process. Assessment of economic performance and capability must, therefore, take into account the organisation and management of assets, not simply the behaviour of volumes. In Table 2.4 the ratio of the growth rates of individual countries to their investment ratios provides a crude first pass at some assessment of the effectiveness of investment and the impact of changes in investment ratios (as calculated from Table 2.3) on rates of growth. For the period as a whole, the United Kingdom required a significantly higher ratio of investment to gross domestic product to achieve a given growth rate, but this situation changed significantly over the sub-periods. While this was markedly true in the golden age, in the 1980s only Canada could achieve a given growth rate with a lower ratio than the United Kingdom. By contrast, the performance of the 1970s was truly bad.

Table 2.5
Business sector investment as a percentage of GDP at 1990 prices

Country	1960–67	1968–73	1974–79	1980–89	1990–94
USA	8.8	9.7	10.1	10.9	10.7
Japan	13.7	18.0	15.9	16.8	20.1
Germany	12.9	12.8	11.2	11.7	13.5
France	11.7	13.0	12.0	11.1	11.7
Italy	13.2	12.5	11.3	10.4	10.7
UK	11.3	12.0	12.2	12.5	12.7
Canada	7.3	7.3	8.4	11.0	11.7

Source: OECD Business Sector Database, 1995, No 2

A crude test of the sensitivity of the United Kingdom growth rate to a rise in the investment ratio is simply to multiply an increased ratio by the relevant coefficient in Table 2.4. In the golden age, if the investment ratio had been the same as Germany, the rate of growth is calculated to be 3.6 per cent as against an actual achieved growth rate of 3.1 per cent. If we look at the 1980s, the German investment ratio would result in an estimated growth rate for the United Kingdom of only 0.08 per cent higher, i.e. 2.48 per cent as compared to an actual growth rate of 2.4 per cent. To argue that British economic performance during the 1980s was held back by low investment, as currently measured, is simply not borne out by the facts. This is not to say that had the investment ratio been higher the rate of growth would not have increased. The performance of the 1970s raises other issues, but again on the basis of the numbers in Table 2.3 and Table 2.4, if the investment ratio had matched that of Germany, the observed growth rate should have actually declined. The conclusion is that after 1973 at least, had the United Kingdom's investment ratio matched that of Germany, a rise in the investment ratio in itself, other things equal, would have had a negligible effect on the rate of growth. It is of course arguable that things are not equal, since a higher rate of investment might have itself improved the way in which capital was used, i.e. led to a rise in the coefficients in Table 2.4. But in the British case there was a significant rise between the 1970s and 1980s. At this level, it needs a great deal more to establish the proposition that the United Kingdom had a poor growth rate as the result of a lack of investment.

The figures in Table 2.3 exclude residential construction but include government investment in other than residential construction. Table 2.5 sets out data that exclude such expenditures and, therefore, focuses on private business investment alone as a percentage of gross domestic product for selected countries. The data show that while Britain lagged the peer group countries in the golden age, the ratio of business investment to gross domestic product 1973–89 was exceeded only by Japan. From the discussion later it is clear that such a performance reflected considerable investment in industry and services outside the manufacturing sector. Again the thesis that British economic performance after 1973 was wholly poor as a result of low investment is simply not supportable. The problem of the 1970s as we have seen, and will see again, raises issues other than those of investment as such.

However, from the point of view of investment and its effects on economic growth, the disaster of the 1970s was not related to the volume of investment but to its effectiveness in sustaining growth. As can be seen from Table 2.4, the ratio of the growth rate to the investment ratio halved between the 1960s and the 1970s. Had its effect on the growth rate been the same as in the 1980s, the growth rate would have been increased from 1.5 per cent to 2.6 per cent between 1974 and 1979. Since, as we saw in Table 1.1 in Chapter 1, the United Kingdom per capita growth and actual growth rate were the same, it is reasonable to suppose that the per capita growth rate over the period 1974–79 would have risen accordingly. In that event, only Japan, Italy and Canada in the peer group would have had faster rates of growth per capita over that period.

Leaving aside the question as to whether Britain's economic growth has been significantly and adversely affected by its rate of physical capital accumulation, there is the second question of whether the British financial system is inherently inimical to investment and economic growth.

Harold Rose (1996) has commented:

> Critics of the British financial system argue that the ideal 'bank-dominated' model exists in Germany. It is said to be reinforced by bank representation on German supervisory boards and by German banks' holding of share votes which are regarded as giving them a degree of credit monitoring power and of corporate governance in general that is absent in Britain (and even in Japan) enabling German banks to lend more with confidence. (Rose, 1996, p. 11)

However Edwards and Fischer (1994) argue that these perceptions are largely fictional. The implicit assumption that German firms have used more bank finance than British firms is simply not true. Moreover, German firms of any standing have multiple arrangements with banks as do companies in the United Kingdom, rather than a set of limited long term relationships. Only a minority of German firms have supervisory boards, and as recent history has amply demonstrated, such arrangements have singularly failed to prevent corporate failure or to secure financial support in times of hardship. The banking industry is still less concentrated than in the United Kingdom and the big three banks that receive most publicity in the area of corporate governance probably account for no more than 15 per cent of bank lending to non-banks in Germany. In addition, as Rose points out:

> ... retained profits are the largest source of company finance in all countries. Debt financing comes second: and whereas the ratio of outstanding debt to book equity is undoubtedly higher in Germany than in Britain in the most recent years for which data are available (1986–90) the share of debt in the total finance used by British companies, including gross retained earnings, was actually higher than that of Germany. (Rose, 1996, p. 12)

Historically, the *prima facie* case for so-called 'bank dominated' financial systems has been based on the belief in the superior economic performance of countries where long-term bank lending has been supposedly prevalent. As demonstrated earlier, at the levels of aggregation discussed so far, the performance of Germany over the last twenty years has not been significantly better than that of countries with equity based systems, as in the Anglo-Saxon world. Moreover, the banking system in Japan, by the standards of most other regulatory systems, has suffered severely since the collapse of the financial bubble in Japan in the late 1980s. It is not for nothing that equity is often referred to as the longest term form of finance.

However, the main criticism of the British financial system has been directed toward fund managers and equity markets. The demand for immediate returns, it is said, pressurises business into undertaking investments with relatively short pay back periods (see Richard Caborn above) as they are under pressure to pay 'excessive' dividends.

A thorough account of why this view is mistaken is provided by Marsh (1990). The starting point that embraces 'short-termism' by banks as well as equity investors stems from the assumption that productive investment in the United Kingdom is limited by the availability of finance. The 'short termist' attitude of investors is supposed to lead to excessively high hurdle rates being set by enterprises undertaking investment, a suggestion that sits uneasily with the observed relatively low rates of return on investment (see Figure 2.3). Insofar as hurdle rates in more recent years may have appeared to be excessive, the more likely cause of this has been the attempt to secure protection against unanticipated increases in inflation which have occurred since 1973. There is no evidence that there has literally been a shortage of finance, or that 'short termism' by investors has resulted in the cost of capital to British firms being higher than for their competitors. There is no evidence for such a conclusion. There is no evidence that British companies have recourse to international capital markets on uncompetitive terms compared with companies in other countries. The globalisation of finance has meant that expected risk-adjusted real rates of interest in the leading markets tend to converge and there is no clear evidence that the long-term risk premium, required by equity investors in Britain, has been higher than elsewhere.

In this context of global financial markets, the suggestion that there are serious shortages of finance or an excessive cost of capital for British companies does not hold up. Still less do the arguments justify a demand for restricted dividend payments in the interests of raising the rate of productive investment. The principal objections to so doing were recognised over forty years ago in 1955 by the Royal Commission on Taxation:

> Restricting dividends does not encourage companies to plough back profits, so much as to retain them. ... Whether companies' retained profits are actually invested in the business depends on wider considerations affecting the economic prospect as a whole, including such inducements as may be offered by other tax measures not forming part of the profits tax itself. The mere retention of profits cannot be rated an economic advantage; on the contrary it would better serve the public interest that a company should be encouraged to distribute those profits which it cannot put to fruitful use, in order that there may be a chance that they may be invested elsewhere. Nor is it advantageous for the economy that the level of dividends be held down. Whatever other considerations bear upon the problem,

the market value of shares in industrial and commercial enterprises is artificially depressed and an obstacle placed in the way of raising new capital. (Royal Commission on Taxation, 1955, p. 159)

Moreover, dividend limitation would ultimately protect managements behind walls of cash, reducing competitive pressure from the market place, in many cases encouraging unnecessary take-over activity and low return projects. If it were really the case that investments were held back by a shortage of finance, dividend limitation, with all its distortions, would be very much what economists call in the jargon a 'second best' solution. The 'first best' solution would be to seek to encourage a higher rate of saving in the economy as a whole. A key difference between Britain, Japan and many of the fast growing economies lies in the rates of saving. Fiddling with dividends would be no solution to the problem if the problem exists.

Figure 2.3
Business sector profitability

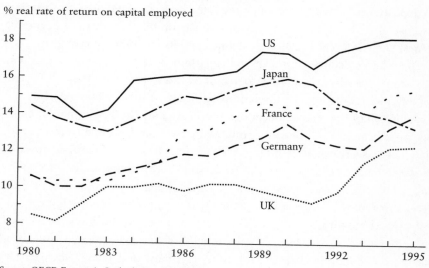

Source: OECD Economic Outlook, December 1996

Unfortunately the attack on the dividends of pension funds introduced in the 1997 July Budget has taken us down this route. The measures introduced to generate additional revenue for the public purse have been justified in the interests of investment and faster economic growth. All the arguments of this section against such a development apply. As described by Graham Searjeant:

The Chancellor excused his £5 billion-a-year grab on dividends paid to pension funds and charities on the grounds that 'the present system encourages companies to pay out dividends rather than reinvest their profits'. In the modern manner, Mr Brown's devastating deterrent to savings was disguised as an incentive to economic growth.

The agenda is an old Labour one. It dates back to the revolution in company tax made in Lord Callaghan's comparable first Labour Budget of 1965 which proved as misguided in its effects as any until Mr Brown's effort on 2 July. The philosophy is simple: dividends bad, investment good. This has only tangential connections to the corporation tax system. (Searjeant, 1997b, p. 29)

SOCIAL CAPABILITY AND HUMAN CAPITAL

A further popular explanation of poor growth performed in the United Kingdom relates to human capital. Economic growth may be defined as the process of creating and exploiting process and product opportunities. The ability to do so depends on the availability of physical and human capital. In turn, the effective use of such resources will depend in part on other features of economic society such as its culture broadly defined and its institutional arrangements.

The relative decline of the United Kingdom since the Second World War has sometimes been ascribed to major cultural characteristics of British society such as the historical relationship between social classes. A common explanation of the relative decline in the 1950s and 1960s was that, in many respects, Britain was a declining imperial power, and coming to terms with that fact was a slow and painful process. Complacency and natural superiority were held to characterise the leadership both economically and politically. The educational system and the class system were supposed to have served Britain well in creating management fit to run an empire, but the values associated with them and the cultural attitudes to business meant that these were not very helpful at generating effective management to lead or sustain an economic charge. Moreover, Germany and Japan, having 'lost' the war, were strongly motivated to 'win' the peace by economic means.

The evidence for claims of this kind is mostly anecdotal and speculative. In many respects there appears to be some truth in the descriptions of British attitudes and social institutions in the 1950s and 1960s. The difficulty, however, lies in translating these views into concrete effects on observed economic performance.

However, in two areas at least, it is important and possible to focus on the specific characteristics of the British institutional and cultural environment and their relevance for growth. First, in the field of industrial relations, and second the development of human capital. As remarked by Oulton (Oulton, 1995) in the context of industrial relations:

> Though it is something of a commonplace amongst financial journalists and economic commentators that trade unions have adversely affected UK economic growth, this proposition is still quite controversial in academic circles. (Oulton, 1995, p. 58)

One might add that it has also been a commonplace among overseas commentators who cite the adversarial nature of British industrial relations compared with a more consensus approach as perceived in Germany and Japan amongst others. While there are important differences in the nature of trade union organisation in this context, this is often seen to characterise industrial relations in the Anglo-Saxon countries in comparison with Continental Europe and Japan.

In the years 1950–1979, trade union membership grew substantially, reaching a peak of 54 per cent of employees at the end of the period. The British system of industrial relations differed in several significant respects from what was to be found in peer group countries. Unlike systems of industry or firm based unions to be found elsewhere, the British system was essentially craft related, resulting in multi-unionism and inter-union conflict in the workplace. There were, of course, large unions in some cases covering a range of occupations. In these unions the practice developed, particularly as seen in the 1970s, of national bargaining followed by individual plant bargaining between management and shop stewards, thereby extending the bases for conflict. Moreover, legally enforceable contracts did not exist and British unions enjoyed a freedom under the law that did not exist elsewhere.

At a theoretical level, the arguments as to why trade unions might affect the growth of productivity largely follow common sense. Productivity improving investment may not be undertaken by management in the absence of any binding commitment from the workforce. It is, therefore, impossible to make a good estimate of the return on the investment, because the return is the subject of further bargaining. This lack of ability to estimate the gains from the investment with some certainty may, therefore, result in an under-provision of investment and so a slower rate of increase in productivity. The argument has been extended by Bean and Crafts (Bean and Crafts, 1996) to a reduction in the incentives for product innovation.

Multi-unionism clearly does open the way to creating difficulties in developing and implementing more efficient management and organisational processes. Agreement has to be general. And it is important to emphasise the extent of bargaining about labour practices and disputes about jurisdiction, rather than focusing on basic rates of pay. For British trade unions, procedures and historical practices have often been as important as money. The situation by the end of the 1970s prompted the view, in many quarters, that managements had either given up, or lost, the right to manage. From a theoretical point of view the position is summed up by Oulton:

> These theoretical arguments suggest the following broad conclusions. Multi-unionism, multi-level bargaining and the absence of binding contracts meant that bargains, which could potentially make all parties better off ... could not be reached by negotiation. (Oulton, 1995, p. 59)

After 1979, the situation began to change in the United Kingdom, and the apparent power of the trade unions declined. In quantitative terms, trade union membership by 1990 had fallen back to its 1960 level of about 40 per cent. Moreover, trade union presence also fell from about two-thirds of all establishments in 1984 to about half in 1990. The explanation of this period of trade union decline is a matter of contention. The Conservative government went down the route of reducing trade union power by legislation. Union recognition rights were restricted, and the closed shop outlawed, together with secondary picketing. The calling of strikes became more difficult as a result of the requirement to hold a ballot.

However, while objections were raised in some quarters to the restriction of trade union powers, others were sceptical about its effects. The fall in trade union participation was ascribed to the impact of the 1979–81 recession and the jump to what appeared to be a higher equilibrium rate of unemployment even after economic recovery. Moreover, the observed increase in productivity growth relative to the 1970s was seen as a one off, upward shift as the result of the shedding of manpower rather than any permanent rise in productivity growth attributable to changes in industrial relations. Further, it is important not to underestimate the importance of the privatisation programme on the relationships between unions and management over a wide range of activities. Industrial actions of the 1970s were dominated by the big public sector unions. But privatisation and the collapse of the coal miners' strike created a new environment that saw the government withdrawing its guarantee from a substantial proportion of economic activity. This factor clearly interacted with legislative change and it is in practice impossible to separate their influences. A change in the climate was signalled by the fact that while almost certainly the effective victory of the miners in 1974 attracted the sympathy of a large proportion of the people, their defeat in 1984 was approved of substantively.

One might add that while the discussion continues, it should be clearly stated that the productivity increases of the early 1980s were not simply the backwash from the recession and the rise in the unemployment rate. As Oulton again remarks:

> When it first became apparent, the productivity improvement was often dismissed as an effect of the 1979–81 recession. In one version, the recession caused a one-off reduction in over-manning. In another version, closures killed off low productivity plants, raising the average productivity of the survivors (the 'batting average' effect). Though both these factors may have played some role, the persistence of the improvement up to and through the most recent recession makes exclusive relevance of such explanations increasingly implausible. (Oulton, 1995, p. 60)

Moreover, as he goes on to point out, productivity increases over the period after 1981 tended to be greater in the industries that had been more heavily unionised in the 1970s.

While, as indicated above, it is a commonplace that industrial relations played some role in the explanation of Britain's growth performance since 1950, it is an equal commonplace that the British education and training system failed the nation over this period. Investment in human capital, like investment in physical capital, has been regarded by many as woefully inadequate.

The initial and substantive problem in reaching conclusions in this matter lies in the definition and measurement of skills and their precise relationships to economic performance. As described below, much of the criticism of education and training in the United Kingdom has stemmed from criticism of the various policy initiatives that have been undertaken over the years, particularly since 1979. The central thrust of such criticisms has been that education and training policies over that period have been left largely to the market place, which has resulted in market failure on a large scale. Since training, in particular, has been seen to become substantially employer based, there is an *a priori* belief that there will be a significant under-investment in training from a social point of view as employers will be unable to appropriate a sufficient proportion of the returns to their investment. Here the 'poaching' argument predominates. A second problem in this argument is that it focuses almost entirely on the supply side of the educational and training question – it does not also focus equally on the behaviour of the demand side.

The so-called 'stylised facts' about education and training in Britain are easy to summarise. The principal difference between the United Kingdom and its peer group lies in the educational qualifications of the lower half of the skill range. For example, while data show that the proportion of managers with degree qualifications is substantially below the peer group, it is at the bottom of the scale that from a formal point of view the inadequacies appear worst. The most striking comparison in Table 2.6 shows that in 1987, 60 per cent of the workforce in United Kingdom manufacturing had no vocational qualifications of any kind, compared with 29 per cent in Germany. The vast majority of the United Kingdom workforce began work with nothing more than a limited number of years of schooling behind them. And since the nature of that schooling is for the most part not concerned with preparing entrants into the workforce for a life of work, it is not surprising that there is *prima facie* concern. However, looking at the workforce as a whole, it is clear that matters are at least moving in the right direction as can be seen in Table 2.7. For the workforce as a whole, the proportion with no qualifications has fallen significantly over the last decade.

Generally speaking, however, the concerns underestimate two factors. The first is the general character of the educational system at all levels; its culture is not geared to meeting the needs of the critics. The second is the perception on the demand side that education and training will not yield an adequate return to those who undertake it. Education, in general, in the United Kingdom has invariably been perceived as a consumption good, that is good if you can get it, but not strictly necessary, unless one enters a profession as such. Unlike the United States for example, education has not traditionally been seen as a ladder to climb up. Neither employers nor the workforce has historically placed great value on the acquisition of skills. In this context, elaborate attempts to increase the supply of education and training have largely come to naught. Until the valuation of skill changes, the supply side policies (on which criticism has mainly been focused) will continue to produce little.

Table 2.6
Vocational qualifications of the manufacturing workforce in UK and Germany, 1987

Highest qualification level	UK %	Germany %
Degree and above	7.2	6.0
Higher intermediate	4.4	8.2
Lower intermediate	28.1	57.2
No vocational qualifications	60.3	28.6

Source: Oulton, 1995

Table 2.7
Highest qualifications held by the UK working age population

Education Group	% of working age population		
	1984	1989	1995
Higher education	12.2	13.5	19.7
A-level or equivalent	21.8	24.0	25.1
O-level or equivalent	15.5	17.7	18.4
Other qualifications	8.7	12.0	15.5
No qualifications	40.0	32.0	21.0
Do not know/did not say	1.8	0.9	0.3

Source: Labour Force Survey, Spring 1996

While as suggested earlier, it is difficult to relate human capital to economic growth in practical terms it is even more difficult to specify in any detail the kinds of skills that are needed in order to promote their delivery. We are left in the unsatisfactory state of intuitively feeling that investment in human capital is of major significance in terms of the growth process, but without knowing what precisely is of importance or what its quantitative impact on the rate of growth might be. The issue has been excellently summed up by Bean and Crafts:

> At present it is quite unclear what has been achieved in terms of human capital formation. Undeniably there have been failings in policy design and incentives to politicians and educational providers to exaggerate the quality of the outputs of the training system have been undoubtedly important. On the other hand real expenditure on training by employers appears to have roughly trebled between 1970 and 1989 and it is difficult to believe that this together with the additional participation in education after 16 does not indicate a higher real accumulation of human capital ... It is possible therefore that the UK has improved its medium term growth prospects somewhat as a result of improved human capital accumulation but this remains to be demonstrated. The quantification of the impact of growth on reforms in this area is highly desirable but not likely to be an easy research project. (Bean and Crafts, 1996, pp. 158–159)

MACROECONOMIC POLICY

As described in Chapter 1, the 1950s and the 1960s in Britain were characterised by what was known as 'stop-go'. The intellectual environment created by John Maynard Keynes suggested that fiscal policy should be used to 'fine tune' the level of demand appropriately to ensure the maintenance of full employment. Fiscal expansion promoted increases in output and employment in the short term, followed by a deterioration in the current account of the balance of payments and some acceleration in the inflation rate. As always, considerable judgement has to be exercised in deciding to what extent these episodes affected the underlying rate of growth during the period. At the time, there were two diametrically opposed points of view. The first argued that had the economy functioned at a somewhat higher rate of unemployment, and hence a lower rate of inflation, economic growth would have been faster. The second took the view that the fluctuations in growth rates that occurred in the 1950s and 1960s were seriously damaging to economic performance, even though they were relatively minor when compared to the 1970s and the early 1990s. The advocates of this view suggested that demand should be run at a consistently high level, and that the pressure to increase real wages would be beneficial thereby forcing companies into investment and technological change.

Whatever the relative merits of the two arguments, it is reasonable to conclude, in the light of what followed in the 1970s and the absolute numbers involved, that the consequences of these policies go nowhere near explaining the significant gap between the growth rate of the United Kingdom and its peer group up to 1973. As suggested in Chapter 1, there are other reasons for anticipating *a priori* the relative decline of Britain that took place. However, the history of the post-war economic years, up to 1960 at least, suggested that, on balance, the policies pursued during the 1950s were destabilising, mainly on the grounds that policy intervention was often mistimed. But the precise consequences of this were not quantified (Dow, 1964).

Moreover, an examination of some of the statistics of the period suggests that, for the most part, the period of the golden age was not one of financial instability compared with episodes in later years. Indeed, financial stability, by and large, was one of its defining features. Table 2.2 sets out data for the United Kingdom fiscal deficit since 1965, which shows that deficits as a percentage of gross domestic product were held reasonably in check. While public expenditure as a proportion of gross domestic product continued to rise, the increase was not out of line with that experienced elsewhere. Moreover, as shown in Table 1.4 in Chapter 1, before the late 1960s and into the early 1970s, the United Kingdom was not a particularly inflationary economy. In the decade of the 1960s, the British inflation rate was marginally below the average for the European Community as it was (based on twelve countries), the United States and Japan. Inflation rates for all countries began to accelerate in the latter part of the 1960s, as a result of monetary expansion, initially led by the United States in its financing of the Vietnam War and followed, after the breakdown of the Bretton Woods system, by Uncle Tom Cobleigh and all (the United Kingdom being in the lead!).

Problems for the United Kingdom began after the devaluation of sterling in 1967 as can be seen in Table 1.4. Inflation performance deteriorated after the devaluation and in the context of what came to be known as the Barber boom. The first oil price shock, OPEC I, was imposed on an inflation performance that was beginning to deteriorate. Fiscal and monetary policy accommodated the shock in real terms rather than seeking to restrain its inflationary consequences. As can be seen in Table 2.2 public expenditure continued to rise as a proportion of GDP, while overall output fell and the public deficit rose.

The behaviour of the relative growth rate is one measure of the volatility of economic behaviour over the periods considered. Figure 2.4 illustrates the behaviour of the real growth rate of gross domestic product in the United Kingdom relative to its European partners. As can be seen by eye the volatility of British output has been greater than that of the European peers. More precisely, the variance of the growth rate of the United Kingdom has also exceeded that of the vast majority of the peer group, although as pointed out by Oulton (Oulton, 1995, p. 63) such a measure suffers from the symmetry with which it treats deviations from both above and below the mean.

Fluctuations in economic activity may have three effects. The first and least interesting is that they may simply time shift output, without affecting the underlying growth rate of potential output. Losses on the downswings are compensated by gains on the upswings. A second effect is that if the recession tends to be longer than the booms, output may be permanently lost although the underlying sustainable growth rate is itself unchanged. Finally, not only may output be permanently lost, so reducing the observed rate of output growth below the underlying rate of growth of potential output, but the underlying rate of growth of output may be itself permanently reduced.

The evidence seems clear that compared to its peer group, the United Kingdom suffered most as the consequence of short booms followed by longer recessions. Recession may be defined as continuing so long as output remains below its previous peak. The length of the recession is then the number of quarters before output equals or exceeds that peak. Taking the period 1970–1994 on a quarterly basis, it is estimated on this definition that in 48 of the 100 quarters the United Kingdom was in recession (Oulton, 1995, p. 65). Germany by contrast was in recession for 21 quarters, the United States for 20, Japan for 14 and France for only 12. Oulton concludes that there is a significant, negative correlation between this measure and rates of economic growth for the countries considered, suggesting that poor cyclical performance had a significant effect on growth rate differentials.

Figure 2.4
UK and European economic growth (annual % change in GDP)

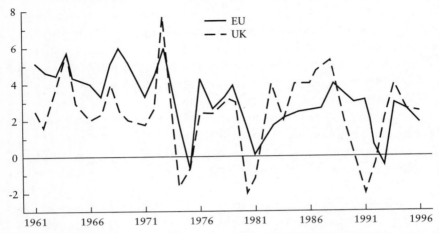

Source: OECD Historical Statistics, 1960–1994, Paris, 1996, Economic Trends, Office for National Statistics, July 1997

This does not, in itself, show that the underlying potential for growth was significantly damaged. Short term effects on investment might be expected to result in longer term deleterious consequences. It is arguable that the evidence suggests that the results of poor macroeconomic policy making are to be seen in the 1970s and the recessions of 1980–81 and 1989–92. Ironically, as seen in Table 2.3 the United Kingdom's ratio of investment to gross domestic product was at its highest in the 1970s, while incremental capital productivity halved as compared with the golden age. Given the recovery in capital productivity observed in the 1980s, back to within striking distance of the golden age, it is not *a priori* obvious that the underlying potential growth rate suffered severe damage. But the data are certainly consistent with the conclusion that poor macroeconomic policy in the 1970s and into the early 1980s had significant effects on the *reported* rate of growth. Oulton (Oulton, 1995, p. 65) suggests that such effects may have been worth about 0.6 per cent on top of the British growth rate. As pointed out earlier in this chapter, had incremental capital productivity in the 1970s been the same as in the golden age, 1 per cent might have been added to the British growth rate in the period 1974–79, bringing it up to the growth rate of Germany over that period.

CONCLUSIONS

The focus of this chapter has been on the economic performance of the United Kingdom in and after the golden age as reflected in the growth of overall output and output per capita. It was argued in Chapter 1 that it is important to distinguish between the different sub-periods that span the period 1960–1989. It was suggested that while the bulk of Britain's relative economic decline had occurred by 1973, the period from 1974 to 1979 was disappointing. Excluding Japan and the United States, 'catch up' by the peer group had largely been completed by 1973, and there is little excuse for the relatively poor performance after 1974 and up to and including 1981. However, between 1981 and 1989 the situation was quite different. The United Kingdom during this period grew significantly faster than the European Union group, shown in Table 2.8, and made up much of the ground lost in the 1970s. Only Japan and Canada grew faster.

Table 2.8
Growth rates of GDP, 1981–89, %

Austria	2.0
Belgium	1.7
Canada	3.3
Denmark	2.1
France	2.2
Germany	2.1
Italy	2.2
Japan	3.9
Netherlands	2.0
Sweden	2.1
Switzerland	2.1
United Kingdom	2.9
United States	2.8

Source: OECD Historical Statistics 1960–1995, Paris, 1997

Economic growth theory as discussed earlier provides alternative conceptual frameworks to try to analyse information that we have about significant economic variables which affect the growth process. But it is difficult in many cases to translate theoretical ideas into practical measurements. This is particularly the case, for example, with regard to innovation and ideas that may be ultimate drivers of the growth process as a result of social capabilities as reflected in culture, social institutions, and the development of human capital. It is small wonder, therefore, that theorists have recourse to stressing some specific aspect of the growth process, and claiming for it the right to be the all important factor that we must influence in order to promote better performance. Small wonder that the factors that are identified tend, in the main, to be of a macroeconomic nature, since when the issue is expressed in macroeconomic terms there appears to be a direct suggestion of appropriate economic policies that might be adopted. If the problem is excessive public expenditure – cut it. If it is too low a level of investment – subsidise it. Or, if the low level of investment is caused by a shortage of finance, create new institutions to provide finance. But if the problem lies in individual performance, such as inefficient management and poor labour relations, it becomes essentially a microeconomic problem for which the economic cure is not so obvious. Similarly, when a cure is identified, it may require a timescale for implementation that is of no interest to short-termist politicians.

In this chapter we have looked at some of the principal factors that have been adduced to explain Britain's relative decline since 1960, in terms of the behaviour of aggregate output. The nostrum of excessive public expenditure and crowding out the private sector does not seem *prima facie* to account for the relative decline in the British economy, at least up to the end of the 1960s. The discipline imparted by the Bretton Woods system largely ensured a concomitant degree of discipline in the conduct of fiscal policy, even allowing for the episodes of 'stop-go' that characterised the period. After the Second World War, the ratio of the national debt in the United Kingdom to gross domestic product fell during the golden age. Public expenditure in the United Kingdom as a proportion of gross domestic product did little more than grow in line with the peer group.

The story of the 1970s is quite different. Beginning with the Barber boom and following the impact of OPEC II, pressure to maintain real levels of public expenditure resulted in inappropriate monetary and fiscal policies. In this sense, it could be argued that in the 1970s excessive public spending impacted on the rate of economic growth, but this was primarily due to the way in which public expenditure was financed. The question, what is the 'optimal' ratio of public expenditure to gross domestic product, is another matter, which is taken up in Chapter 5. The story of the 1980s up to the Lawson boom of 1988 is of a continuous attempt to restore public finances, reduce fiscal deficits and lower the rate of inflation. An improvement in stabilisation policy relative to the 1970s was associated with a significant improvement in the rate of economic growth.

The most common hypothesis about Britain's relative economic decline relates in some way to the rate of investment, with the initial emphasis on the notion that British investment over the respective periods was 'low'. Excluding residential construction, and using the actual incremental capital productivity derived from the United Kingdom's actual performance, some crude idea of the sensitivity of the British growth rate is set out in Table 2.3. We consider what the British growth rate might have been, if Britain had experienced the investment ratios of the peer group members. Looking at Germany and France, its principal comparators, we see that there is a marked contrast between the three periods. Given the British marginal productivity of capital, the British growth rate relative to Germany would have been increased in the golden years from 3.1 per cent to 3.7 per cent and given the French investment ratio from 3.1 per cent to 3.4 per cent. For the years 1973 onwards, the impact of these substitutions is negligible. For the period 1981–89, the growth rate would have improved by 0.2 per cent for both German and French investment ratios.

Calculations of this kind are crude to say the least, but they serve on a *prima facie* basis to discredit the general proposition discussed earlier that British economic performance has been dismal since 1973 as the direct result of a shortfall of investment. As argued earlier, even given the fact that since 1973 the British investment ratio has been moderately below the peer group, the suggestion that this has been due to short termism and a shortage of finance cannot be substantiated.

It has also been argued that it is plausible, but difficult to prove, that a failure to accumulate human capital has occurred. On the face of it, anecdotal evidence added to the incidence of forms of qualification suggests that the inadequacy of the British labour force was a significant factor in Britain's relative decline. But as already emphasised it would have to be established that this was a major factor accounting for the relative decline of the United Kingdom in the 1950s and 1960s. The events of the 1970s have little to do with this, since there are other convincing explanations, while in the 1980s British performance relative to the peer group was eminently respectable, despite the persistent attempts of a variety of commentators to prove otherwise.

The explanation of the relative decline of the United Kingdom over the golden years remains crucial. It has been argued here that most of it followed a perfectly reasonable course of events that entailed the inevitable economic catch up of those members of the peer group that found themselves so far behind in 1950. The performance of the 1970s can indeed be pronounced disappointing, but it is unnecessary to go much further than to cite industrial relations and the inappropriate conduct of fiscal and monetary policy to account for the disappointment. The catch-up period of the 1980s may, on a first pass at least, be attributed to the removal of some of the negative factors of the 1970s rather than any major shift in the rate of accumulation of physical and human capital. The restoration of the prerogative of management in a different labour and fiscal environment could go a long way to account for the observed improvement up to the recession of the early 1990s.

There is a serious paradox at the heart of trying to explain both the absolute and relative performance of the British economy; we have either too many explanations or too few. Many are put forward as candidates; a list on a blank sheet of paper may include low investment, lack of finance, excessive public spending, high taxation, poor industrial relations, low investment in human capital, low savings, not enough infrastructure and poor macroeconomic policy. Given that the 1970s constitute some sort of aberration that can be explained in terms of the arguments above, if we exclude the 1970s and combine together the golden age and the 1980s, the British average growth rate of 2.8 per cent compares with the average German growth rate of 3.2 per cent. Germany is the comparator that we are repeatedly told we should be like. Given that Germany in the 1950s recovered much faster than other peer group countries such as France and Italy, over this period of comparison, Germany may indeed be taken as par for the course. But given the fact that Britain grew faster than Germany over the 1980s, it is clear that once again we are back to explaining the difference in the golden age rather than any consistent underperformance.

CHAPTER 3

MANUFACTURING INDUSTRY, TRADE AND COMPETITIVENESS

INTRODUCTION

In the two previous chapters, the discussion of economic performance and economic growth has been cast entirely in aggregate terms. The principal focus of attention has been the gross domestic product, in absolute terms and in terms of gross domestic product per capita. However, over the last twenty years or so, many commentators and critics have linked performance to the behaviour of manufacturing industry, both in relation to total output and in relation to the manufacturing performance of the OECD peer group. Britain's perceived failure as a manufacturing nation has been set at the heart of its perceived general economic problems. The thesis of this chapter is that this perception is fundamentally mistaken, and that adherence to such a view is liable to lead to serious errors of judgement in economic policy.

None of this is to suggest that manufacturing industry is not a fundamental and important sector of economic activity in Britain. It is, however, to suggest that there is nothing particularly unique about it in economic terms. As long ago as 1776 the great British economist Adam Smith was arguing that manufacturing industry itself was basically dependent on the produce of agriculture without which there would not be the basic food and raw materials that enabled manufacturing to take place. Over two hundred years later a House of Lords Select Committee concluded:

> First the services sector is very dependent on manufacturing. As one witness said, 'The growth of the service area is not only tied to its own competitiveness within the service area itself ... but it is totally dependent on the growth of the manufacturing industry to use the services it provides'. (House of Lords, 1985, p. 42)

To the extent that service industries are defined in terms of services to manufacturing, the statement is tautological. Cleaning factory windows requires factories. But in a wider sense the statement is palpably untrue. It is the case that we know less than we would like about inter-sectoral flows. Much evidence is anecdotal. But we know for example that sales of modern electronic equipment, including computers and telecommunications, have been made to service industries on a large scale. Activities such as tourism lead to orders for cars, ships and aeroplanes, while tourism is a major customer of the construction industry. To say that the developing service sector depends on manufacturing industry is no more or less true than the statement made in Adam Smith's time, that manufacturing industry was essentially dependent on economic activity in agriculture.

As we shall see later, one of the most frequently presented arguments for the unique importance of manufacturing industry relates to the determination of the trade balance and the current account of the balance of payments. To quote again from the House of Lords Select Committee:

> Manufacturing even now represents over a fifth of all activity in the United Kingdom and it provides over 40% of our overseas earnings. Its performance is therefore crucial in an economy which depends upon imports of foods and raw materials. (House of Lords, 1985, p. 11)

Moreover their Lordships went on to assert that:

> The Committee fully recognise that the growth of GDP is the important objective. But sustainable growth has not been possible without a favourable trade balance in manufacturing and manufacturing output would be expected to grow faster with a favourable balance in manufacturing than without. Manufacturing products are tradeable in the world while many services are not. (House of Lords, 1985, p. 42)

A more contemporary version of this story has emerged over the last decade in the shape of a demand for increased 'competitiveness'. To quote a Government White Paper, Britain must compete in the world otherwise we shall not survive. Britain is fighting for its life, and the performance of manufacturing industry is the key to salvation. Manufacturing industry, trade and competitiveness are seen to be inextricably bound up together.

To put these arguments and assertions into perspective we examine the role of manufacturing in the economy and its implications in particular for the balance of payments and trade. We consider the importance of the idea of 'competitiveness' and the behaviour of the supply side of the economy. Finally, we look in some detail at the actual behaviour of manufacturing in Britain both absolutely and in relation to its peers, and essay some prognosis as to its future. But first we look at the ideas before examining the facts.

ECONOMIC GROWTH AND MANUFACTURING INDUSTRY

It was the late Nicholas Kaldor, the distinguished British economist, who first focused on the link between economic growth and manufacturing industry in his influential inaugural lecture at the University of Cambridge in 1966 (Kaldor, 1966). His general thesis was that differences in rates of economic growth were largely attributable to differences in the *stages of economic development* 'rather than in the realm of personal (or rather individual) abilities or incentives' (Kaldor, 1966, p. 3).

In the light of the discussion of growth theory in the last chapter, it is clear that this assertion would be rather difficult to swallow today. However, Kaldor believed that a fast rate of economic growth was primarily associated with a fast rate of growth of the secondary sector of the economy, principally the manufacturing sector. The trouble with the British economy, he alleged, was that in terms of sector balance it had reached 'premature maturity' ahead of other countries. The rise in the importance of the service sector was inhibiting the recorded rate of economic growth.

The unique importance of manufacturing industry in the growth process was said to be derived from the fact that unlike the primary sector of the economy (i.e. agriculture) the manufacturing sector exhibited:

> ... the existence of economies of scale or increasing returns which causes productivity to increase in response to, and as a by-product of the increase in total output. (Kaldor, 1966, p. 8)

Innovation was seen by Kaldor to be concentrated in the manufacturing sector with subsequent spill-overs, or external benefits to the other sectors of the economy. The interplay of static and dynamic factors caused returns to increase with an increase in the size of manufacturing activities. The centrepiece of this phenomenon was the 'learning curve', down which the economy had to travel, '... which means that productivity tends to grow, the faster output expands' (Kaldor, 1966, p. 9).

It was, Kaldor said, of the utmost importance that this process was to be seen as a 'macro-phenomenon':

> ... just because so much of the economies of scale emerge as a result of increased differentiation, the emergence of new processes and new subsidiary industries. (Kaldor, 1966, p. 10)

Thus manufacturing industry was perceived as the *engine* of growth. In the late 1960s the argument was sufficiently persuasive to encourage the Labour government under Harold Wilson to introduce a Selective Employment Tax on service industries to lower the relative costs of employment in manufacturing (later repealed).

Kaldor was uncertain as to how to apportion the explanation of *differences* between the growth rates of countries, between the behaviour of demand factors and supply factors. To begin with, and in line with the rationale of the Selective Employment Tax, he was inclined to emphasise the shortage of labour as being a critical factor, an idea that was curiously enough reflected in a contribution by Bacon and Eltis, a decade later, under the title, *Too Few Producers*. But he quickly moved on to a second idea which he expressed in 1971 (Kaldor, 1971) that manufacturing was important, in particular, because of its export component.

The idea here was not related to the so-called 'balance of payments constraint' argument that is discussed below. Rather it emphasised what came to be known as 'export-led' growth:

> My main criticism of the philosophy underlying the White Paper (of 1944) and of the post-War policies of economic management that were built on it, is that it treated the problem of full employment and (implicitly) of growth, as one of internal demand management, and not one of exports and of international competitiveness. (Kaldor, 1971, p. 5)

With one bound, Kaldor had reached forward to the contemporary discussion of economic growth and competitiveness. But he was not quite there. The new twist that he introduced at the time was the argument that fiscal policy, rather than being used to generate the full employment level of demand, was to be the key instrument for maintaining equilibrium in the balance of payments, by determining the rate of growth of imports. The overall rate of growth of output was to be determined by the rate of growth of exports, which was in turn to be determined by setting the exchange rate. The essence of this approach was the idea that the exchange rate could be used together with fiscal policy as instruments to determine both the desired growth rate and equilibrium in the balance of payments.

The trouble with all this, as with much of the theorising about the macroeconomy in the 1950s and 1960s, is that it left the rate of inflation undetermined. Inflation was the skeleton in the cupboard. It was presumed to be set by some kind of administered prices and incomes policy which was for many (*mea culpa*) a favourite nostrum of the time. The importance of this was that it appeared to enable governments to determine the *real exchange rate* and therefore to determine the real rate of growth of exports. It implied that manipulating the *nominal exchange rate* would result in permanent real effects on the underlying rate of growth of the economy.

Events that followed the publication of these ideas conspired to put the issues it raised on the back-burner. Monetary and fiscal expansion in Britain after 1970, followed by the dramatic increase in the price of oil, was reflected in record inflation and a deeper recession in Britain than was experienced by most. However, as the dust began to settle in 1976, with some semblance of economic recovery, the question relating to the performance and the future of manufacturing industry came back onto the agenda in the form of the so-called problem of *de-industrialisation*.

The general problem might be described as the progressive weakening of the manufacturing sector of the economy. How is weakness to be defined? A starting point might be to consider the share of manufacturing employment and output in total employment and output. These appear to be reasonable *domestic* measures of the *relative* importance of the manufacturing sector to the national economy. However, if falling ratios simply reflected a change in the relative performance of manufacturing in the economy, accompanied by a 'satisfactory' overall rate of growth of total output, why should there be any concern? The answer might be that given by Kaldor initially, namely that the overall rate of growth is driven by manufacturing and so a falling share of manufacturing must imply a falling rate of economic growth in the future. At one level this is simply arithmetic. If 'manufacturing' has a faster rate of growth of productivity than 'services', a falling share of manufacturing will lower the overall rate of growth of productivity which is a weighted average of the two.

However, the emphasis at the time shifted to the importance of the external dimension, which had been introduced by Kaldor's second thoughts on the subject. The argument was well explained by Arjit Singh:

> The manufacturing sector is the major source of foreign exchange earnings on the current account. More importantly ... it is the main means through which an improvement in the balance of payments could be thought sufficient to correct the existing disequilibrium. Therefore, given the normal level of the other components of the balance of payments we may define an efficient manufacturing sector as one which *(currently as well as potentially) not only satisfies the demands of consumers at home, but is also able to sell enough of its products abroad to pay for the nation's import requirements.* This is however subject to the important restriction that an *'efficient' manufacturing sector must be able to achieve these objectives at socially acceptable levels of output, employment and the exchange rate.* (Singh, 1977, p. 128)

He went on to argue that:

> In operational terms, a structural problem can arise in this sense if the manufacturing sector, without losing price and cost competitiveness is unable to export enough for the full employment level of imports. (Singh, 1977, p. 128)

In the 1980s the issue of the relationship between the balance of payments and manufacturing became inextricably mixed up with the impact of the coming of North Sea oil. As recorded in Chapter 1, following the recession of 1980–1981, the consequence of North Sea oil was to drive up the real exchange rate, which impacted negatively on manufacturing exports. The current account however moved into surplus. As far back as 1977, Singh had issued a dire warning as to what might be the shape of things to come after the full benefits of oil had been achieved:

> But there is at least one component of visible trade (minerals, fuels etc.) which may be expected to show an enormous improvement over the next few years as a consequence of North Sea oil. Depending on the size of the surplus the country would then have a balance of payments equilibrium at full employment and at desired levels of real income and exchange rate even if the trading performance of the manufacturing sector continued to decline. This however is not a sustainable position in the long run, since unless the manufacturing sector improves and becomes more dynamic, it may not be able to pay for the full employment level of imports at a later stage when the oil runs out. (Singh, 1977, p. 133)

As we saw earlier, by 1985 these fears were absorbing the Select Committee on Trade of the House of Lords. It would be encapsulated in the question 'What are we to do when the oil runs out?'

MANUFACTURING OUTPUT AND EMPLOYMENT

For the moment let us leave on one side the questions of what happens 'when the oil runs out' and the inter-relationship of manufacturing industry with the balance of trade. Let us return to the significance of the role of manufacturing industry within the closed economy, i.e. the economy ignoring the role of external trade.

The initial Kaldor argument, as presented above, suggested that irrespective of external relationships, manufacturing industry had a special significance as the engine of economic growth and implicitly as a key factor in generating full employment. Neither of these propositions would be true even if we confined ourselves to the limitations of the so-called 'closed economy' ignoring foreign trade.

In the first place the structure of economic output is in the longer run determined by the pattern of economic demand. As can be seen in Tables 3.1 and 3.2, the relative decline in the share of manufacturing industry in both output and employment is a widespread phenomenon in the G7 countries and other mature economies of the OECD. While the ratios differ between countries over time, there is a clear trend in all of these countries which shows a relative decline in manufacturing and a relative increase in the importance of service industries. Leaving aside issues of competitiveness and supply side aspects of these economies, this shift in economic structure can be largely accounted for by a shift in the structure of both public and private demand. In the mature and developed countries of the OECD, at the margin, individual expenditures measured in terms of the dollar, the pound, and the deutschmark are increasingly spent on what are conventionally defined as service products. The demand for manufactured products of some kind or other is falling relative to the demand for health, education, travel and tourism and more sophisticated and sometimes intangible products that have been generated by the revolution in information technology. This process cannot be reversed and will continue well into the twenty-first century. Meanwhile, behind these developments in the mature industrial economies, the manufacturing component of the so-called developing and emerging economies will inevitably rise. The successful ones will converge on the more mature economies, an issue that we shall discuss later in this chapter.

The reversal of this process for the mature economies is impossible. The growth and development of the knowledge based world have indeed made it more and more difficult to distinguish between 'goods' and 'services'. The concept of a 'service' has always been more basic than that of a 'good'. A toothbrush is a good, but its primary function is to deliver a service, namely the cleaning of teeth. As an object in itself it has no value. In this sense, manufactured goods are often less fundamental than loaves of bread, and indeed less fundamental than telephone lines in achieving communications. In some instances, attempts have been made to sustain the cult of the importance of manufacturing by redefining what have been commonly treated as 'services' as 'manufactured products'.

The perceived importance of manufacturing industry and its relative decline on both sides of the Atlantic have also been influenced by history and emotion. In the case of Britain, there is a widespread belief that its historical economic strength was entirely dependent on manufacturing and a relative decline in manufacturing must therefore equate to a relative decline overall in the country's economic significance and standard of living. The issues here were well captured by David Henderson in his Reith Lectures where he detected what he described as 'Soap Opera in High Places' (Henderson, 1986, Chapter 1). Part of the emotion he attributes to two ideas, structural *snobbery* and *essentialism*. An illustration of the former in an American context is given by a quotation from the Chairman of the US International Trade Commission. Speaking of the need for US industry to modernise he opined that:

> I don't believe myself that this nation is going to become a nation of hamburger stands, Chinese restaurants, laundries, banks and computer operations. I think we have to have some sort of manufacturing sector. (Henderson, 1986, p. 21)

Table 3.1
Distribution of total output, %

	1960	1974	1985	1990	1995
USA					
Manufacturing	28.0	23.3	20.0	18.7	18.0[a]
Services	57.9	62.9	66.8	69.9	71.9
Other industry	14.1	13.8	13.2	11.4	10.1
Japan					
Manufacturing	34.6	33.6	29.5	28.2	24.7
Services	42.7	49.7	55.8	56.3	60.0
Other industry	22.7	16.7	14.7	15.5	15.3
Germany					
Manufacturing	40.3	36.0	31.7	30.6	24.1
Services	41.0	51.2	57.7	59.8	65.8
Other industry	18.7	12.8	10.6	9.6	10.1
UK					
Manufacturing	32.1	27.1	21.6	20.3	18.2[a]
Services	53.8	60.1	62.9	67.8	71.1[a]
Other industry	14.1	12.8	15.5	11.9	10.7
Canada					
Manufacturing	–	19.7	17.2	15.9	14.4[b]
Services	–	62.3	65.7	69.6	72.1[b]
Other industry	–	18.0	17.1	14.5	13.5
EU					
Manufacturing	32.2	29.3	24.5	23.2	20.6
Services	47.9	54.8	61.4	64.3	67.9
Other industry	19.9	15.9	14.1	12.5	11.5
OECD					
Manufacturing	29.7	26.7	22.9	21.6	19.8
Services	52.6	57.5	62.6	65.3	68.2
Other industry	17.7	15.8	14.5	13.1	12.0

[a] 1994, [b] 1992

Source: OECD Historical Statistics, 1960–95, Paris, 1997

Table 3.2
Distribution of total employment, %

	1960	1974	1985	1990	1995
USA					
Manufacturing	26.5	24.2	19.8	18.0	16.4
Services	56.2	63.4	68.8	70.9	73.1
Other industry	17.3	12.4	11.4	11.1	10.5
Japan					
Manufacturing	21.3	27.2	25.0	24.1	22.5
Services	41.3	50.1	56.4	58.7	60.7
Other industry	37.4	22.7	18.6	17.2	16.8
Germany					
Manufacturing	34.3	35.8	32.3	31.6	27.0
Services	39.1	46.3	54.4	56.7	59.1
Other industry	26.6	17.9	13.3	11.7	13.9
UK					
Manufacturing	38.4	34.6	27.7	25.5	22.1
Services	47.6	55.1	63.0	66.0	70.5
Other industry	14.0	10.3	9.3	8.5	7.4
Canada					
Manufacturing	24.6	21.7	17.3	16.0	15.3
Services	54.1	63.1	69.5	71.1	73.3
Other industry	21.3	15.2	13.2	12.9	11.4
EU					
Manufacturing	28.9	29.7	25.0	23.6	18.5
Services	39.0	47.9	57.4	60.7	64.3
Other industry	32.1	22.4	17.6	15.7	17.2
OECD					
Manufacturing	26.0	26.6	22.3	20.9	17.8
Services	43.1	52.1	60.1	62.8	64.6
Other industry	30.9	21.3	17.6	16.3	17.6

Source: OECD Historical Statistics, 1960–95, Paris, 1997

Clearly the last sentence of this quotation is eminently reasonable. But the implied distaste for the service sector expressed here is also a manifestation of structural snobbery and essentialism. But in a wider context, the desirability of having a manufacturing capability is not really the issue. The issue is whether there is in a sense a *unique* requirement for a role to be played by manufacturing industry beyond simply meeting the expressed demands for its products. Whereas Adam Smith saw the supply of agricultural produce and raw materials as 'essential', the modern world, at least as far as the mature industrial economies are concerned, in some quarters thinks differently. Henderson gives us another revealing quotation, from US Congressman Gingell:

> We now occupy the position of a colony with Japan: we send them raw materials and they send us finished products ... That's a very clever way of increasing Japanese prosperity at the expense of the United States. (Henderson, 1986, p. 21)

As Table 3.2 shows, the relative share of employment in manufacturing in the mature economies has been declining everywhere over the last quarter of a century. Evidently the decline has been greater and faster in the Anglo-Saxon world as compared with Continental Europe and Japan. Nevertheless, the trend is the same. On the other side of the coin, growth and development in the service industries in the United States have been leading the world. Indeed, Britain's overall economic performance could have been significantly improved over the period if its service industries had grown faster. As we saw earlier it is becoming more evident that the growth of manufacturing capability is being driven increasingly by the demand for services rather than the other way around.

On reflection this is not very surprising, as the history of the relationship between agriculture and manufacturing industry suggests. The agricultural revolution in Britain with its major gains in agricultural efficiency laid the basis for the so-called industrial revolution of the nineteenth century. It is equally reasonable to forecast that a fall in the share of manufacturing is almost inevitably driven by technological change which enables productive capability to outstrip demand, and changes in the pattern of demand as consumers seek to exercise their expenditure over things other than those that are simply produced in factories. The impact of technology suggests that it may also be the case that the share of manufacturing employment may fall faster in the future than the share of manufacturing output. There may be cyclical fluctuations, but the trends are clear for the mature economies. The issue as to whether Britain has fared worse in this process than others is another matter. But looked at simply from the point of view of economic growth and employment, and leaving the external issues on one side, there is no doubt that there is no general case for the idea that manufacturing industry is unique or engaged in some sense in more worthy economic activity.

THE BALANCE OF PAYMENTS AS A CONSTRAINT ON GROWTH

As discussed earlier, the prime concern of Arjit Singh and the Select Committee of the House of Lords in 1985 was with the contribution of manufacturing industry to the UK balance of payments. This theme was developed as recently as 1992 by the economist Tony Thirlwall, who expressed in modern dress the idea that economic growth in Britain would be constrained by problems of the balance of payments. In a world of perfect capital mobility – the ability to borrow to finance current account deficits – the sense that a poor current account performance would constrain the growth of output suggested that the country had some kind of solvency constraint. This problem is exemplified by Charles Bean:

> The phrase external constraint is open to a variety of interpretation. It is here construed narrowly as reflecting the countries' ability to borrow to cover a current account deficit. (Bean, 1991, p. 202)

But if capital mobility is not present, as it was not in the period prior to the 1980s, the external constraint is seen as a failure to generate sufficient international liquidity to finance a necessary level of imports. The argument as put forward by Thirlwall reflects the ideas put forward by Singh and the House of Lords Select Committee:

> Demand, determined by export performance and the balance of payments position governs output growth but supply side policies such as investment, technology, research and development effort, education and skills etc. determine the income elasticities of exports and therefore how fast exports grow as world income grows. The view that I cannot accept is that a mere augmentation of the supply of resources *will necessarily improve the growth performance of a country if it does not at the same time improve the long run balance of payments position* [author's italics]. If exports remain static and imports rise, the deficit on the balance of payments will be unsustainable and therefore demand will have to be restricted and resources remain underutilised. It is in this sense that the balance of payments becomes the ultimate constraint on growth. (Thirlwall, 1992, p. 141)

This echoes the earlier statement by the House of Lords Select Committee to the effect that sustainable growth is not possible without a favourable trade balance in manufactures. Here it is alleged that the growth rate cannot be improved unless there is an improvement in the balance of payments. More recently, Alistair Darling (then Shadow Labour Party Minister for Trade and Industry) asserted that the British manufacturing base was too small to support an adequate level of sustainable growth.

The implication of Thirlwall's analysis and the concerns expressed by the House of Lords Committee is that the structural relationships that relate together the level of domestic economic activity and the behaviour of imports and exports make it *impossible* to achieve both internal equilibrium (a balance between domestic demand and supply at a 'reasonable' level of unemployment) and external equilibrium (a 'satisfactory' balance of payments). Since external equilibrium has to be observed, it is the domestic equilibrium that will be constrained. In the absence of a sufficient rate of growth of exports (largely provided by manufacturing industry) the economy will be condemned to lower rates of economic growth and higher rates of unemployment than would otherwise be achieved without the presence of this 'external' constraint. The performance of manufacturing industry, therefore, becomes central to the overall growth performance of the economy.

There are two immediate reasons why the arguments of the House of Lords Select Committee and Tony Thirlwall are fatally flawed. The first is the obvious one, namely, since trade deficits and surpluses must add up for the world as a whole, these propositions cannot be general without asserting that improvements in growth rates cannot be shared. Economic growth would become a zero-sum game, which must be nonsense. The idea that it might be is also related to the view that international trade is a game of this kind, in which there will inevitably be winners and losers.

The second reason for dismissing the argument is that it also rests on the assumption (or the assertion) that there is some *unique* level or rate of growth of imports that must obtain when the economy is at something like 'full employment'. A similar assertion underlies the analysis of Arjit Singh described earlier. But this conclusion is only established by ruling out adjustment mechanisms such as changes in real exchange rates which may affect the *composition* of total output at any level of unemployment. The level of income alone does not determine how demand is allocated between domestic output and imports. There is nothing inevitable about the import content of the overall expenditure of the economy.

If we abandon for a moment the assumption that there is a unique relationship between the rate of growth of imports and the rate of growth of income, are there any other reasons for supposing that there is, in a significant sense, the serious possibility that a country like Britain may be 'balance of payments constrained'? In order to discuss this further, we need to take on board the accounting relationships that hold between the current account of the balance of payments, domestic savings and investment, the capital account of the balance of payments and the change in foreign exchange reserves.

In general we have

$$CUR \equiv S - I \equiv CAP + \Delta R$$
$$CUR \equiv \text{the current account}$$

where

S = domestic savings (public and private)
I = domestic investment (public and private)
CAP = the capital account
ΔR = the change in foreign exchange reserves

In an accounting sense the balance of payments always 'balances'. This is no more than to say that the numbers across the balance of payments must add up. A current account deficit must be financed either by an inflow of foreign capital, an outflow of foreign exchange, or some combination of the two. This is to be distinguished from the economist's idea of *external equilibrium* in the balance of payments, which indicates a 'satisfactory' state of affairs in association with a stable exchange rate, stable prices and a 'satisfactory' level of employment.

If we start, for the sake of argument, from such a happy state, it is clear that expressing the balance of payments in the form set out above suggests that changes in the balance of payments, and the emergence of disequilibrium can emanate from a number of different sources. Typically those who have been concerned with the relationships between manufactured exports and the current account have focused on changes in the structure of traded goods relationships. Thus a sudden upward shift in export demand would have to be balanced by an outflow of capital, an increase in foreign exchange reserves or both. The role of saving and investment decisions in affecting the behaviour of the current account has long been well recognised. It is arguable for example that the trade imbalance between Japan and the United States is not primarily driven by relative competitiveness, that may be adjusted simply by appreciating the yen and depreciating the dollar. It derives primarily from the fact that, relatively speaking, Japan saves a great deal and the

United States saves very little. As can be seen from the balance of payments account, a rise in domestic savings relative to domestic investment will result in an improvement in the current account. Finally, the change in reserves can be interpreted in terms of changes in a country's desire to acquire or reduce holdings of money, an idea that underlies the so-called monetary theory of the balance of payments. Its proponents argue that the balance of payments is inherently a monetary phenomenon (which it is) but go on to add that the outcome of the balance of payments is largely independent of what is happening to real trade. It follows from this analysis that if we start from what is regarded as a 'satisfactory' position in the balance of payments, disturbances may come from shocks that are derived from several different sources – from changes in factor productivity and technology, from shifts in decisions to save and to invest, and shifts in the demand to hold or dispose of money.

At the time of writing, the last major crisis that developed in the United Kingdom economy occurred in the late 1980s, following the major expansion in the economy in 1988. The resultant current account deficit was not attributable to a sudden and dramatic decline in the structural competitiveness of British industry (even allowing for the fact that some fall in the real exchange rate might have been justified by the fall in oil prices in 1986). As in other post-war British episodes, the problem arose as the result of excess demand and a collapse in net (not gross) private saving. Private sector debt grew rapidly.

Most previous episodes had resulted from a reduction in public rather than private saving. This so-called privatisation of the deficit in 1988, it was argued, should not have been a worry since it would eventually correct itself. This proposition was unfortunately muddled with another proposition, namely that such deficits do not matter. This was wrong on two counts. The first is that the shock was largely due to the conduct of public policy, and did not arise from some spontaneous increase in private sector demand. Secondly, large departures from equilibrium subject the economy to major welfare costs as adjustments take place. Therefore such movements do matter.

Against this background, one wonders how can the balance of payments be a constraint on economic growth, in the absence of a fixed relationship between the rate of growth of imports and total output? Provided fiscal and monetary policy is conducted on a prudent basis, there is little evidence that economic fluctuations have, on the whole, reflected autonomous shifts of any magnitude in private spending behaviour. It should be possible, therefore, in principle to restrict disturbances from arising in the savings and investment account.

To summarise, a balance of payments constraint may be interpreted in terms of the ability or inability of an individual country to finance its current deficit. This is not what has been meant traditionally by a balance of payments constraint – nor is it the problem that some have presented in modern dress. Those who are concerned about this issue rest their case on the unique relationship between imports and output at an acceptable level of employment. By implication this argument posits that conventional trade adjustment processes, which depend on movements in real exchange rates, will not 'work' in the sense that adjustment will either not take place at all, or only over a sufficiently long period as to be socially unacceptable. It is this belief that gave rise to the question 'what do we do when the oil runs out?' There is no evidence in fact to refute the traditional proposition that there is always a real exchange rate that is consistent with both internal and external balance. The fear of balance of payments constrained growth has neither a theoretical nor a practical foundation, from which it also follows that there is no unique role for manufacturing industry in dispelling it.

THE BALANCE OF PAYMENTS IN THE POST-WAR PERIOD

In previous sections we have considered the ideas that have underlain *the proposition* that economic growth in Britain has been constrained by the balance of payments and that that constraint can only be broken by a major improvement in the economic performance of manufacturing industry. In the 1950s and 1960s the apparent empirical basis for such an idea was simply derived. Over short time periods, growth appeared to be slow and unemployment rose modestly by the standards of the day. Fiscal expansion was put in place and eventually imports rose faster than exports and the current account of the balance of payments deteriorated. Having stamped on the accelerator, the policy makers then had to step on the brakes. The result was described as 'stop-go'. It was interpreted as demonstrating the existence of a balance of payments (current account) constraint on economic growth, in the sense that the authorities were limited in their ability to pump up the rate of growth of demand.

There were those who believed that the constraint was derived essentially from the fact that the exchange rate was pegged in the context of the Bretton Woods system, in which case a major devaluation of the currency or, better still perhaps, a floating exchange rate would remove the constraint. This view was based unfortunately on rudimentary thinking about the determinants of the inflation rate. There was a failure to see that current account deficits (under pegged exchange rates) and inflation (under floating rates) are simply two sides of the same coin. They both reflected policy shocks emanating from the conduct of fiscal and monetary policies that pushed the rate of growth of demand beyond the ability of the supply side of the economy to respond. The current account constraint theory turned a supply side/labour market problem into a so-called balance of payments problem. As pointed out in the last chapter, the intellectual pressure to represent economic growth as a macroeconomic rather than a microeconomic phenomenon is powerful. The former problem, which is largely microeconomic in character, is difficult to deal with precisely, and invariably calls for changes that are often painful, requiring changes in attitudes with results that can only be expected in a long distant future. Political short-termism is itself a potent force. The latter suggests quick fixes, such as export subsidies, protectionism and exchange rate manipulation. It is not surprising that the balance of payments constraint hypothesis had many adherents, although, it must be said, far fewer today than in the past.

The behaviour of the current account of the United Kingdom relative to gross domestic product is depicted in Figure 3.1. The periods of significant deterioration in the current account, as so defined, are seen clearly in the 1960s, the 1970s and the late 1980s and their origins are formally the same, namely, the generation of an excessively rapid growth of domestic demand. In the case of the first two periods, the responsibility for the deterioration was associated primarily with a significant decrease in public net saving, or to put it another way, a too rapid expansion in public expenditure. As already recorded, the problems of the late 1980s had emanated from a different source, namely the decline of net private saving, but as argued, this was not caused by a spontaneous shift in private spending, but by a major relaxation in monetary policy. Figure 3.1 also points up clearly the major improvement in the current account of the early and mid-1980s as a result of the impact of North Sea oil.

Since the breakdown of Bretton Woods in 1971, current account behaviour in the United Kingdom has been dominated by the behaviour of supply side shocks to the economy resulting from changes in oil prices, and the conduct of monetary and fiscal policy. Over the period of the 1970s, economic performance was a major disappointment. However, as we saw earlier, there is little evidence that performance was influenced or constrained by the balance of payments as such. Its behaviour was an outcome of events and policies rather than a cause of anything *per se*.

Figure 3.1
The current account (% of nominal GDP)

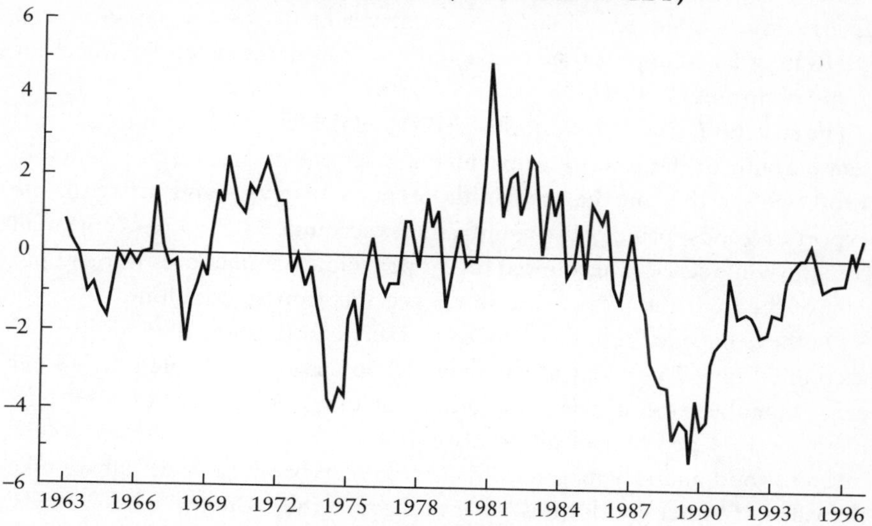

Source: Economic Trends, Office for National Statistics, July 1997

Having said that, there is little doubt that had manufacturing industry performed better in the 1970s and in the early 1980s with regard to export growth and import substitution then the overall economic performance in Britain could have been significantly improved. But this has little or nothing to do with the impact of manufacturing on the balance of payments as such, or with the uniqueness of manufacturing as the engine of growth. Still less would it have been the case that better manufacturing performance would have enabled Britain to achieve the level of imports and food required at 'full' employment as suggested by earlier references. Even as late as 1992, it was asserted that:

> It is commonly observed that the economy requires a strong tradeable goods sector to support our consumption of imports. Correspondingly the UK's balance of payments deficit is said to reflect our growing inability to do this. (Davis, Flanders and Star, 1992, p. 46)

On the assumption that this is intended to mean more than simply the fact that imports in general have to be paid for by something, it is best interpreted in terms of the 'full employment' level of imports, a concept which we have argued, at a theoretical level, has little meaning. It also has little meaning at a practical level, since statements of this kind ignore completely the major change in the structure of the current account of the balance of payments of the United Kingdom over the last forty years. This is ironic, as we shall see later, because special attention has been paid to the rising share of manufactures in total imports. The quotation from the sources given earlier still characterise the United Kingdom as a country which exports manufactured goods in order to import food to eat and raw materials to keep the wheels of industry turning.

The structure, since 1960, of the credits and debits that determine the current account of the balance of payments is set out in Table 3.3. Starting in 1960, we see that on the credit side (exports of goods and services), the export of goods, principally manufactures, accounted for 63 per cent of all receipts while services accounted for 37 per cent. Manufactures were 52 per cent of the total and 77 per cent of the receipts from goods alone.

On the debit side (imports of goods and services) imports of goods in 1960 accounted for 67 per cent of payments while services accounted for 33 per cent. Manufactured imports accounted for only 23 per cent of total payments and 34 per cent of all goods imported. The category 'other goods' includes food and raw materials. As can be seen from Table 3.3. if we take the value of 'other goods' plus 'oil' as reflecting the economy's 'basic needs' we see that they were roughly equal to the value of manufactured exports in 1960. Under these circumstances, it might appear reasonable to conclude that in 1960 the United Kingdom exported manufactured goods to pay for food and imports required in the processes of production.

Over thirty years later the situation on the debit side has changed dramatically. On the credit side, following the fall in revenues after 1986, the situation as far as the goods account is concerned was almost identical to that of 1960; 82 per cent of the revenue from the sale of goods was attributable to manufactures. However, the ratio of revenues from goods relative to receipts from services had fallen materially. Putting matters the other way round, receipts from so-called invisible payments had risen from 37 per cent to nearly half the total. It remains a puzzle why there is a contemporary view that contributions from services can never substitute for earnings from manufacturing when to a large extent they already have.

However, the major change on the visible account has been the rise in imports of manufactures. For total manufactures, i.e. both finished and semi-finished goods, the proportion of manufactured imports, in total imports of goods, rose from 34 per cent to 82 per cent in 1995. Imports of other goods fell to only 12 per cent of the total value of imports of goods. Reflecting a similar development on the credit side of the current account, the ratio of payments on goods account also fell relative to receipts from services, from 67 per cent to 54 per cent. Payments of interest, profits and dividends rose from 7 per cent in 1960 to 28 per cent of total debits on current account by 1995.

Table 3.3
The current account of the balance of payments, £m (%)

EXPORTS	1960	%	1970	%	1980	%	1990	%	1995	%
Visible Exports (fob)										
Manufactures										
Semi-manufactures	1311.0	(22)	2782.0	(21)	14152.0	(16)	28796.0	(13)	43437.0	(15)
Finished manufactures	1756.0	(30)	4100.0	(31)	20727.0	(23)	53613.0	(25)	83783.0	(28)
Oil	104.2	(2)	180.0	(1)	6118.0	(7)	7484.0	(3)	8687.0	(3)
Other goods	565.8	(10)	1088.0	(8)	6392.0	(7)	11825.0	(5)	16439.0	(5)
Total visibles	3737.0	(63)	8150.0	(62)	47389.0	(54)	101718.0	(47)	152346.0	(51)
Invisible Exports										
Services	1419.0	(24)	3379.0	(26)	15647.0	(18)	31447.0	(15)	45254.0	(15)
Interest, profit and dividends	671.0	(11)	1494.0	(11)	23531.0	(27)	79106.0	(37)	93139.0	(32)
Transfers	117.0	(2)	230.0	(2)	1881.0	(2)	4032.0	(2)	6135.0	(2)
Total Invisibles	2207.0	(37)	5103.0	(38)	41059.0	(46)	114585.0	(53)	144528.0	(49)
TOTAL CREDITS	5944.0	(100)	13253.0	(100)	88448.0	(100)	216303.0	(100)	296874.0	(100)

Table 3.3

The current account of the balance of payments, £m (%) *(continued)*

IMPORTS	1960	%	1970	%	1980	%	1990	%	1995	%
Visible Imports (fob)										
Manufactures										
Semi-manufactures	922.0	(15)	2323.0	(19)	12561.0	(15)	31556.0	(13)	45035.0	(15)
Finished manufactures	474.0	(8)	1997.0	(16)	16871.0	(20)	62500.0	(27)	90180.0	(30)
Oil	480.0	(8)	676.0	(5)	5818.0	(7)	5955.0	(3)	4457.0	(2)
Other goods	2262.0	(37)	3188.0	(26)	10811.0	(13)	20516.0	(9)	24302.0	(8)
Total visibles	4138.0	(67)	8184.0	(66)	46061.0	(54)	120527.0	(51)	163974.0	(55)
Invisible Imports										
Services	1411.0	(23)	2963.0	(24)	11878.0	(14)	27758.0	(12)	39112.0	(13)
Interest, profit and dividends	438.0	(7)	898.0	(7)	23750.0	(28)	77837.0	(33)	83567.0	(28)
Transfers	185.0	(3)	412.0	(3)	3876.0	(5)	8928.0	(4)	13113.0	(4)
Total Invisibles	2034.0	(33)	4273.0	(34)	39504.0	(46)	114523.0	(49)	135792.0	(45)
TOTAL DEBITS	6172.0	(100)	12457.0	(100)	85565.0	(100)	235050.0	(100)	299766.0	(100)

Source: UK Balance of Payments, Pink Books (various)

These dramatic changes in structure have received insufficient atttention in the discussion relating to the performance of the current account. Financial liberalisation has fundamentally altered the impact of capital flows on current account behaviour. On the credit side, receipts from profits, interest and dividends have risen from 11 per cent in 1960 to 32 per cent in 1995. On the goods side, it is no longer remotely true that Britain exchanges manufactured goods for food and raw materials. The statement that the United Kingdom needs to export manufactured goods to 'pay its way in the world' is totally meaningless. What the United Kingdom does now is to export manufactured goods, primarily to buy manufactured goods. The next question is why has this come about, and should we be as concerned about it as many people are?

GROWTH, TRADE AND COMPETITIVENESS

Before addressing this question, it may be helpful to begin with some observations about the nature and importance of overseas trade.

The international economic framework that followed the Bretton Woods Agreement in 1944 (described in Chapter 1) was established on the clear assumption that free trade was essential for the prosperity of the world. This commitment to free trade was led and strongly supported by the United States for two principal reasons.

The first was simply the historical judgement that the international developments in the world economy after the crash in 1929 were a disaster. America had imposed a major tariff on industrial products, the infamous Hawley-Smoot tariff, in 1930. But by 1934, given the establishment of a Democratic administration with free trade sympathies, protectionist attitudes in the United States were already on the wane. By 1944, the attitude of the United States executive was already pro-free trade. This view was not based on any particular intellectual framework. It was derived simply from the fact that the protectionist philosophy of the early 1930s had failed to deliver what had been expected of it.

While this was undoubtedly a factor that helped to account for the initial enthusiasm of the United States for free trade after the war, that in itself was not sufficient to sustain its interest over the next quarter of a century and after. The second motivating force for such an interest rested on the belief that free trade, and its role in promoting economic prosperity across the world, was an essential element in American foreign policy. It was possible for the United States for a long period to run two horses in parallel: a belief in the importance of the gains from trade in a free trading world that increased prosperity, and a belief that increasing prosperity under the umbrella of the Pax Americana would provide a solid defence against the possible encroachment of the Communist world. Economic prosperity and the defence of the free market system went forth hand in hand.

Over the years of Bretton Woods, world trade grew rapidly, consistently faster than the rate of growth of gross domestic product in the world at large. This has continued to the present day (see Table 1.3, Chapter 1). This was inevitably accompanied as a matter of arithmetic by a significant rise in the ratio of tradeable goods to total goods for the countries and groups of countries referred to in Table 3.4.

Table 3.4
Exports of goods and services as % of GDP

	1960–73	1974–79	1980–89	1990–95
USA	5.5	8.5	8.6	10.5
Japan	10.2	12.6	12.9	9.8
Germany	18.4	23.7	27.9	24.3
France	14.3	20.2	22.2	22.7
Italy	15.2	22.4	21.4	22.3
UK	21.0	28.2	26.2	25.4
Canada	20.2	24.5	27.1	29.7
EC	19.6	25.4	27.9	27.3
OECD	12.7	16.7	18.1	18.2

Source: OECD Historical Statistics, 1960–95, Paris, 1997

There is little doubt that the economic performance of the golden years in the industrial world, discussed earlier, owed much to the liberalisation and growth of trade that took place over the period. Catching up, cheap raw materials, cheap energy, and financial stability were all significant in creating a favourable environment for growth for the major industrial economies. But it is also difficult not to believe on *prima facie* grounds that the liberalisation of trade was equally of crucial importance.

However, as matters stand today, at no time since the Second World War has the principle of free trade been under such threat. After the war, the free trade principle was seen to be almost self-evident. But in more recent times, the struggle to complete the so-called Uruguay round of tariff reductions and to establish the new World Trade Organization reflects the decline in the general belief that free trade is 'a good thing'. In looking ahead into the future and assessing Britain's role in international trade, and trading arrangements, it is necessary to understand why this has taken place.

There are principally four reasons why attitudes to trade have changed. The first is due to the macroeconomic instability that followed the collapse of the Bretton Woods exchange rate arrangements and the oil price shocks of the 1970s. As was the case in the 1930s, the wide fluctuations in both nominal and real exchange rates over the last quarter of a century have provided ammunition for those supporting more general demands for protection and for some form of managed trade. In the United States, for example, the major deterioration in the current account in the middle 1980s was attributed by many to serious structural weakness in the American economy, rather than simply to a massive loss of competitiveness brought about by an overvalued dollar. The recessions of the 1970s and the 1980s, in particular, raised questions of survival for particular industries. Adjustments to changing trading patterns, easier to accommodate on the back of a steady rise in prosperity, became individual disasters in a rollercoaster world.

Secondly, concerns have been raised in many quarters by the impact of the increased competitiveness of Japan and the newly developing countries. In the West, there has developed a major presumption that with respect to large parts of its traditional high volume manufacturing activities in technologically based products, textiles, a wide range of metal and engineering activities, and shipping, it has become inherently uncompetitive. This has led in both Europe and the United States to calls for protection, particularly for blue collar workers exposed increasingly to international competition. The globalisation of trade and the transfer of technology are seen by some as a threat to the material prosperity of the West.

Thirdly, the very success of European trade integration has generated suspicions about the ultimate objectives of the Union itself. On the face of it, the Union's progress toward the single market has been based on the free trade principle as a means of realising internal prosperity. But some outside the Union have raised the fear of Fortress Europe – closing off the access for those outside the Union to its supposedly new and expanding market. To potential injury has been added perceived injury in the shape of the Union's Common Agricultural Policy.

Finally, there is little doubt that, rational or otherwise, the attitude of the United States to free trade has been influenced by its internal perception of its relative decline in economic importance. Between the 1960s and the 1990s, the gross domestic product of the United States as a ratio to world gross domestic product has fallen from about a third to something over 20 per cent. This relative decline concerns many Americans. In addition, this is linked to the fact that with the ending of the Cold War (if not long before) the promotion of free trade ceased to be seen as an element in American security policy.

The bottom line that derives from the factors just enumerated has been a significant weakening of the *political* case for free trade. But on top of this, in recent years, new theoretical ideas have been developed that have sought to undermine the *economic* case for free trade.

Put very simply, the so-called classical theory of trade supposed that the world was a highly competitive place in which the principle of comparative advantage, specialisation of production and exchange of goods and services between countries would lead to higher levels of output and collectively greater welfare. The conclusions from this simple model, first clearly enunciated by David Ricardo in the early nineteenth century, were powerful indeed – they supported the proposition that free trade between nations was a universal good.

The starting point of what has come to be known as the New Strategic Trade Theory is that the world is not in the main perfectly competitive. It is inhabited by large oligopolistic companies who enjoy increasing economies of scale in production. These economies of scale and market imperfections have a great deal to do with why trade takes place. Just so. The next stage in the argument is to borrow recent developments in the analysis of competitive behaviour, drawn from industrial economics, which compare policy moves by governments to the strategic moves made by rival firms. Thus it has been suggested that individual countries may gain permanent advantage by playing 'games' with taxes, subsidies and protective devices rather than following the free trade rules.

It is true that once imperfect competition and economies of scale are introduced into the analysis, it is no longer possible to prove with any generality that free trade is a universal good. Moreover, it raises the idea that comparative advantages in trade do not fall like the gentle rain from heaven. Comparative advantage may be created. However, empirical studies of trade under the new assumptions, far from destroying the case for trade, suggest that in many cases the benefits of trade may be even greater than was previously supposed. Moreover, it is quite unclear that governments have the required knowledge and capability to create comparative advantage and competitiveness. While some believe that the New Strategic Trade Theory provides a new agenda for government actions, others sceptically regard the process as an attempt to provide the old Emperor with some new clothes to justify the populist attitudes to trade of the past.

These ideas have been supplemented by a serious misunderstanding about the nature of globalisation, the nature of trade, and the meaning of competitiveness. The issues have been elegantly set out in a series of publications by the American economist Paul Krugman (Krugman, 1994a, 1994b, 1994c, 1995).

The first point to make is that the expansion of world trade is not to be explained simply in terms of something called 'globalisation'. World trade as a share of world output reached a peak in 1913, which it did not reach again until 1969. In the 1970s, the share of trade rose above its historical peak in 1913 and has remained relatively stable ever since. This points to the fact that variations in the trade ratio over the last hundred years have been seriously affected by the political framework within which trade has taken place. More specifically, the growth of trade between the Second World War and the mid-1970s had a great deal to do with the positive liberalisation of trade rather than some hidden force called 'globalisation'. As noted by the American investment guru, George Soros, this means that the current economic order is not inevitable. It can unravel if the wrong political decisions are taken. In this context, the key issue is protectionism (Soros, 1995).

The second point is that those who have focused on the ideas of 'globalisation' and 'competitiveness' in many cases see the development of trade as some kind of economic war between nations rather than the process of allocating resources efficiently to mutual advantage on the basis of liberal economic principles. The implication of treating trade as a battle leads to the idea that in the process of trade between countries there are 'winners' and 'losers'. This idea is not only misleading but also dangerous, as it tends to lead to the promotion of policies that are discriminatory in nature and designed to benefit specific interest groups. As was recognised by the United States after the Second World War, such policies engender not simply economic but also political conflict. It is sad that in large measure it has forgotten this. International trade is not a zero-sum game, although many current attitudes to trade imply that it is.

The third point is that winning some kind of trade war is not a precondition for economic growth and increases in living standards. The key issue is simply the increase in domestic productivity. Trade performance is not *per se* of importance. Ultimately trade performance is a byproduct of domestic economic efficiency. Real living standards rise as the result of absolute increases in domestic productivity, not relative to how fast other people's productivity grows. As Krugman remarks:

> Even though world trade is greater than ever before, national living standards are overwhelmingly determined by domestic factors rather than by some competition for world markets. (Krugman, 1994c, p. 34)

The issue may be put further in perspective by excluding any reference to international trade at all, and simply talking about the level of world demand. As a matter of arithmetic again, those countries whose share of world demand is increasing will by definition be growing at a faster rate than the world average. Clearly, if by competitiveness we simply mean domestic economic efficiency (which affects both exports and imports) then competitiveness in a general sense is a factor in determining the absolute rate of economic growth. A falling share of world demand, in itself, is not necessarily a cause for concern, as other countries might be expected to raise their relative standards of living. Just as it was argued in previous chapters that it was quite unreasonable to expect the standard of living in the United Kingdom relative to its peers to have been sustained over the early post-war levels, so too it was unreasonable to expect that the United States should have continued to have generated something of the order of a third of the world's gross domestic product.

These factors are relevant to an assessment of the concerns expressed about the 'globalisation' of trade and the perceived decline of 'competitiveness' in the OECD economies. The simple version of the story argues that globalisation is leading to the transfer of technology from countries of the so-called 'North' to countries of the 'South'. The 'South' has low labour costs, and this combined with the transfer of new technology means that the ability of the North to compete in many of its traditional markets has been eroded, and this has led to widespread unemployment, particularly among unskilled workers. One of the most careful exponents of this view, Adrian Wood, has set out his stall as follows:

> Expansion of trade has linked the labour of developed countries (the North) more closely with developing countries (the South). This greater economic intimacy has had large benefits, raising average living standards in the North and accelerating development in the South. But it has hurt unskilled workers in the North, reducing their wages and pushing them out of jobs. Northern governments must take action to solve this problem. Otherwise, the North will continue to suffer from rising inequality and mass unemployment, and the South from barriers to trade. (Wood, 1994, p. 1)

The problem to which Wood is referring may be exemplified by the numbers in Table 3.5. In the top half of the Table we show the change in the share of world imports of manufacturing between 1970 and 1992. While in 1970 the South accounted for only 5 per cent of world imports of manufactures, by 1990 that proportion had risen to nearly 16 per cent. The bottom half of the Table shows the increase in the share of manufactures in the South's exports to the North. In 1992, 82.2 per cent of the exports of the

North to the South were manufactures. By 1992, the exports of manufactures from the South to the North had risen from about 15 per cent in 1980 to 56 per cent. In 1992, 66 per cent of the exports to the United States from the South were manufactures. The definitions of 'North' and 'South' for this purpose are set out in Table 3.6. There is little doubt that trade in manufactures has become a significantly increasing proportion of the North's imports from the South.

Table 3.5
World trade in manufactures

Share of world imports of manufactures (%)			
	North	South	Eastern Europe
1970	84.4	5.5	9.5
1980	82.3	9.7	7.2
1990	79.1	15.9	3.1
1992	77.7	18.2	1.6

Share of manufactured exports in North/South trade (%)					
	North	South	Japan	Europe	USA
1970	78.7	15.4	7.8	11.0	27.7
1980	79.2	15.1	7.6	13.5	21.1
1990	80.5	53.8	35.0	50.2	66.0
1992	82.2	56.4	36.9	54.4	65.9

Source: UNCTAD Handbook of International Trade and Development Statistics, 1994

None of this should, on the face of it, be any cause for alarm for the developed countries. Firstly, as can be seen from Table 3.7, the proportion of total exports from the North to the North and the South respectively has shown virtually little change over the twenty year period. The jump in 1980 was solely due to changes in oil prices, and by 1992 the situation had more or less returned to normal. The major change, however, is the significant acceleration in trade between the countries of the South, as shown by the rise in the share of the South's exports to itself. New markets have been opening up between the fast growing countries of the South which in turn offers opportunities for the North.

Secondly, following on these developments concerns about globalisation, technology transfer and competitiveness do not take account of their effect on the real incomes of the South. Such increases in productivity and efficiency brought about by these factors will, as all history has shown, be reflected in increased real income levels and standards of living. The success of the South enhances world demand. As already emphasised this is not a zero-sum game.

Table 3.6
Definitions of the 'North' and the 'South'

Developed market economies ('The North')	
Australia	Italy
Austria	Japan
Belgium	Luxembourg
Canada	Netherlands
Denmark	New Zealand
Faroe Islands	Norway
Finland	Portugal
France	South Africa
Germany	Spain
Gibraltar	Sweden
Greece	Switzerland
Iceland	United Kingdom
Ireland	United States
Israel	
	(27)

Developing countries and territories ('The South')

All countries other than those listed above and those defined as included in Eastern Europe, i.e. all countries other than those above in Africa, America, Asia, Europe and Oceania plus socialist countries of Asia (China, N. Korea, Mongolia and Vietnam).

Source: UNCTAD Handbook of International Trade and Development Statistics, 1994

Thirdly, the quantitative size of the impact, to date at least, of these changes on output and employment in the North has not been significant enough to account for the perceived problems of unemployment and inequality. In addition, the timing is wrong. For the United Kingdom and Germany, the percentage of gross domestic product exposed to manufacturing imports from the South was of the order of about 2.5 per cent and for the United States about 3 per cent. The big surge in manufactured exports from the South to the North took place in the middle and late 1980s. As regards European unemployment the big rise in unemployment took place between 1973 and 1984. As far as the United States is concerned, the failure of real wages of blue collar workers to rise has been associated with a poor productivity performance that began around the early 1970s. None of the evidence suggests a *prima facie* case for attributing many of the perceived problems of the United States, the European Union and the United Kingdom to the impact of the South.

Table 3.7
Exports of the North and South by destination, %

		North	South
North	1970	76.4	19.2
	1980	70.8	24.0
	1990	77.5	19.5
	1992	74.7	20.5
South	1970	71.6	19.9
	1980	69.3	25.1
	1990	63.1	27.2
	1992	60.5	31.1

Source: UNCTAD Handbook of International Trade and Development Statistics, 1994

THE PERFORMANCE OF MANUFACTURING INDUSTRY

The decline in the share of manufacturing in total output is a phenomenon that encompasses all the major industrial countries, albeit in different degrees. The relative decline has been fastest in the United Kingdom and in the United States. Relative employment in manufacturing industry has been declining correspondingly. The data for the G7, relating to the structure of output, and aggregate data for the European Union and the OECD have been set out in Table 3.1.

The thesis developed in the previous sections asserts that there is nothing unique about manufacturing industry as a source of economic growth. This is so if we focus on the direct impact of manufacturing on the growth of total output and employment. The idea that its uniqueness in the growth process also derives from its contribution to the balance of payments is equally erroneous. There is no case for some special treatment of manufacturing from an economic policy point of view relative to other sectors of economic activity.

This is not to downgrade the *importance* of manufacturing either in the past or in the future. As we shall see, there is little doubt that had the performance of the manufacturing sector since the war been much better, this would have contributed to the overall rate of economic growth. Moreover, it is to be hoped, and expected, that manufacturing will continue to contribute to the economy in a more efficient way than it has in the past, particularly in the years of the 1970s and early 1980s.

The history of manufacturing output since the Second World War is illustrated in Figure 3.2. As can be seen, allowing for some small disturbances along the way, output grew steadily, if not spectacularly, between 1948 and the boom year of 1973. Clearly, the other countries in the peer group grew markedly more rapidly in line with the differences in overall growth rates that we have already examined in previous chapters. The relative performance of manufacturing over this period reflects, as with total output, the catching up of the peer group. As argued earlier with respect to total output, much of this was to be expected, although it will no doubt be argued by many that even given the catch-up, the performance of British manufacturing industry should have been better for similar reasons to those discussed in the last chapter.

Figure 3.2
Index of production: manufacturing (1990=100)

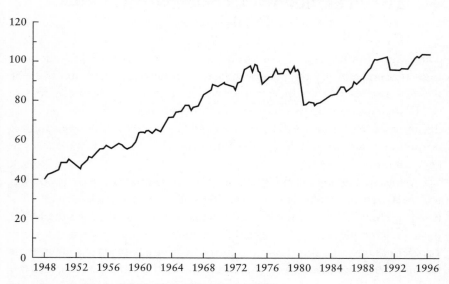

Source: Economic Trends, Office for National Statistics, July 1997

Be that as it may, there is no doubt that the performance of manufacturing between 1973 and 1981 was seriously disappointing. The contrast between the years before 1973 and those after is visually striking. The trend of manufacturing output between 1973 and 1979 was negative, as illustrated in Figure 1.7 in Chapter 1. During the 1970s, the United Kingdom was the only member of the peer group that saw manufacturing output fall absolutely.

Reasons for the relative underperformance of manufacturing, other than the catch-up of the early years, embrace similar factors to those discussed in the last chapter with regard to the growth of total output. The lack of education, investment in training, insufficient expenditure on research and development and a punitive tax system have all been prayed in aid. In very general terms, relatively poor performance has been blamed on a lack of investment linked to the behaviour of the financial system.

Whatever the merits of these considerations as part of any contribution for economic improvement in the United Kingdom, none of them serves to explain the dramatic and violent deterioration of manufacturing industry performance in the period 1973–81 as compared with the prior years. Looking at Figure 3.2, it is as if some severe force had caused a step-down, from the steady progress before 1973 to a resumption of a significant upward trend after the bottom of the recession in 1981. The impact of the oil price shocks required an adjustment in real wages that was not forthcoming.

While some of the factors adduced to explain performance might plausibly be expected to have long term effects, the explanation of the short term behaviour of the 1970s must be sought elsewhere. The popular story of inadequate investment fails to impress, since the investment ratio of the middle 1970s was at its post-war peak. The explanation must be found rooted in the cyclical factors affecting output, combined with a disastrous deterioration in industrial relations which began with, and continued after, the miners' strike of 1974, with severe strike action, particularly in the public sector. Strike first and negotiate after became the fashion of the day.

Trade union behaviour over this period was driven to some degree by what in retrospect was a major failure of macroeconomic policy. The implications of ending the Bretton Woods Agreement were not properly understood. It did not mean that since monetary policy was no longer geared to maintaining parity with the dollar it could be used recklessly (by both Conservative and Labour governments) in an attempt to promote growth or shore up jobs. The consequence was the massive rate of inflation in the United Kingdom relative to the peer group, and after both oil price shocks, substantively deeper recessions. All this is sufficient to account for most of the poor performance of the 1970s. Control of the economy was not regained until the Budget of 1981 which tightened fiscal policy at a time of rising unemployment.

The contrast between these three historical periods, before 1973, the 1970s and the middle to late 1980s, is highlighted by the behaviour of manufacturing productivity over the period as set out in Table 3.8. In each of the periods recorded, manufacturing output per hour in British manufacturing grew at about 4 per cent a year. The out-turn for the 1970s of 1 per cent stands out like a sore thumb. To a Man from Mars, the data would suggest that in the United Kingdom, manufacturing productivity tends to grow on average at about 4 per cent, but the 1970s constituted an aberration that needs an explanation all of its own. That explanation has little to do with the long term factors that may have potentially significant impact on the growth rate.

Table 3.8
Growth of output per hour in manufacturing, %, 12 countries:
selected periods

	1960–73	1973–79	1979–89	1979–94
USA	3.28	1.41	2.34	2.47
Canada	4.44	2.03	1.45	1.81
Japan	9.59	5.15	4.58	4.18
Belgium	6.69	5.83	4.16	3.73*
Denmark	6.22	4.09	1.28	1.68
France	6.55	4.39	3.28	3.04
Germany	5.71	4.21	1.83	2.22
Italy	6.14	5.60	3.86	3.91
Netherlands	7.15	5.32	3.40	3.04
Norway	4.69	2.21	2.03	2.06
Sweden	6.25	2.65	2.53	2.87
UK	4.14	1.01	4.13	3.95

* 1979–93

Source: US Department of Labor, BLS News, September 1995 (except US 1960–73, from BLS News, August 1991)

This perception is highly relevant in the context of the debate as to whether the economic and social reforms carried out under the governments of Margaret Thatcher had any serious impact on the supply side of the economy. Did the improvement in manufacturing industry from 1981 consititute a 'mirage' or a 'miracle'? The sensible answer is neither. First, there is no doubt that serious change did take place, and the minimum that might be asserted is that there was a return to business as usual. That in itself is not to be underestimated. To write off what happened as being no better than the

1950s and 1960s is to miss the point. The second issue that is less clear, but perhaps becoming clearer since 1990, is whether the improvement in manufacturing that was seen was simply a one-off phenomenon resulting from the more efficient use of existing resources. Of change there is no doubt. While manufacturing output did not regain its 1979 level until 1987, that output was delivered with one third fewer people.

The answer to this depends to a large extent on the performance of manufacturing industry management. Has there been a permanent shift in the overall capability of management and the workforce? There are two important reasons why this may be expected to be the case. Firstly, for whatever reasons, the climate of industrial relations since the 1970s and particularly following the second miners' strike has changed. To the extent that that is reasonably permanent, there is hope. Secondly, it is important to realise what a significant change in the economic environment has been brought about by the abolition of exchange control and the increase in the mobility of capital. The globalisation of finance has imposed a different set of pressures on both managements and government that are not easily reversible without a serious reversion to protectionism.

It is against this background that we can return to the question, 'what shall we do when the oil runs out?', and take note of the serious warning from Arjit Singh quoted earlier. The fall in oil prices in 1986 was quite dramatic. The price of oil halved. As Nigel Lawson, the Chancellor of the Exchequer at the time, remarked, if we could lose half our oil revenues overnight and survive reasonably well, we should be able to deal with the other half. Despite the fall in oil prices and the maturity of the North Sea, there is still no evidence that the United Kingdom economy is faced with the kind of balance of payments constraint discussed earlier.

Many critics, however, have placed great weight on the rise in manufactured imports as a sign of a structural competitive weakness in British manufacturing. Looking at manufactured exports (in Figure 3.3) the United Kingdom's share of world manufactured exports fell from 10.75 per cent in 1966 to 6 per cent in 1981. After that the share stabilised during the 1980s for the first time since the Second World War, although there was a further very modest decline during the recession of the 1990s.

However, it is argued, that while this is so, the rise in imports of manufactures is a cause for concern because it implies that there are serious structural problems with manufacturing which will come home to roost in the future. In fact there are several reasons why imports of manufactures relative to exports might have been expected to increase significantly in the 1980s, apart from longer term structural issues of competition.

The first is the obvious impact of the coming of North Sea oil on the real exchange rate. Figure 1.8 shows the behaviour of the exchange rate relative to its purchasing power parity over the period. For our purposes this may be construed as the real exchange rate. The loss of competitiveness in this sense clearly made imports cheaper. Indeed, as argued in Chapter 1, only by importing more or exporting capital could the benefits of North Sea oil be enjoyed. Recent research (Anderton, 1996) seems to demonstrate the presence of 'hysteresis', namely that if competitiveness is lost through a temporary rise in the real exchange rate, the consequences have some degree of permanence. A fall in the exchange rate does not return the status quo. Trading relationships and sources of supply may be permanently altered to some extent.

The second is that, as the previous discussion suggested, the idea that the United Kingdom is an exporter of manufactures in order to buy food and

Figure 3.3
UK share of world trade in manufactures

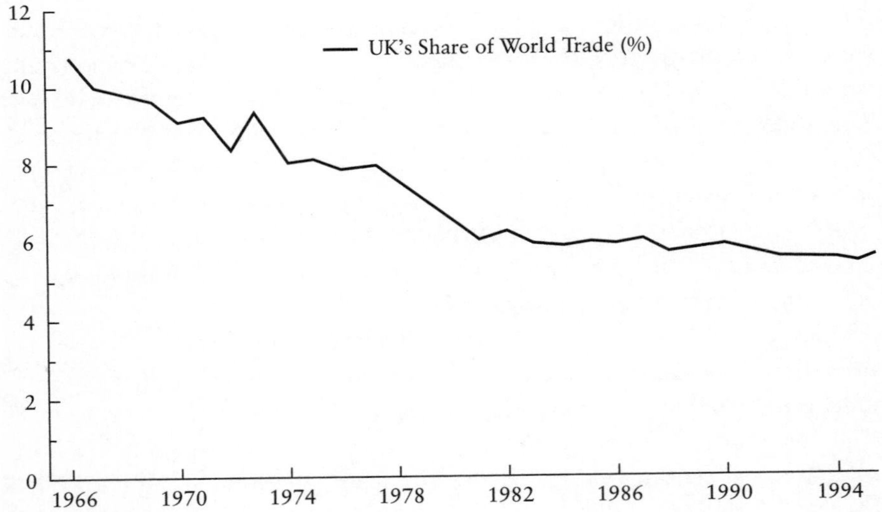

Source: OECD Economic Outlook (various)

raw materials is quite out of date. The growth of world trade in the peer group consists largely of *intra* rather than *inter* trade. We no longer exchange manufactures for food, but manufactures for manufactures. Table 3.9 (p. 112) demonstrates clearly that the rise in the share of manufactures in imports is not a British phenomenon. It traverses the countries of the G7.

The twin forces of imperfect competition and economies of scale, referred to earlier, have been changing the structure of trade. The major industrial countries exchange cars for cars and machine tools for machine tools. It is no longer principally a world that trades cloth for wine as described by David Ricardo in the early nineteenth century. Given a higher income elasticity of demand for manufactured goods relative to foodstuffs and a declining technical ratio between raw materials and real output, countries that began as major sellers of manufactured goods would be expected to spend an increasing proportion of their export receipts on manufactured imports.

As far as the United Kingdom is concerned, the surge in manufacturing imports in the latter part of the 1980s is not ascribable to any significant decline in long term competitiveness, but to the over-expansion of demand in the 1988 boom. Ironically, this expansion in manufactured imports occurred just at the time that the recovery of manufactured productivity referred to earlier was in full swing. Timing is everything!

The myth that manufacturing industry holds the key to economic growth and equilibrium in the balance of payments at full employment holds no water. Looking over the historical facts, the period of the 1970s must be seen as an aberration in a story of otherwise steady if unspectacular progress. Relative to the peer group, British manufacturing industry has been competitive at least based on measures of aggregate manufacturing output and trade performance. Plausible as it may seem to some, there is no evidence from the behaviour of productivity and trade in the 1990s that Britain is suffering either from a balance of payments constraint (brought about by the decline in oil revenues) or from some long term structural paralysis. The strong growth of British manufacturing productivity in the 1980s was followed by continued gains during the recession of the early 1990s. Between 1990 and 1993, productivity rose by over 10 per cent. Much of the productivity gap with our European competitors has been closed (Eltis and Higham, 1995). Profitability, a key factor in the decline of the 1970s, has been largely restored. In addition, as has been demonstrated frequently in recent years, Britain has become a major target for inward manufacturing investment. The idea that British manufacturing industry is in terminal decline has never been less true since the Second World War.

All of this could of course be reversed. The return of serious inflation, a significant change in the ability of management to manage, and a retreat to the corporatist ambitions of the 1970s would all contribute to a reversal of the gains that have been achieved since the early 1980s. To this extent, the outcome is always uncertain. But at this stage, at least there is a case for some degree of optimism.

Table 3.9
Imports of manufactured goods (% total visible imports by value)

	1960	1965	1970	1975	1980	1985	1990
USA	49	56	68	56	62	81	82
Japan	–	23	30	20	23	29	50
Germany	45	54	61	58	59	62	77
France	–	51	63	63	58	62	61
Italy	–	51	54	46	50	53	68
UK	34	40	53	53	64	69	78

Source: OECD Economic Surveys (France, Germany, Italy and Japan), Statistical Abstract of the United States (USA), Pink Books (various) (UK)

CHAPTER 4

UNEMPLOYMENT AND INFLATION

INTRODUCTION

The behaviour of the British economy since the Second World War, as analysed in the previous chapters, makes it clear that the behaviour of economic activity and growth has been materially affected by macroeconomic policy. The conduct of fiscal and monetary policy has played a central role in our explanation of the behaviour of the economy.

As we have seen, the economic performance of the 1970s contrasted dramatically with what had gone before. The interaction of the oil price shocks with the way in which stabilisation policy was conducted accounts, in a proximate sense, for the acceleration in unemployment and the wide fluctuations in the inflation rate that characterised the period. In Britain, matters were compounded by certain institutional factors, in particular the response of organised labour to the change in economic conditions; but there is little doubt from where the proximate impulse came.

Most industrial countries experienced a rise in unemployment and an acceleration in the inflation rate, although the quantitative effects varied significantly between them. Table 4.1 illustrates the behaviour of unemployment rates and inflation rates for the G7 countries since 1960. In Europe, unemployment rose steadily and the inflation rates in Europe exceeded those in America and Japan, with the notable exception of West Germany (as it then was). By 1984, unemployment in Europe exceeded 10 per cent, in contrast to America and Japan. By the middle of the 1990s, unemployment in America had fallen close to its post-war low, while unemployment in Europe had reached an initial post-war peak.

The fact that, generally, economic growth does not proceed smoothly has been known for many years. Serious works on trade cycles go back to the nineteenth century. Periods of boom and bust have characterised the past on a number of occasions, with concomitant variations in unemployment and changes in prices. These fluctuations and depressions have varied in magnitude, the most famous of which is probably the so-called Great Depression that followed the downturn of the American economy in 1929, and a severe deepening of the decline in 1930. The years of the depression of the 1930s left their mark across the world, and as we saw in Chapter 1, had profound effects on the design of the post-war trading regime that was developed at Bretton Woods.

Table 4.1
Unemployment* and inflation rates, %

	1960–73	1973–79	1979–89	1997
USA				
Unemployment	4.8	6.7	7.2	5.1
Inflation	3.2	8.5	5.5	2.2
Japan				
Unemployment	1.3	1.9	2.5	3.3
Inflation	6.2	9.9	2.5	1.7
Germany				
Unemployment	0.8	3.4	6.8	11.2
Inflation	3.3	4.6	2.9	1.5
France				
Unemployment	2.0	4.5	9.0	12.7
Inflation	4.6	10.7	7.3	1.7
Italy				
Unemployment	5.3	6.6	9.9	12.1
Inflation	3.9	16.7	11.2	2.1
UK				
Unemployment	1.9	4.2	9.5	6.3
Inflation	5.1	15.6	7.4	2.3
Canada				
Unemployment	5.0	7.2	9.3	9.5
Inflation	3.3	9.2	6.5	1.2
G7 countries				
Unemployment	3.1	4.9	6.9	6.8
Inflation	3.5	12.1	8.4	2.0
EU(15)				
Unemployment	2.3	4.6	9.2	11.3
Inflation	4.5	11.9	7.3	1.9
OECD				
Unemployment	3.2	5.0	7.2	7.3
Inflation	4.1	10.7	8.9	4.0

* as % of labour force

Source: OECD Historical Statistics, 1960–95, Paris 1997 and OECD Economic Outlook, June 1997

The interesting aspect of the Great Depression in the United States does not arise simply from the economic downturn of 1929. Prior to 1929, America had experienced rapid growth, throughout most of the 1920s, cul-minating in 1927 and 1928 in an extremely strong investment performance, particularly in residential construction. Given the historical background of economic growth in the past, it was not, therefore, entirely surprising that the economy should pause for breath in 1929. The important question is not why was there a pause in 1929, but why in 1930 and afterwards did the downturn became an economic disaster almost without precedent? Much has been made in popular mythology about the consequences of the stock-market boom coming to an end, with ruined brokers leaping out of windows in Wall Street. However, the impact of the stockmarket collapse on the total economy has been generally overrated. The initial fall in the market was no greater than that which occurred in Wall Street in the fall of 1987. We need to look elsewhere for an explanation of events.

KEYNESIANISM

In the face of the Great Depression of the 1930s, economists and others struggled to find an explanation for the cause of events. The most notable of these was, of course, John Maynard Keynes. In 1936, he published what became known in short as *The General Theory* (Keynes, 1936), which has been described as the most important publication in the social sciences since Marx's *Das Kapital*. Keynes and Marx shared the distinction of having a major impact on the way in which the issues they discussed were viewed by those who came after them. They also shared the fact that, in their different ways, their theories were fatally flawed, in large measure because events overtook them. In Keynes's case it was the problem of inflation, in Marx's the fact that limited liability enabled capital to be subdivided.

The essence of Keynes's explanation of the Great Depression started with the idea that so-called capitalist or market economies are essentially unstable. It has already been pointed out in this chapter that it was well known that fluctuations took place. Insofar as the Great Depression was akin to what had gone before, it simply exhibited much greater severity. It was the economic equivalent of the two-hundred-year storm.

This instability, said Keynes, arose from fluctuations in the rate of investment. Entrepreneurs (for reasons Keynes does not clearly explain) were subject to periods of pessimism which affected what Keynes called their 'animal spirits'. Excessive optimism could lead to overinvestment and excess capacity, resulting in the reverse – pessimism and low investment. This in turn would reduce the level of demand, resulting in depression and rising unemployment. In order to prevent this, it was necessary for government to intervene by itself investing *contra* cyclically to offset the fall in private investment. This call for what he described as the 'socialisation of investment' (nothing to do with socialism) was the only policy recommendation that came out of the *General Theory* itself. Later Keynes's followers extended the analysis to include changes in general government spending and in taxes as part of the fiscal tool kit that was deemed necessary to maintain the level of demand.

In simple terms, economies deviate from their longer term growth paths as a result of shocks. Such shocks are customarily divided into demand shocks, supply shocks, and policy shocks. Keynes focused on the first of these, demand shocks, believing that fluctuations in economic activity were caused by an internal failure of private spending. Such failures were regarded as endemic to a free market economy. However, a different historical interpretation of the depth of the Great Depression has been offered by the American economists, Milton Friedman and Anna Schwartz (see Chapter 1), which focuses on the prime role of policy failure on the part of the Federal Reserve.

Apart from the focus on private investment as the driver of the economic system, the other major development that arose from Keynes's *General Theory* was the redefinition of the nature of unemployment. Keynes's predecessors and contemporaries argued that if unemployment existed, it must be because the price of labour was excessive – it was above the market clearing rate. For Keynes, people did not choose to offer their services at a given price on a 'take-it-or-leave-it' basis. The unemployed were willing to take jobs at below the rate in the market place. They were unemployed because there were no jobs available at any price. Hence, the only reason there was unemployment was a lack of effective demand. The unemployed were *involuntarily unemployed* and the key to reducing their number was simply to raise the overall level of expenditure.

In the United Kingdom these ideas swept the board, and provided the background for macroeconomic discussion in both the political parties, Conservative and Labour; we were all Keynesians then. When discussed in the post-war period, after Keynes's death, it was recognised that trying to maintain full employment or accelerating growth did tend to run up against two other problems, the rate of inflation and the current account of the balance of payments. Up to and including the 1970s, the principal macroeconomic strategy was to try to maintain what was thought to be the full employment level of demand, and the faster rate of growth of demand consistent with supply side constraints, by the use of fiscal and monetary policy. In Britain at least, few challenged the idea that government should and could legitimately set real unemployment targets that were achievable by the use of such policies.

While Keynes's ideas had much impact in the Anglo-Saxon world and in the Scandinavian countries and the Netherlands, they had little currency elsewhere, notably in Germany and Japan. The economic achievements of these countries had nothing to do with the application of Keynesian ideas. Ironically, and contrary to more popular mythology, nor did they have anything to do with Britain's economic performance in the 1950s and 1960s. The boon of monetary stability over those years was derived from adherence to the discipline imposed by the Bretton Woods system of pegged exchange rates. It was only in the 1970s that Keynesianism was really put to the test by both Conservative and Labour governments with the disastrous consequences that we have already studied. The issue was famously summed up by the then Labour Prime Minister, James Callaghan, in a speech to the Labour Party Conference in 1976:

> We used to think that you could just spend your way out of a recession and increase employment by cutting taxes and boosting government spending: I tell you in all candour that that option no longer exists, and that insofar as it ever did exist, it worked by infecting inflation into the economy. And each time that has happened, the average level of unemployment has risen. Higher inflation followed by higher unemployment. That is the history of the last twenty years.

MONETARISM

The intellectual dominance of the ideas of Keynes, in economic thinking in Britain, if not as the mythology has insisted their positive influence on economic management, began to come under pressure in the early 1970s. The challenge continued throughout the decade. In the United States, the ideas of Keynes did not achieve the same dominance as in the United Kingdom. Nevertheless, amongst intellectuals they were important. In a practical sense, they had little relevance until the Kennedy era when attempts were made to use such ideas as a basis for policy making. But in the United States, as in Germany, the separation of economic powers and the relative independence of the central bank made it difficult to apply the ideas of so-called demand management, particularly with regard to fiscal policy.

By the 1960s it was increasingly recognised that inflation and the current account of the balance of payments were presenting significant problems for what might be described as 'naive Keynesianism'. Indeed, as described in the last chapter, the view had emerged that economic growth in Britain suffered from an external constraint. At the same time it was believed, as the result of a number of statistical studies, that there existed a significant long term trade off between the unemployment rate and the rate of inflation. Lower unemployment meant higher inflation. Notice the implied direction of causation. The presumption was not that high inflation was detrimental to employment. Quite the contrary. More employment – lower unemployment – could be achieved only if inflation were higher. Given this view, it was hard to explain at that time why one should be worried about inflation at all.

The theoretical underpinning of this argument was given short shrift in Milton Friedman's presidential address to the American Economic Association in 1968 (Friedman, 1968). He argued that the failure of the previous analysis lay in not taking into account the importance of people's expectations. The relationship between unemployment and the inflation rate (the trade off) was constructed for a given rate of expected inflation. A rise in people's expectations about future inflation raised the rate of inflation that would occur at any given rate of unemployment. And Friedman went further. In the long run, the rate of unemployment had no effect on inflation at all, once the actual rate of inflation had caught up with the expected rate. This seemed at first sight to leave the inflation rate without a sponsor, yet another example of the Cheshire Cat whose grin remained behind while the corporeal entity had vanished. Not so, said Friedman, because common sense tells the person in the street that what drives inflation and inflationary expectations are changes in the money supply. Ultimately, unemployment is not the arbiter of the inflation rate, it is changes in the supply of money relative to changes in the volume of economic activity or output. Ultimately, inflation is not a *real* phenomenon that is permanently affected by the unemployment rate, but a *monetary* phenomenon that is governed by what is happening to the monetary stance. Therefore, while in the short run, when the economy is disturbed, unemployment interacts with the inflation rate, in the long run there is no trade off. Thus, while exceptionally high unemployment may be needed to bring the inflation rate down, long term price stability is not connected to any particular level of unemployment.

These theories led to the creation of a new -ism, 'monetarism'. In many quarters of contemporary Britain, 'monetarism' became a term of abuse. It either represented a particularly ossified and singular view of how an economy works, or reflected a particular set of political attitudes, or probably both together. But while the theoretical arguments led to forms of monetarism as described above, the force of practical affairs was pushing in the same direction.

With the collapse of Bretton Woods in 1971, the post-war monetary system came at least to a formal end. For all practical purposes, it was under increasing pressure throughout the 1960s starting with developments in the United States associated with President Kennedy. In 1971 President Nixon, by suspending the convertibility of the dollar into gold, simply shot a dying duck. For a year or two it continued to flap its wings, but finally (with the exception of those who joined what was known as the 'European snake in the tunnel') the duck died and currencies floated free. At the same time, the statistical basis of the inflation/unemployment trade off theory was undermined by the fact that in the 1970s, instead of unemployment and inflation being negatively related as they had been before, both unemployment and inflation rose together. A new term was coined to describe what was happening – 'stagflation'. Stagflation was the empirical realisation of Friedman's analysis; inflationary expectations rose as unemployment also rose. Thus both intellectually and empirically the so-called Keynesian consensus in Britain that had underlain the approach to economic policy on both sides of the House of Commons was undermined. In the context of British politics, it was the late Keith Joseph who blew the whistle and deserted Edward Heath to support Margaret Thatcher for the leadership of the Conservative Party.

What is meant by 'monetarism' is both inadvertently and, in some cases, deliberately misunderstood. Sometimes it is confused with the proposition that the quantity of money (however measured) is the most significant economic variable that should drive the conduct of economic policy. It is believed to reflect a dogmatic adherence to some sort of mumbo jumbo about the money supply. A second source of confusion stems from the idea that monetarists believe that only the rate of inflation matters, so that monetarists are unconcerned about the rate of unemployment.

There are several different versions of 'monetarism' which, from an intellectual point of view, come with a variety of different bells and whistles attached. First, there are the so-called new classical school of monetarists. Second, the conventional monetarists and third the international monetarists. But broadly speaking they share certain basic ideas that, ironically, at the outset have nothing to do with money at all. The behaviour of money is a consequence of the basic economic argument. Indeed, the practical monetarist would concur with the nineteenth-century classical economist, John Stuart Mill, who observed:

> There cannot ... be intrinsically a more insignificant thing, in the economy of society, than money; ... like many other kinds of machinery, it only exerts a distinct and independent influence of its own when it gets out of order. (Mill, 1929, p. 488)

To begin with, the monetarist rejects the Keynesian starting point, that it is spending behaviour (or level of *demand*) that principally causes change in economic activity. The monetarist also focuses on the behaviour of *supply*. Questions are asked as to why people want to work and on what terms, what effect does their productivity have on their employment, and why should anyone want to employ anyone in the first place? To sum up, labour markets and the way in which they work become a central part of the analysis of both the behaviour of output and levels of employment. Supply side behaviour, for example, as manifested by changing technology and by the institutional behaviour of organised labour, becomes relevant to the process of job creation.

Secondly, monetarists believe that for much of the time (some believe for all of the time) it is impossible to target real economic objectives (such as a given number of unemployed, or a given rate of growth of real output) by the use of fiscal and monetary policy. This is sometimes described by economists as a belief in the long run *neutrality of money*. You cannot generate permanent, real gains in the economy by simply expanding the money supply. One might temper that by saying that it is possible to envisage Keynesian type unemployment as a result of a demand shock, for which Keynesian remedies would indeed be appropriate. It then becomes an empirical question as to how frequently cyclical disturbances in the major industrial countries are indeed due to demand shocks.

Monetarists have tended to place greater weight than Keynesians on the importance of monetary policy. Curiously, Keynes himself in his earlier years placed strong emphasis on it as well. Monetarists tend to be sceptical about the discretionary use of fiscal policy in order to manipulate the level of expenditure in the short run. They are inclined to the view that the fiscal framework of government spending and taxation should be geared to the supply side of the economy particularly with regard to incentives and risk taking. Finally, monetarist analysis tends to look at the longer rather than the shorter term behaviour of the economy, which raises the question as to how long the 'longer term' is meant to be, a question that is usually tacked on to Keynes's pronouncement that 'in the long run we are all dead'.

On the other side of the coin, monetarists do not say that inflation is the only important economic objective. What they do sometimes imply is that in the longer run, unemployment can only be reduced by expansionary monetary and fiscal policy in special circumstances. In the main, a significant reduction in equilibrium unemployment may require important changes in the supply side of the system and, therefore, supply side policies. Moreover, for the reasons discussed, the last thing that monetarists advocate is massive unemployment to hold down the inflation rate, since it is a core part of their perception of the world that in the long run there is no trade off between the two.

THE RE-EMERGENCE OF UNEMPLOYMENT

In the United Kingdom at least, if not universally, the economic consensus of the 1950s and into the 1960s was that effectively the unemployment problem had been solved. As can be seen from Table 4.1, the G7 world as a whole experienced what could reasonably be described as full employment during this period. In Britain at least, it was believed that in the event that unemployment did rise as the result of demand shocks, the problem could be easily dealt with using Keynesian recipes. Today that optimism has disappeared. Even at the time it was not fully understood what policy constraints the Bretton Woods Agreement placed on its subscribers. But as we have recounted, both intellectual developments and the subsequent course of events have had profound effects on the approaches to the conduct of macroeconomic policy that are shared by most governments in the OECD countries today.

Table 4.1 demonstrates that the behaviour of unemployment in the OECD countries from the early 1970s onwards has varied significantly between countries. To begin with, we may distinguish between unemployment behaviour in the United States, Japan, the European Union and other countries of industrial Europe.

The United States data show us that, by and large, there is no evidence of any significant trend in American unemployment. Indeed, by the middle 1990s, unemployment in the United States had fallen to a virtual post-war low. At the same time (see Figure 1.5) employment growth throughout the period after 1970 was strong relative to the peer group. On the face of it, it would appear that unemployment in America was positively correlated with fluctuations in the rate of growth of output; increases in periods of recession were offset by falls in periods of recovery. However, another significant feature of this period has been focused on in the course of the discussion of unemployment in the OECD, namely, the significant increase in the degree of income inequality that has taken place. The real wages of so-called blue-collar workers in the United States have been virtually stationary since the middle 1970s, and the evidence seems to suggest that at the bottom end of the income scale real incomes have actually fallen.

The situation in Japan is difficult to compare with the other principal economies of the OECD, because of significant differences in the institutional framework of employment and a problem of measuring the unemployment rate. Japan has been regarded as different from other major countries because of its long and continuing commitment to what has been called 'life-time' employment reinforced by a collective search for harmony. While there has certainly been commitment to such a concept by large scale businesses and institutions, these are supported by a significant separate layer of economic activity which supplies the major businesses. In recession, the bulk of any labour adjustment is effectively absorbed by this second tier of mostly family businesses, which is augmented by the entry and exit of women from the labour force. Accordingly, it is reasonable to take a some-what sceptical view of the official rate of unemployment that is published in Japan. In addition, it has become evident in recent years that Japanese industry and financial institutions are suffering massive over-manning and require major structural adjustments going forward. Consequently, there is what may be described as substantial 'disguised unemployment' which of course does not appear in the official figures. However, as Figure 1.5 shows, over the period as a whole, Japan did steadily create jobs, although at a less rapid rate than the United States.

Turning to Europe, a contrast has often been drawn between the behaviour of unemployment among the members of the European Union, and other mature non-member economies, such as Sweden, Austria, Switzer-land and Norway. Whereas unemployment in the Union trended strongly upward (see Table 4.1) between the mid-1970s and mid-1980s, this was not true for those other countries. However, the most recent experience of the 1990s suggests that similar issues to those facing EU members are now fac-ing non-member countries.

From Figure 1.5 we see that, while the United States and Japan created significant new jobs during the quarter-century since 1970, employment in the Union and in the United Kingdom remained flat until it started to move up in the mid-1980s. Meanwhile, the trend rate of unemployment moved upwards. How can we explain this increase, particularly in contrast to the experience of the United States?

For much of the period since the early 1970s, the unemployment rate in the United Kingdom was in line with or marginally worse than the Union average depending on which criteria you chose. By the mid-1990s, it had fallen significantly below the average. But for current purposes of discussion we can associate it with the general problems that have beset the Union membership.

In analysing the behaviour of European unemployment, it is important at the outset to distinguish between the 'cyclical' and non-cyclical or 'struc-tural' components of the unemployment rate. If unemployment is simply 'cyclical' in nature, it is more likely to correspond to the kind of demand induced unemployment that Keynes had in mind. While cyclical unemployment, in itself, would not necessarily justify an interventionist, stabilisation policy (as that would depend on the nature of the shock causing a downturn) it would at least be reasonable to assume that it would be eliminated as the economy recovered. In this context, it can be argued that during some periods the conduct of macroeconomic policy across the Union has aggravated the unemployment problem. For example, in the case of the United Kingdom unemployment was higher than it would otherwise have been, given the nature of the stance of stabilisation policy put in place by the Thatcher government in order to reduce the inflation rate. Nonetheless, it has been widely agreed that the problem of unemployment in the Union, *pace* Keynes, is not primarily associated with a lack of effective demand.

To quote the Annual Economic Report of the European Commission:

> ... since that part (the cyclical) of unemployment is currently estimated to represent only 2% of the labour force, it will be far from enough to bring unemployment down to acceptable levels, and to reach the unemployment target ... (The European Economy, 1995, p. 129)

This analysis by the Commission leads us to distinguish between the *actual* unemployment rate at a given moment in time, and what economists describe as the *equilibrium* rate of unemployment. Fluctuations in expenditure (from whatever source of shock) will cause deviations from equilibrium in the unemployment rate. A trend increase in the unemployment rate of the kind observed in the European Union, however, suggests almost certainly that over time the equilibrium rate of unemployment has been shifting upwards.

It is also important, from an historical point of view, that what has been regarded as an *upward shift* in the equilibrium rate in the Union took place in the period between the mid-1970s and the mid-1980s. After the mid-1980s unemployment fell to rise again during the early and mid-1990s. The problem over this period would appear to be, not so much the *creation* of unemployment, as its *persistence*. This issue of timing is important in reviewing the status of alternative explanations of the rise in European unemployment. It also relates to the significance of particular kinds of economic influence in accounting for the creation of unemployment and/or its persistence.

The proximate cause of the rise in European unemployment in the 1970s must be found initially in the two oil price shocks in 1973 and 1978. A careful study of European unemployment published by the Centre of Economic Policy Research (CEPR, 1995) remarked:

> At a proximate level it seems obvious ... that the two oil price shocks must share part of the blame, because the coincidence of timing is just too great for it to be otherwise. (CEPR, 1995, p. 31)

The oil price shocks of the 1970s reflect a general disturbance which is not industry specific nor does it focus on a particular industrial segment of the labour force. The impact of the oil shocks on inflation and the general level of demand (for a given set of policy responses) impacted in a general sense on unemployment across the Union. Again, in a proximate sense, the rise in unemployment across the Union, and indeed elsewhere, can be associated quite simply with pressure on profitability. If we compare the Union with the United States, we can see that the interaction of the oil price shocks with rigidities in real unit labour costs created a general pressure for corporate restructuring which forced firms to become more efficient in the face of declining profitability. In the United Kingdom this process began in the 1970s and continued throughout the 1980s and into the 1990s. During the 1980s, in the United Kingdom some 2.5 million jobs were eliminated in manufacturing industry alone.

These developments reflected *general* reasons why unemployment in Europe rose. However, there are two other hypotheses which have been advanced to explain the tendency for jobs to be eliminated and, therefore, other things being equal, for unemployment to rise.

The first of these is the argument discussed in the last chapter, that the rise in unemployment, particularly in manufacturing industry, where most of the jobs have been lost, has been due to the increase in competition from the 'Third World' or 'The South'. The most immediate reasons for dismissing this argument are twofold. First, as pointed out earlier, the major rise in European unemployment, associated with an upward shift in the equilibrium unemployment rate, occurred in the decade between the mid-1970s and the mid-1980s. Over this period, the quantitative significance of imports of manufactures by the Union from the South was negligible. This is not to say that this might not be a problem in the future (although, as we saw, there are arguments as to why that might not be the case). Secondly, as the European Commission itself in an earlier White Paper stated:

> The world economy has continued to grow over recent years and a number of developing countries have experienced very high rates of growth. The preserve of new vibrant economies in Asia, and soon in Eastern Europe, constitutes a huge opportunity and not a threat to our standards of living. (European Commission, 1993, p. 39)

The second hypothesis concerns the impact of 'changes in technology'. Initially we have a problem in defining exactly what this means. Technological change may imply the ability to raise production as the result of new knowledge and process change. The impact on employment clearly depends on how fast the demand for output is growing relative to the productivity increase. For goods that are not responsive to increases in income, the result may be no change in volume but a loss of jobs; job displacement may result in a given sector of the economy. But the story clearly does not end there. The question then arises as to whether the surplus labour will not be re-employed in other sectors, and if so why not. History has tended to show that despite fears regularly expressed down the years, rising productivity does not lead permanently to higher rates of unemployment (as mistakenly forecast by Karl Marx). At one level this is not very surprising as rising productivity is simply the way in which living standards rise and real income grows overall.

However, technical change can cause significant changes in the product mix as innovations occur over time. Such changes inevitably give rise to changes in the pattern of demand across different sectors of the economy and require changes in relevant skills. Thus, the interaction of both product and process innovation reacts in complex ways on the actual level and distribution of employment. The speed with which labour is reallocated between growing and static or declining economic activities becomes crucial.

The CEPR Report of 1995 emphasises the difficulty of direct testing of hypotheses associated with technology and unemployment. A commonly held view suggests that the increased income inequality in the United States and the high unemployment rates in Europe, both of which result from changes in technology, are in effect two sides of the same coin. The explanation offered is that over the last twenty years the USA has seen technological change biased in favour of 'skilled' rather than 'unskilled' labour. As labour markets in the United States are relatively flexible, new jobs have been created in low paid service industries. 'Full employment' has been maintained but this has been accompanied by a radical increase in the dispersion of post-tax incomes. The real wages of so-called 'blue collar' workers have been relatively static.

The pressure of technical change in Europe has been similar, but the outcome in terms of labour markets has been very different. As labour markets in Europe have been extremely rigid and inflexible, the result of technological change has only partially affected the income distribution. Unlike the USA the principal effect has been one of increasing unemployment. From this it has been concluded that the two situations are equally bad; the Europeans have 'no jobs', the lower tail of the American income distribution has 'bad jobs'.

On this issue, the CEPR Report suggested that:

> as well as being consistent with the evolution of wages, this thesis also apparently fits with the evolution of unemployment rates by skill ... it is also consistent with more detailed micro-economic work on the source of widening wage differentials

in the United States which traces it to shifts in relative demands (that furthermore are not simply the result of a changing industrial structure) rather than supplies. All this is circumstantial evidence ... There is, however, no direct evidence that suggests that technological progress has been biased against unskilled workers in the recent past. (CEPR Report, 1995, p. 50)

The impact of technology on *unemployment rates* is unclear. However, there is clearly a *prima facie* case for its effect on *income distribution*. As persuasively argued by Peter Drucker (Drucker, 1993) we have been witnessing over the last twenty years or more the coming of a new industrial revolution. The age of mass production has been coming to an end. Semi-skilled supervision, the technical worker, is replacing the unskilled worker. Formerly the machine drove the man, enabling relatively unskilled workers on assembly lines to generate middle class incomes. This is by and large no longer true. The man drives the machine. Economies of scale in production are no longer so crucial. The days of Henry Ford are over. As we see with the United States such developments need not result in unemployment if labour markets are sufficiently flexible.

Unemployment rates of the unskilled have always been materially larger than those of the skilled. But that in itself may not appear very surprising. What is perhaps surprising in the context of the discussion of the impact of technological change on unskilled unemployment rates is that the unemployment rate of unskilled labour relative to the unemployment rate of the skilled has shown no significant increase since the mid-1970s, as can be seen in Table 4.2. If looked at in terms of educational qualifications, the unemployment rates for both skilled and unskilled employees roughly trebled during the recession of the 1970s and the recession of the early 1990s. However, as demonstrated by Haskel (1996), the relative incomes of the skilled and the unskilled have changed significantly over this period, not simply where relatively large proportions of unskilled labour are employed but generally across different sectors of manufacturing industry. Haskel tests and rejects hypotheses relating to Third World competition or a decline in trade union power, particularly since 1979. He reaches the conclusion that new technology, particularly information technology, has played an important role in raising the relative incomes of skilled labour. The earnings of skilled labour in manufacturing industries where information technology is particularly important, such as office machinery and food processing, have risen much more than in industries where it matters less.

Table 4.2
Male unemployment rates % by qualification

	1975–78	1979–82	1983–86	1987–90	1991–93
Total unemployment rate	4.4	7.7	10.5	7.5	11.4
1 rate for those with A-levels/ higher education	2.0	3.9	4.7	4.0	6.3
2 rate for those with no qualification	6.4	12.2	18.2	13.5	17.4
Ratio 2:1	3.2	3.1	3.9	3.4	2.8

Source: Nickell and Bell, 1995, General Household Survey

As already argued, the *proximate* causes of rising unemployment in Europe which occurred in the mid-1970s are not hard to find, but they have nothing to do with the impact of technological change or competition from the Third World. The shocks of the 1970s and the macroeconomic policies that accompanied them put pressure on corporate profits which forced companies to become more efficient and raise productivity faster than demand. The central question which concerns British and European economists is not so much what caused the initial increase in unemployment but why, as the European economy recovered, the rise in unemployment was not reversed.

The most characteristic feature of unemployment in Europe and in the United Kingdom has been its persistence, coupled with the fact that a major proportion of the unemployed fall into the category of being long term unemployed lasting over a year and more. It has been suggested that the European labour market is in fact less sclerotic than it sometimes appears. The flexibility of the market, with movement of labour between jobs, in Europe is concealed relative to the United States by the fact that job changes more often take place from job to job rather than via a period in unemployment. The conclusion is that job insecurity is in fact greater in the United States than in Europe but the average period of unemployment is substantially less. Thus, while the probability of becoming unemployed in the United States is greater than in Europe, the probability of remaining unemployed for a considerable period is correspondingly less.

To some degree, hysteresis may affect the behaviour of unemployment over time, as the probability of being re-employed is believed to decline significantly as the period of unemployment becomes prolonged. But this is hardly likely to account for much of what we see in the European context.

Given that factors such as technological change and global competition affect both the United States and Europe, the difference between them with regard to the creation of jobs must be accounted for in other ways.

Much attention has been focused on the response of the unemployed in seeking and offering themselves for work. The persistence of European unemployment has been attributable to the existence of excessively high minimum wages in some countries, to over-regulation of labour markets, so increasing the costs of hiring, and certainly those of separation. Relatively high levels of unemployment benefits discourage the search process and the willingness to accept less well paid jobs than those from which the unemployed have been displaced. This has particularly impacted on the creation of jobs in service industries where the progress of the United States has been most striking. The European Commission commented in 1993 that:

> The relatively high cost of unskilled labour is speeding up the rationalisation of investment and holding back job creation in services. This has resulted in the loss of millions of jobs. (European Commission, 1993, p. 11)

Welfare systems in Continental Europe have not been supportive of the process of job creation. Moreover, as will be seen in Chapter 5, they pose serious fiscal difficulties for many countries going forward. But as the CEPR Report points out, the employment related welfare systems of Continental European countries have not changed substantively since the 1960s. They are not in themselves *causes* of the rise in the rate of unemployment but materially affect its *persistence*. As the Report noted at its outset:

> Europe's relatively ... regulated labour markets and generous welfare provisions were forged on the back of the optimistic expectation engendered by the Golden Age, but have turned out to be less suited to a world of low growth and high unemployment. Instead of relaxing these provisions on the lines of the US market, however, European governments have predominantly chosen to maintain social cohesion by retaining or even strengthening the existing structure. (CEPR, 1995, p. 1)

The conclusion must be that the persistence of unemployment in Europe, relative to the United States, has been sustained by the behaviour of labour markets and their interaction with the welfare system. This is clearly not the whole story with regard to the levels of unemployment since as we have seen, since the 1970s while the equilibrium unemployment rate appears to have shifted upward, there have been significant fluctuations around it. Moreover, the failure to create more jobs in service industries may reflect other supply side problems. The creation of unemployment has been driven by mistakes in the conduct of monetary and fiscal policy. But persistence is rooted in labour market behaviour supported by fiscal and regulatory environments that have failed to provide incentives to work. If we wish to change behaviour we should change the reward system.

UNEMPLOYMENT POLICIES

From this discussion we see that while there is much debate as to the reasons for the existence of high unemployment in the G7 countries relative to the United States, agreement as to why this is so is insufficiently precise to lead easily to agreed policies for correcting the situation. There is however a general presumption that the core of the problem is structural rather than simply cyclical. While we have focused on unemployment in the European Union, it is worth noting the contrast in North America between Canada and the United States. Over the post-war period as a whole the Canadian unemployment rate has been higher than all members of the G7 with the exception of Italy.

By definition, the core problem of structural unemployment cannot be resolved by the manipulation of stabilisation policy. This is not to say that demand management policies have no part to play in the unemployment story. On the contrary, as we have argued earlier, inappropriate macroeconomic policies are themselves part of the process which combined with other factors has ratcheted up unemployment rates in many countries. As will be argued later, the goal of financial stability is an important one. Inappropriate stabilisation policies may incur major real costs in the process of correction which could potentially have serious longer run consequences for productivity and growth. Some fall in unemployment was to be expected as the world recovers from the recession of the early 1990s and we have seen this occurring in a number of places. But there is little prospect that renewed growth alone in the mature OECD economies will in itself be sufficient to reverse the tide of the last quarter of a century. The high water mark for unemployment for many major industrial economies is now much further up the beach.

This is the case despite the fact that some have argued that in Continental Europe and elsewhere the conduct of monetary policy has been more important in sustaining high unemployment than the previous discussion leads one to suppose. The central issue concerns the impact of the Bundesbank on real interest rates in Europe, following the reunification of Germany. A further factor that also serves to keep real interest rates high is the existence of significant fiscal deficits and the fear that much of the debt will be monetised in the foreseeable future. The other side of the coin is the fear of the reverse, namely that fiscal retrenchment in anticipation of a single European currency would mitigate against significant economic recovery as we approach the end of the century.

Despite these considerations, there is a widely held view that structural issues lie at the heart of the problem faced by these industrial countries which are currently suffering exceptionally high unemployment. The value of employment depends on the productivity of labour and its price. These are the key factors that determine the relationship between employment and the rate of growth of demand. There are two, not mutually exclusive, approaches to dealing with what is virtually a tautology: for a given rate of growth of demand, one choice is to lower the cost of labour; at a given level of productivity, the second choice is to raise the level of productivity itself.

Excessive regulation of labour markets combined with institutional rigidities make it difficult to ensure the smooth transfer of labour between different occupations. In the modern world the pace of change is probably faster than it has ever been, and the need for flexibility and speed of adaptation is consequently greater. Regulation raises the cost of hiring and separation. Payroll taxes are levied in order to pay for unemployment benefits. A vicious circle develops because such taxes raise the cost of labour to the employer and, in turn, inhibit the reduction of unemployment as the price of labour rises, while at the same time reducing the incentive to seek work. The loading of payroll taxes, pension costs, and high costs of hiring and separation may all serve to raise the effective price of labour to the employer. The problem becomes even more acute when the long term growth of the economy is slower than in the past and when, in many occupations, the value of unskilled labour is diminished. The deregulation of labour markets is an important necessary condition if not a sufficient one to reduce long term unemployment. Institutional rigidities created by the existence of powerful trade unions can inhibit the creation of jobs in two ways. The first, particularly important in the United Kingdom history until the 1980s, was the ability of unions to frustrate productivity increases by restrictive practices so diminishing the future value of employed labour and reducing the competitiveness of companies. The second concerns the maintenance of wage levels in particular occupations discouraging the employment of additional labour and discriminating between the employed and the unemployed, the so-called insider/outsider problem.

These issues have all been fully discussed, not only in the CEPR Report referred to above, but also in a major study published in 1994 by the OECD (OECD, 1994). This report, like the discussion above, focused on the labour market. But a subsequent study carried out by McKinsey (McKinsey, 1994) has emphasised the role of regulation in creating product market barriers and thereby reducing the ability of individual industries to adapt to change.

This study concluded that while capital market barriers seemed relatively unimportant, product markets in Continental Europe are affected by measures designed to preserve existing jobs, protect the environment, and generally inhibit competition by creating barriers to entry. Retailing is selected as an industry beset by classic zoning regulations, restrictions on opening hours and other anti-competitive practices. In America, the retail sector has been a major contributor to job creation. In banking, while deregulation in the United States led to the loss of many jobs in conventional banking, it also encouraged the creation of even more jobs in financial services. In the area of multi-media, countries such as France have extensive regulations which inhibit competition, particularly from abroad, and which prevent job growth. It should be noted that these are all examples of regulation affecting the service sector, an area where Europe is far behind what has been achieved in the United States.

A more controversial issue, believed by many to be a significant part of Europe's unemployment problem, is the minimum wage. In France, for example, over the last twenty-five years the statutory minimum wage created by the law of January 1970 has risen by over 100 per cent in real terms. It has, in fact, increased significantly more rapidly than the average wage. There is, it is argued, a *prima facie* case for believing that the behaviour of the minimum wage has had significant consequences for unskilled if not for skilled employment.

In economic theory it is possible to conceive of a situation in which the setting of a minimum wage at a particular level not only does no harm, but actually encourages employment. The idea requires certain special assumptions but it is not clear that these are sufficiently convincing to dispel the intuitive belief that raising the price of the product (if that is the result of a minimum wage) reduces the demand for it. Clearly, what effect a minimum wage has depends on where it is set relative to the going market rate. If it is below the market rate or more or less equal to it, clearly it serves no purpose. In terms of money of the day, if it is above the going rate in the market this will simply raise money costs. If the workers being paid higher rates in *money terms* are also to benefit in *real terms*, which must be the object of the exercise, this can only be the case if the affected industries are able to raise their product prices so lowering real wages elsewhere. If that is not possible the result will be to lower employment. Equally, no real benefit will be achieved if others resist the fall in real wages and raise their wages and prices. A different result might be achieved if as the result of imposing a minimum wage, the productivity of the affected workers also increased. Why that should be the case is not clear, although this outcome has been suggested by some economists. If the argument holds that is sometimes put, that minimum wages are not to be feared because they will do no positive harm to anyone, then by the same token they will not do much good either. The upshot may, therefore, be what many perceive as a significant problem in Continental Europe, namely that minimum wage levels exceed the market clearing rate and so sustain the unemployment level.

The emotional case for setting minimum wages must turn on the belief that market wage rates are concomitant with what may be described as 'poverty'. As already pointed out, it is not clear that minimum wage rates would succeed in raising real living standards for the lowest paid workers in any case. Moreover, it has been argued for many years that it is important not to confuse the 'poor' with the 'low paid'. Minimum wages will benefit low wage earners in middle-class families. A minimum wage is badly focused. The general conclusion is that if it is the 'poor' that one is concerned about, setting minimum wages is an inefficient way of going about it. Far better to concentrate on providing a minimum *income*, rather than a minimum *wage*, thus separating the issue of welfare from the functioning of the labour market.

Proposals to alleviate unemployment have often contained suggestions to the effect that work should be shared in some sense. The basic fallacy in such proposals is that they make the implicit assumption that the amount of work is in some sense 'fixed'. But there are also practical considerations. If labour costs are not to be increased by job sharing, then those already employed must be willing to enjoy more leisure and to take home less pay. Except in the event of compulsion it is difficult to see why this should be common behaviour. If compulsion were applied, a whole series of new issues come onto the table with regard to the nature of free markets and the pricing of labour. Such a scenario would require the imposition of some kind of command economy. Moreover, overhead costs to the firm may rise if the firm has to employ two people where there was only one before. Finally, job sharing which reduces unemployment below its equilibrium rate will create inflationary pressure resulting in restrictive policies to reduce inflation, so returning the unemployment rate to its original level. Similar objections can be made to arguments for early retirement.

Although no one has yet come up with a universally acclaimed scheme, perhaps the most promising direction of thought lies in attempts to use unemployment benefits as employment subsidies, so reducing the costs of labour to the employer. Such schemes are, generally, strongly opposed by trade unions and are often described as 'workfare'. The problem is to create a workable scheme that is not open to simply the displacement of the employed at the expense of the cheaper unemployed. One problem is, therefore, one of moral hazard. Those such as the late James Meade have sought to distinguish between the market price of labour and income (the point made above with regard to minimum wage legislation). It is also related to the problem of attempting to reconcile the need to lower the cost of labour nearer to the market clearing level, while at the same time avoiding the rise in the inequality of take home pay, such as is seen in the United States. Apart from moral hazard, such schemes may turn out to be seen as prohibitively expensive as they must certainly involve minimum income guarantees. The principle, however, is not dissimilar to the idea of Family Credit. The cost would come in the universality.

As pointed out earlier, the relationship between employment and aggregate demand is determined by the price of labour and its productivity. While there are inevitably disagreements about the deregulation of labour markets and issues such as minimum wage legislation, there is broad agreement across a wide spectrum in the importance of investing in education and training as part of the process of reducing unemployment. The argument is appealing. Whereas much of the previous discussion has been concerned with considering how to bring the price of labour into line with the market clearing rate, rather than focusing on the fact that labour rates may be too high, let us focus on increasing employee skills and raising labour productivity. This should yield the benefits of a high-wage, high skilled economy. Education and training are seen to be critical to this process.

There are several serious difficulties with this scenario, insofar as it relates to unemployment as such. It has clear relevance to the question of the distribution of income. Upgrading the skills of workers may, indeed, result in higher overall productivity, economic growth and standards of living, although even here the tea leaves are hard to read.

As far as unemployment is concerned, much of the discussion of this chapter has contrasted unemployment experience between the European Union and the United States. It has been very different. Also, as pointed out, the experience of Canada has been much more like Europe than the United States. It is difficult to believe that these major differences in unemployment behaviour can be explained by differences in investment in, or systems of, education and training. It is a stylised fact that the United Kingdom labour force is the most uneducated and untrained among our peer group. Yet as discussed in earlier chapters, Britain's economic performance since the early 1980s has been at least comparable with the economic performance of the OECD countries outside the United States and Japan. Indeed, given the perception of investment levels in skill development in Britain, if education and training are so important (and absent) how is it that, as far as the United

Kingdom is concerned, economic performance over the last fifteen years or so has not been that bad? Moreover, as far as unemployment is concerned, Britain's experience of unemployment during the 1980s was not dissimilar to the European average and more recently has been significantly better.

There are three further problems with being optimistic about the effects of education and training on unemployment. The first is that we do not know with any precision what forms of education and training are most needed. It has been argued that the American system of education has great advantages in its generality, with specific skills focused within institutions and corporations. The idea of simply preparing people for a job or making them more employable lacks focus and falls uncomfortably between the two. What are we going to teach the unskilled and the unemployed?

The second is that education and training are almost everywhere discussed in terms of supply. But what is often missing, particularly in Britain, is demand, as pointed out in Chapter 2. It might be argued that this is changing and has changed as the increased dispersion of income reflects higher personal returns on acquired skills. But to encourage the unskilled and the unemployed to learn skills there must be a perception that acquiring skills will be rewarded in the market place. It is not evident in several different countries' schemes designed to encourage the acquisition of skills, that skill acquisition is met with rewards. It is not seen as sensible to train for the army unless there is a war to fight.

Finally, while specific skills may be acquired in the short term, the impact of education on human capital is a long term issue and, as indicated, in part a cultural one. From a policy point of view this time dimension may be the critical one for reasons other than simply economic performance. There are undoubtedly strong reasons for both education and training, but it would be foolish to suppose that such investments will have a rapid effect on the skill base of the economy and the unemployed.

THE LABOUR MARKET AND UNEMPLOYMENT IN BRITAIN

The discussion of the previous sections has focused on the general question of unemployment, its development, particularly in the European Union, and possible policies for its alleviation. We must now look at these issues from the specific point of view of the United Kingdom economy.

The general discussion has suggested that the functioning of labour markets is of central importance in accounting for the differences in unemployment behaviour between the European Union and the United States. It has been generally agreed, as we have recorded, that Europe is faced with a structural problem that affects what we have described as core unemployment. At the back of all this is the fact that real interest rates in Europe have remained high throughout the slowdown in growth of the early 1990s. Where does Britain fit into this picture?

The central question for both the United Kingdom and the industrial economies with relatively high unemployment is the extent to which the underlying problem stems from the ability of the labour markets to adapt to changing economic circumstances. Is it that there is some kind of structural problem that could never be solved by the efficient behaviour of markets for both products and labour? Or is it simply that markets do not fail, they are not allowed to work? If the latter is the case, then the failure to reduce unemployment is largely self-inflicted. Not in a Keynesian sense which concentrates on a lack of effective *demand*, but because the *supply* side of the economy does not operate well. Labour markets are inhibited from responding to the changing patterns of product, process and the need for skills.

Optimism for the view that high unemployment in Europe and, from a relative point of view, in the United Kingdom stems from the fact that, historically, technological and social changes have always been accompanied by dire warnings about the long term effects on employment. Technological unemployment has been an unfulfilled prediction for centuries. Is high unemployment in the major industrial countries a reflection of the struggle between the realities of what markets would dictate if left to themselves, and the unreality of what appears socially desirable to politicians, policy makers, trade union leaders and other wishful thinkers? Are we simply wringing our hands because we will not permit markets to function effectively because we cannot accept the reality of the pricing of different kinds of labour?

It is against these ideas and thoughts that we must calibrate the behaviour of employment and unemployment in Britain, and the behaviour of the labour market. As seen in Table 4.1, the pattern of behaviour of unemployment in Britain following the oil price shocks of the 1970s is similar to that exhibited by the other 'high unemployment' countries. But it is important to differentiate the behaviour of the United Kingdom in this respect from the Europe peer group for two reasons.

The first is that the major change in both unemployment and employment in Britain did not occur until the late 1970s and particularly the early 1980s. As we can see in Table 4.1, unemployment in Britain for the period 1973–79 was the third lowest in the G7 countries after Japan (*sui generis*) and what was then the Federal Republic of Germany. The major upsurge in unemployment of the early 1980s resulted in the fact that while unemployment in Britain in the 1970s was below that in France, and significantly below that in Italy, in the years 1983–86 the unemployment rate in Britain was the worst in the G7. Between 1979 and 1983 employment in Britain fell dramatically. The principal reason for this was the fall in manufacturing output, which declined 15 per cent from the peak of 1979. Unlike its Continental peers, Britain experienced a large shake up in manufacturing industry which began a period of rapid increase in manufacturing productivity, the like of which had not been seen since the golden age. An interpretation of the nature of this upturn in manufacturing productivity has been given in the last chapter.

The second is that between 1984 and 1990 *employment* in Britain grew faster than any country in the G7, with the notable exception of the United States. Indeed by 1990 unemployment in Britain had fallen to 5.5 per cent, half the rate of Italy, 60 per cent of the unemployment rate in France and below the unemployment rate of Germany, before reunification. However, following the downturn of the early 1990s, unemployment again rose to a peak of 10.7 per cent in 1993. Thereafter unemployment has fallen continually towards the figure of 5.5 per cent that was achieved at the end of the 1980s. Meanwhile, between 1990 and 1996, unemployment rates in other European countries continued to trend upwards.

How are we to interpret these relative movements in unemployment rates? As far as the United Kingdom is concerned the evidence would seem to suggest that a substantial proportion of the rise in unemployment between 1990 and 1993 was essentially the result of recession, which has been substantially reversed by the subsequent recovery in the rate of growth of output. As pointed out above, it is arguable that higher unemployment in the other countries of the Union has resulted from the pressure of real interest rates caused by German reunification, and a desire for fiscal rectitude ahead of the decision to establish a single currency. But these are relatively recent phenomena. They do not account for the failure of unemployment in the Union to show similar falls to that experienced in the United Kingdom over that period.

The comparison suggests that unemployment in Britain has been more cyclical since the mid-1980s than in other countries of the G7 other than in the United States. Unemployment fell significantly in the expansionary period of the 1980s, rose again during the recession of the 1990s, and fell again as the economy recovered. The key question is, did something significant happen in the early 1980s that changed the situation in Britain from having the highest unemployment rate in the G7 to having one of the lowest rates?

One hypothesis is simply that the shake-out of the recession of 1981, the reduction in trade union power, the deregulation of the labour market and the absence of such generous unemployment benefits as existed in Continental Europe resulted in an increased flexibility in the labour market in Britain. Contrary to much anecdotal evidence, academic research has not generally supported this view, although there are considerable differences of opinion. On the other side it is argued that the relatively poor performance of Continental Europe *vis-à-vis* Britain is not due to differences in labour market behaviour and structural problems, but simply results from the fact that Continental Europe did not experience the economic boom of the 1980s in comparison with the United Kingdom. Subsequently, in the 1990s, economic activity in Europe was unusually depressed as the result of restrictive monetary policy in particular. All this would imply a much greater importance for the role of demand in determining the unemployment rate in both Britain and Continental Europe than was suggested in an earlier discussion.

It is difficult, however, not to believe that the dramatic events of the early 1980s have had significant effects on the way labour markets have functioned in Britain in recent years. In earlier chapters, the impact of industrial relations was identified as a key factor in explaining poor performance in the 1970s and into the 1980s. We have seen that productivity improvement was greater during the 1980s in those industries that were heavily unionised. Falling unemployment in the 1990s has appeared to be consistent with relatively benign inflation, falsifying many predictions. To argue that there has been no significant change in the United Kingdom labour market puts excessive emphasis on the role of demand during the later 1980s and the 1990s.

Insofar as unemployment experience in Britain, since the mid-1980s, has been better than her major European peers, and that to a significant extent this performance has been related to increased labour market flexibility, further measures to reduce flexibility should be avoided. These include the introduction of a minimum wage and further regulation of labour markets via the Social Chapter of the Maastricht agreement. Here an argument similar to the minimum wage applies. Advocates of minimum wages and the Social Chapter seek to persuade employees that they will have no adverse effects. But if they do not lead to significant change, it is questionable why they are undertaken in the first place. There is no evidence that minimum wage rates, as exist in Europe, have increased job protection. The higher costs of labour borne by employers will now make the task of bringing down unemployment even greater than it was. The advocates of such developments do not spell out the economic benefits, merely arguing that the economic costs will not be that great. As discussed in Chapter 6, signing the

Social Chapter, as Britain has now done, has written a blank cheque for future restrictions on the labour market that will inevitably come.

All this is concerned with aggregate employment and unemployment, and takes no note of the changing nature of employment and its structure. In this context, it is argued, irrespective of the behaviour of aggregate employment, there are important qualitative considerations that must be taken into account. A number of major concerns have been expressed.

The first relates to the extent to which employment has been increased over the last sixteen years by the creation of part-time employment replacing full-time employment, and the extent to which temporary contractual relations of one type or another have replaced permanent ones. On the first issue, there is no doubt that part-time employment of one kind or another has risen significantly over the last forty-five years in the United Kingdom from about 4 per cent in 1951 to some 22 per cent in 1996. But it is worth making the point that this has been a long term trend with a particularly rapid growth in part-time employment in the 1960s. Indeed, by 1971, part-time employment had already risen to nearly a fifth of all employment. During the period of rapid expansion in employment in Britain from 1984 to 1990, the ratio of temporary to total employment did not change. However, between 1991 and 1996, it rose from 5.3 per cent to 7.1 per cent. A study conducted by Peter Robinson for the European Commission (Robinson, 1996) concluded that the changing structure of employment reflected long term trends in the economy, but with a major acceleration in the fall of permanent, full-time employment in the recession of the 1980s. (The overall results are presented in Table 4.3.) This fall reflected the massive shake-out in manufacturing employment which, between 1979 and 1987, fell by some 2.5m. Many of those who lost their jobs sixteen years ago have since retired and/or exited from the labour force. The jobs that have replaced them (since total employment in 1990 was 5 per cent above that in 1979) have been associated with a significant rise in the self-employed and those employed in service industries. Robinson concludes that, given the magnitudes of the structural changes that occurred particularly in the early 1980s, labour markets have done reasonably well, and have shown recent signs of adapting successfully to those changes. It should be noted that:

> It is sometimes alleged that employees take part-time jobs because full time employment – which they would prefer – is not available. However, most part-time work is voluntarily entered into, with only one-in-eight of those in part-time employment in 1996 saying that this was because they could not find full time work. (Robinson, 1996, p. 14)

Table 4.3
Length of time in present employment (employees of working age)

	1975	1984	1989	1993
Men (%)				
less than 6 months	5.5	7.4	8.8	7.0
6–12 months	7.5	7.3	8.1	6.8
1–2 years	6.8	7.5	10.1	8.4
2–5 years	18.2	18.4	18.4	22.2
5–10 years	20.9	22.0	16.8	19.8
10–20 years	21.6	22.6	23.7	21.9
20+ years	19.6	14.0	14.1	13.9
Median (years)	7.9	7.1	6.4	6.4
Women (%)				
less than 6 months	9.1	11.2	12.9	8.7
6–12 months	12.1	10.3	11.2	8.7
1–2 years	11.2	10.9	13.7	11.6
2–5 years	27.9	24.6	23.0	27.7
5–10 years	21.8	23.5	17.3	21.8
10–20 years	12.5	16.0	17.7	16.9
20+ years	5.5	3.6	4.2	4.6
Median (years)	3.9	4.1	3.6	4.3

Source: Labour Force Survey, P. Gregg and J. Wadsworth, 1995

The nature and patterns of employment over time have been influenced by changes in the structure of economic activity, and in turn these have affected the demand for different skills and so in turn have affected occupational structure. The major changes in the industrial structure of employment in Britain over the last quarter century are set out in Table 4.4.

The principal feature of Table 4.4 is the fall in the share of employment in manufacturing industry from about a third in 1971 to a fifth in 1996. The major increases have occurred in business and financial services, and public and social services, rather than in areas such as distribution, hotels and catering. The absolute fall in manufacturing employment has been the principal cause of the decline in the share of manual jobs in total employment. While the decline accelerated in the first half of the 1980s the share of manual jobs in total employment has been trending down since 1951.

There are two myths that have surrounded these changes, particularly over the last decade. The first is that jobs in manufacturing have been replaced by low paid jobs in the service sector. But as Table 4.5 shows, the major expansion in jobs has been in those areas where relatively well paid managerial, professional and technical jobs are concentrated, and not in the sectors dominated by less skilled and lower paid service jobs. The same phenomenon, incidentally, has occurred in the United States. The second relates to permanent or life-time employment. Robinson concludes as the result of his study that:

> There is little evidence to sustain the assertion that there has been a significant and ongoing decline in permanent or 'lifetime' employment. Since 1975 there has been a decline in the average job tenure of men, but a slight increase in the average job tenure of women, with much of the secular change for men associated with the effects of the 1979–83 recession which saw the elimination of many long-tenure manual jobs in manufacturing ... It is worth noting ... that the early 1990s' recession did not see any further decline in average job tenure for either men or women. (Robinson, 1996, p. 15)

In addition, Robinson points out that:

> The significant dislocation caused by the early 1980s' recession in Britain is to a large extent water under the bridge. The pace of change in the structure of employment is now moderate enough and the supply response in education great enough to be sanguine that a downward path for unemployment in Britain in the rest of the 1990s will not be spoiled by any severe imbalance between the demand for and supply of labour in different occupational groups with different educational requirements. (Robinson, 1996, p. 17)

As can be seen from Table 4.6, over the last decade there has been a significant upgrading of the skill base of the labour force at least as measured in terms of qualifications:

> With the stock of qualification in the workforce rising strongly there is every reason to think that structural unemployment caused by mismatch between the characteristics of the working age population and the employment that is available is falling. As such, it should be possible for total unemployment to fall perhaps to 5 per cent or less without this causing any significant increase in wage inflation. (Robinson, 1996, p. 17)

This judgement must be conditional on the sensible conduct of macroeconomic policy, and the absence of major internal and external shocks to the economy for the remainder of the century. Such policies combined with a continued adaptation of the labour markets in Britain to changes in the econonomy are the key to the behaviour of unemployment. The only threat to such a scenario would be the adoption of welfare systems under labour practices that currently exist in various formats in the other major countries of the European Union and particularly France and Germany. To this extent, the prospects for employment in Britain as we approach the millennium are in ourselves and not in our stars. There are no quick fixes, but a need to follow the trends that, at the time of writing at least, have distinguished the United Kingdom from its Continental peers.

Table 4.4
Changes in the industrial structure of employment in Britain

	% of total employment						Annualised % point change			
	1971	1979	1984	1984*	1990	1996	1971–79	1979–84	1984–90	1990–96
Primary/Utilities	6.4	5.5	5.2	4.8	3.8	3.0	−0.11	−0.06	−0.17	−0.13
Manufacturing	33.9	29.5	23.5	23.3	21.1	19.4	−0.55	−1.20	−0.37	−0.28
Construction	6.4	6.3	6.4	8.2	8.3	6.9	−0.01	0.02	0.02	−0.23
Distribution/Transport	24.4	25.1	26.6	26.6	26.5	26.3	0.09	0.30	0.02	−0.03
Business Financial Service	6.0	7.0	9.2	10.5	13.2	14.0	0.13	0.44	0.45	0.13
Public Social Service	22.8	26.5	29.2	26.7	27.1	30.4	0.46	0.54	0.07	0.55

Source: 1971–1984 Workforce in Employment Series, SIC (80); 1984–1996 Labour Force Survey, Spring, SIC (92)

Table 4.5
Changes in the occupational structure of employment

Occupation	% of total employment				Annualised % point change		
	1979	1984	1990	1996	1979–84	1984–90	1990–96
Managers/Administrators		12.5	13.8	15.9		0.22	0.35
Professional		8.9	9.2	10.7		0.05	0.25
Associate Prof. & Technical		7.7	8.8	9.6		0.18	0.13
Professional/Managerial/Technical	*24.1*	*29.1*	*31.8*	*36.2*	*1.00*	*0.45*	*0.73*
Clerical/Secretarial	16.8	16.1	17.0	14.9	-0.14	0.15	-0.35
Personal/Protective Services	6.6	7.3	7.5	10.7	0.14	0.03	0.53
Sales	6.3	7.0	7.5	8.0	0.14	0.08	0.08
Service	*29.7*	*30.4*	*32.00*	*33.6*	*0.14*	*0.27*	*0.27*
Craft and Related		17.7	16.0	12.4		-0.28	-0.60
Plant and Machine Operatives		11.6	10.7	9.6		-0.15	-0.18
Other Occupations		11.3	9.6	8.2		-0.28	-0.23
Manual	*46.2*	*40.6*	*36.3*	*30.2*	*-1.12*	*-0.72*	*-1.01*

Source: 1979–1996 Labour Force Survey, SOC classification. Data for 1984–90 reclassified to SOC using mapping provided by Peter Elias from the Institute of Employment Research, Warwick University

Table 4.6
The highest qualifications held by the working age population

Education Group	% of working age population		
	1984	1989	1995
Higher education	12.2	13.5	19.7
A-level or equivalent	21.8	24.0	25.1
O-level or equivalent	15.5	17.7	18.4
Other qualifications	8.7	12.0	15.5
No qualifications	40.0	32.0	21.0
Do not know/did not say	1.8	0.9	0.3

Source: Labour Force Survey, Spring, 1996

INFLATION

The issue of unemployment clearly cannot be discussed without relating changes in unemployment to the inflation rate.

The starting point for a discussion of inflation is whether or not it matters. There are many who do not believe that it does. Perhaps not so many as those who, while being prepared to believe that excessive inflation is a cost, still maintain that the control of inflation is of less significance than other economic objectives such as unemployment or the rate of economic growth. One of the theses of this chapter is that there are no choices between inflation and unemployment in the long run. In the short term they can be closely related, when the economy is in a state of disequilibrium. In the long run there may be no relationship between them at all. Others belong to the school of thought that says that while excessive inflation may be regarded as damaging, a certain amount of inflation actually does you good. It will be argued that all these presumptions are wrong.

The conventional approach to the costs of inflation at the macroeconomic level starts with the familiar distinction between 'anticipated' and 'unanticipated' inflation. If inflation is fully anticipated, shall we say at an annual rate of 5 per cent, what are the costs? On the face of it the costs appear minimal. More frequent trips to the bank may be necessary to obtain cash and it will be necessary to change the publication of prices. Such costs are dismissed as 'shoe leather' costs and 'menu' costs. They are relatively trivial.

Meanwhile, it is assumed that significant economic problems can be dealt with by a process of indexation. The trouble with this is that indexation would always be substantially less than perfect. Institutional sluggishness may prevent nominal interest rates adapting quickly enough to stabilise real interest rates. Contractual agreements such as wage bargains may only be indexed with a lag. Tax adjustments may not be fast enough to eliminate the problem of fiscal drag. Capital taxes will also need to be adjusted sufficiently rapidly to offset the taxation of paper rather than real gains in the value of assets. In practice, as always, some will be able to protect themselves more effectively than others. So, leaving aside the fact that fully anticipated inflation over a significant time period is a myth, even were it to occur, problems would come trailing in its wake.

It would be more generally agreed (although not unanimously) that there are potentially, significantly higher costs associated with unanticipated inflation, and clearly how important they are depends on how fast the actual rate of inflation is. Confusion between nominal and real rates of interest makes it difficult to assess the cost of capital, and the required rate of return on investment. Unfair redistribution takes place between lenders and borrowers; the borrowers borrowing in one money and paying back in another. This way, many in Britain have made gains in the housing market since the Second World War. Income is redistributed between those who can defend themselves against inflation and those who cannot, often the loss of the old being the gain of the younger in full time employment. Finally, fluctuations in the inflation rate create a general climate of uncertainty through the implied variation in the value of money, which, in a general sense, has important consequences for rational economic calculation and the efficient allocation of resources. Note that these are essentially microeconomic costs of inflation. The macroeconomic costs of inflation are discussed below.

The post-war consensus among economists about economic policy in Britain, and the way in which inflation was determined, reflected two strains of thought. The first, developed in the 1950s, focused on what was called 'cost' inflation, determined by imported inflation from changes in world raw material and food prices primarily, and by the power of organised labour to determine wage setting. As far as the latter was concerned, it was implicitly accepted that to a large extent Britain was on a 'labour standard' in that, the level of money wages having been set, the government would create sufficient demand to maintain full employment at the given level of wages. This led to the idea of 'prices and incomes' policies which sought to contain inflation by doing deals with organised labour. Variations of such policies persisted up until the demise of the Labour government led by James Callaghan in 1979. Such policies were implemented or attempted to be implemented by both Conservative and Labour governments, by Macmillan and Heath for the Conservatives and by Wilson and Callaghan for Labour. The fact of the matter is, and always was, that trade unions only cause inflation in the long run if governments permit them to do so by attempting to sustain output and employment by adopting accommodating fiscal and monetary policies. Otherwise labour ultimately simply prices itself out of work.

The second stream of thought emphasised, as we saw earlier, the relationship between the inflation rate and the unemployment rate. Trade union power and unemployment were seen to be the principal inflation drivers and there was concern throughout the 1960s as to how policy might be adapted to deal with them, and in particular how to reconcile so-called full employment with stable prices. Some combination of the carrot (in the form of concessions to the unions in relation to the policy making process) and the stick (in the form of trying to avoid overheating the economy) appealed to a wide spectrum of opinion, although there were significant differences between those who believed that joint government with the unions was inevitable, and those who believed that it was possible to stabilise prices by running a higher if reasonably acceptable level of unemployment in relation to the supposedly overfull employment of the 1950s and 1960s.

It has already been explained how ideas about the distribution of power in a society and the course of events sought to undermine this consensus during the turbulent years of the 1970s and the early 1980s. Whereas, today, probably a majority of people would deny that they could be described as monetarists, nevertheless there is wide acceptance that monetary policy has a major role, if not the complete role, in determining the inflation rate. This proposition is well established elsewhere, particularly in Germany and in practical terms in the United States. However, while this is so, there remains in some quarters doubt about the emphasis of monetary policy on the determination of inflation rates. There are arguments for and against which are discussed below.

Those who start with the presumption that monetary stability in the economy is of major importance do so in part because, first, they believe that the costs of unanticipated inflation of the kind we saw in the 1970s are large. They subscribe broadly speaking to the view espoused by John Stuart Mill in the quotation given earlier. There are, therefore, it is believed direct benefits of stable prices in creating a satisfactory environment for the pursuit of steady growth and rising prosperity. Secondly, there is an important benefit from the existence of price stability, namely the lack of the need to go through the pain and experience the welfare costs of adjustment when inflation gets out of hand. We have argued earlier in this book that the conduct of macroeconomic policy has been extremely costly to the British economy.

It has impacted on observed growth during particular periods such as the late 1970s and early 1980s, and the recession of the early 1990s. Whether the task of putting the inflationary genie back in the bottle is greeted with enthusiasm or without enthusiasm, major social costs in terms of employment and output are experienced. Thus there is a flipside to price and monetary stability, namely the avoidance of such costs which are damaging both in the short and in the long run. As has been pointed out many times, this does not of itself imply that, in relation to some agreed measure of price inflation, the ultimate policy target should be one of zero. This is in part a technical point in that observed inflation when measured at levels such as 2 per cent or less inevitably fails to take on board the increase in the quality of goods and services over time. The current popular assessment of the acceptable inflation rate is that it should be at a rate that does not seriously impact on the making of economic and business decisions.

Those who take a rather different view of the importance of price and monetary stability appear to do so on two broad, not necessarily mutually exclusive grounds.

The first is rooted in the idea, which has a considerable ancestry, that some degree of inflation (unspecified usually) is actually good for employment and good for growth. The traditional view in populist form was along the lines of the idea that inflation oiled the wheels of the economy, keeping employees happy with increases in money wages and house prices and firms happy with rising profits. A little bit of what you fancied did you good. The problems with this idea are twofold. First, it implies that economic agents learn very little over long periods of time about the distinction between real and nominal changes in incomes and earnings. This is not credible (although assumed by Keynes in setting out his *General Theory*). Economic agents do learn. And the issue is two way since, after a period of rapid inflation, they find it difficult to adjust their expectations downward, for example building substantial inflation risks into investment hurdle rates, even when inflation has slowed and is reasonably expected to stay lower. Secondly, history tells us that, like an alcoholic at a party who is proposing to take only one drink, it is difficult to prevent the resultant binge. Only a commitment to firm abstinence is likely to do the trick, and to establish the credibility necessary to restrain inflationary expectations.

The second major concern is that a focus on price and monetary stability leads inevitably to a neglect of important issues such as output and employment. This may be particularly felt in a period in which inflation has been significantly reduced but unemployment remains high. Insofar as a central aim of stabilisation policy is the steady growth of nominal demand in line with the overall growth of output it suggests that explicit consideration of the behaviour of inflation will lead to a deflationary bias at the expense of encouraging the growth of output and a reduction in the unemployment rate. Given the history of stabilisation policy in the United Kingdom over the last forty years, there is no evidence that this has occurred over any significant period. On the contrary, such policies appear to have had a persistent inflationary bias, even in the case of governments who have professed total commitment to price stability. This is palpably evident, for example, in the episodes of demand induced inflation presided over by Conservative governments in Britain. In Britain, at any rate, there is no evidence that an obsession with inflation has blinded governments to the possibility of encouraging growth in real output in line with productive potential. There still remain those who believe that a significant impact may be made on unemployment by demand expansion in an old fashioned Keynesian sense. But supporters of such views tend to believe that inflation is of relatively little importance anyway.

Supporters of this line of thought have sought comfort in the idea that, after nearly thirty years of fluctuations and a steady growth in prices, inflation has somehow been defeated. The exemplar of this is the contribution of Roger Bootle (Bootle, 1996), which argues that globalisation, increased competition in markets and other structural changes have all brought about a new economic environment in which inflation will continue to be benign. There are two issues here. The first, which has been discussed earlier, is whether inflation is in some sense a real phenomenon rather than a monetary one. (For further consideration of these matters see the contribution of Congdon, 1992.) The second issue is how we think economic policy in the future will be conducted, both inside and outside the United Kingdom.

There is little doubt that structural changes in the economy, such as the decline in the power of organised labour, and the increased competitiveness of particular markets may affect the dynamics and speed of adjustment of the inflationary process. But the fundamentals of what determine the inflation rate remain the same. Whatever the changes in the shorter term impact of variations in nominal exchange rates and wage rates, ultimately stable prices can only be guaranteed by stable monetary conditions. Insofar as that is the case it will remain largely true that the future course of inflation in the United Kingdom will be determined both by domestic monetary policy and by inflationary conditions in the world outside.

There is an analogy, here, with the question of trade that was discussed in the last chapter. There we recorded the arguments that structural changes arising from so-called globalisation accounted, in the main, for the significant expansion in world trade over recent decades. In fact, the deregulation of trade as a matter of policy in both the North and the South plays a large part in the story. In the cases of both inflation and trade, a prosperous and stable future is not guaranteed by structural changes in either the domestic or the world economy. It can only be achieved by the application of sensible policies.

Having said that, it is possible to be optimistic about the future of inflation to the extent that governments around the world have realised the costs involved in dealing with the inflationary cat, once it gets out of the bag; the cat quickly becomes a tiger. As the basis for a sensible approach to the conduct of stabilisation policy, the idea that inflation is defeated in some sense is a foolish one. The price of monetary stability is one of eternal vigilance. There are no alternatives if it is to be achieved.

CHAPTER 5

PUBLIC FINANCE AND THE ROLE OF THE STATE

INTRODUCTION

The rise in the power and influence of the state, as measured by the share of public expenditure in gross domestic product, has been a key feature of the history of the industrial nations during the twentieth century. In the nineteenth century public expenditure was largely confined to the provision of 'public goods' such as defence and law and order, some involvement in the public services (e.g. post offices) and the payment of interest on the public debt. In the twentieth century the state has entered into the provision of services such as education and health, financed pensions and implemented a major expansion in social security and welfare payments. For some of the major industrial countries the figures are given in Table 5.1, for the period beginning in 1913. More recent experience for the G7 countries is set out in Table 5.2. While peaking in the early 1990s, the rate of increase in the expenditure ratio has fallen since the mid-1980s.

The rise in public spending has been financed in part by increases in taxation in the longer term, and in part by borrowing. For the more recent period, since 1981, the effect of such borrowing on the debt ratios of the G7 countries is given in Table 5.3. The average debt ratio between 1981 and 1994 rose from 43.4 per cent to 70 per cent. Only in the United Kingdom case is the debt ratio lower at the end of the period than at the beginning, but that as can be seen masks a significant fall between 1981 and 1990, followed by a rapid rise in the early years of the 1990s.

These developments have raised a number of issues that have been much debated, and which will continue to be the focus of attention. While not clearly distinct, it is useful at the outset to distinguish between the macro and the microeconomic aspects of public expenditure. The macroeconomic aspects of public spending relate to its effect on the level of demand, and the consequences of the financing of spending for the fiscal deficit, the money supply and interest rates. The microeconomic aspects of public spending relate to the specific provision of goods and services by the state, and the use of tax and subsidy to affect the distribution of income and welfare. Such developments have consequences for the allocation of economic resources, the level of welfare and the incentive structure that is put in place.

Table 5.1
Government outlays as a percentage of GDP*

	1913	1929	1938	1990
USA	8.0	10.0	19.8	36.2
Japan	14.2	18.8	30.3	31.9
Germany	17.7	30.6	42.4	45.7
France	8.9	12.4	23.2	49.9
Netherlands	8.2	11.2	21.7	57.5
UK	13.3	23.8	28.8	42.3

* net current plus capital outlays

Source: A. Maddison, *The World Economy in the Twentieth Century*, OECD, Paris, 1989, and OECD Historical Statistics, 1960–95, Paris, 1997

The increase in the influence of the state, and the consequent effects on public indebtedness, has in recent years raised concerns on a number of fronts. At a very general level it has been argued that the frontier of the state should be rolled back, and greater responsibility handed back to individuals in the private sector. The reduction of taxation has been at the heart of such beliefs. Reductions in public spending are necessary in order to reduce taxation, which will lead to greater incentives for risk taking and economic efficiency. Such a philosophy underlay what could be described as Reaganomics in the United States and Thatcherism in the United Kingdom. Such ideas have also been associated with criticism of 'big government' and a demand for less government (and in some extreme cases for 'minimal' government).

Table 5.2
Government outlays as a percentage of GDP[a]

	1960–67	1968–73	1974–79	1980–89	1990–96[b]
USA	28.3	29.1	32.2	35.3	33.5
Japan	18.7	19.5	28.4	32.7	33.4
Germany	35.7	37.5	47.5	47.8	48.4
France	37.4	38.0	43.3	50.2	52.6
Italy	31.9	33.7	42.9	49.3	53.9
UK	34.7	36.7	44.4	44.9	42.1
Canada	29.3	31.6	39.2	45.0	47.7
G7	29.8	30.7	36.1	39.5	39.2
EU(15)	33.9	35.6	43.8	48.7	49.8
OECD	29.5	30.5	36.6	40.5	40.5

[a] net current plus capital outlays
[b] 1996 estimated

Source: OECD Historical Statistics, 1960–95, Paris, 1997 & OECD Economic Outlook, December 1996

Table 5.3
Gross public debt as % of nominal GDP

	1983	1985	1986	1987	1988	1989	1990	1991	1992	1993	1994	1995
Canada	55.2	64.1	67.8	68.4	68.1	69.2	72.5	79.4	87.2	99.4	97.2	99.6
France	35.3	38.6	39.3	40.7	40.6	40.6	40.2	41.0	45.7	52.7	55.9	60.0
Germany	41.1	42.5	42.5	43.8	44.4	43.2	45.5	44.4	45.8	51.9	51.6	61.6
Italy	70.2	82.3	86.4	90.6	92.8	95.7	104.5	108.4	114.7	116.3	122.4	122.0
Japan	63.8	67.0	70.5	72.5	70.9	68.7	65.1	62.3	63.5	67.9	73.2	80.7
UK	53.4	58.9	57.9	55.6	49.3	42.9	39.3	40.6	47.6	56.6	54.3	60.0
USA	43.6	49.1	51.8	53.3	53.8	54.2	55.6	59.6	62.0	63.5	63.7	64.3
Total G7 Countries	49.5	54.6	57.0	58.4	58.1	57.6	58.3	60.2	63.4	66.9	68.6	72.1

Source: OECD Economic Outlook, December 1996

A further strand in the argument for public expenditure reductions in the industrial countries is the belief that public expenditure ratios have reached a level where there is continuous tension between public expenditure and the willingness of the taxpayer to finance it. If governments are not prepared to raise taxes to the level required to fund a given level of public spending, then they must borrow. At some point this will materially affect interest rates. In particular, real interest rates will be significantly higher than they would otherwise have been. While there are no simple correlations between government deficits, the debt ratio, and real interest rates, levels of real interest rates in recent years (in contrast, for example, with the 1970s) have been affected by the generally higher expenditure ratios and debt ratios in the OECD countries. (Witness, for example, the consequences of the unification of Germany for German real interest rates.) In addition, large deficits and rising debt ratios increase the risk that governments will reduce their liabilities in real terms by imposing the tax for which parliaments do not vote – namely inflation. Governments in danger of not being able to meet their obligations by taxing and borrowing at 'reasonable' rates may resort to the printing press.

Finally, whatever view one takes about the current situation with regard to public expenditure and debt in the OECD countries, a further issue is now being raised with regard to such ratios going forward, particularly in the context of demographic changes affecting the cost of medical care and the provision of pensions. The problems that these may bring have triggered a demand for a re-examination of the role of the state as a provider and a greater responsibility being given to individuals in the private sector.

The subsequent discussion of this chapter is predicated on a number of assumptions. The first is that the discussion of the role and nature of public expenditure and the role of the state is confined in the main to the OECD countries. Secondly, we will assume that a private sector exists in the economy, as reflected in the clear delineation of property rights. Thirdly, such an assumption rules out any discussion of the role of government in terms of an overarching view about the moral imperatives of public ownership or the comparison of socialism and capitalism. The spirit of the analysis is to seek for some guidelines that will enable us to comment on the issues of the kind just raised, which are representative of concerns about public spending at the present time. At the heart of it all is the problem as posed by Edmund Burke:

> One of the finest problems in legislation, namely to determine what the State ought to take upon itself, to direct by the public wisdom, and what it ought to leave with as little interference as possible to individual exertion. (Burke, 1926, p. 40)

In much recent discussion, these issues have been obscured by general arguments reflecting attitudes towards free market behaviour and the role of government. What is suggested below is that the issues must be examined on a case by case basis. In principle, such an approach could equally lead to a demand for more public expenditure rather than less.

THE STATE AND THE ECONOMY

In the light of much of today's discussion about the role of so-called free markets, and the relationship between the private and the public sector, it is ironic that the impulse toward individualism, individual responsibility and a reduction in the power of the state came over 400 years ago from a desire for individual freedom. The state for this purpose was of course represented by the Church and the Monarchy. The reformation in Europe was not simply the reflection of a spiritual change as such, but a reflection of a desire for the independent right of the citizen to make choices. This development was a precursor to the development of commercial and market based systems that ultimately led the English economic historian, R.H. Tawney, to link the Protestant ethic to the rise of capitalism (Tawney, 1926).

The significance of the role of the individual in the market place was famously exemplified many years later by Adam Smith:

> But man has almost constant occasion for the help of his brethren and it is in vain for him to expect it from their benevolence only. He will be more likely to prevail if he can interest their self-love in his favour and show them that it is for their own advantage to do for him what he requires of them.... It is not from the benevolence of the butcher, the brewer or the baker that we can expect our dinner but from their regard to their own interest. (Smith, 1776, p. 18)

This led to the depiction of Adam Smith as the inventor of the 'invisible hand' which, if left to itself would most efficiently allocate economic resources to the general advantage of all. To coin a later phrase, Smith was supposed to be in favour of the doctrine of 'laissez-faire'. Those who have read Smith's comments on government elsewhere in the *Wealth of Nations* and equally his other major work on *The Theory of Moral Sentiment* will appreciate that Smith said no such thing. But he maintained a healthy scepticism both with regard to the behaviour of individuals in the market place, and with regard to those individuals (or groups of individuals) who professed to be acting 'in the public interest'.

By the early part of the twentieth century, economic orthodoxy suggested a significant role for government in the provision of public goods and services, such goods and services as were appropriately supplied on a collective basis. Some form of Welfare State in Britain had begun with Lloyd George's Budget in 1909, with the introduction of the old age pension. But orthodox views in the 1930s were still in line with traditional values. It was not until the 1940s and the coming of the Beveridge Report, the education White Paper of 1944 and the election of a Labour government in 1945 that the Welfare State as we know it today came into existence.

In a well known lecture in 1926, John Maynard Keynes, under the title of 'The End of Laissez Faire', attacked what he saw were orthodox commitments to a hands off policy as far as the economy was concerned (Keynes, 1926). The apparent intellectual justification for these criticisms had to wait for another decade with the publication of the *General Theory*. In the *General Theory*, as we have seen, Keynes suggested only one form of policy intervention in the economy by government, namely the implementation of counter-cyclical investment, which was described in the last chapter as the 'socialisation of investment'. This was, however, far from advocating any form of state intervention, other than at the level of aggregate demand. On the contrary, when focusing on the microeconomic behaviour of the economy – the behaviour of individual markets – Keynes was comfortable in the belief that markets functioned relatively efficiently and, indeed, that a belief in the market was also a belief in the individual. As Keynes wrote:

> But above all, individualism, if it can be purged of its defects and its abuses, is the best safeguard of personal liberty in the sense that compared with any other system, it greatly widens the field for the exercise of personal choice. It is also the best safeguard of the variety of life, which emerges precisely from this extended field of personal choice, and the loss of which is the greatest of all the losses of the homogeneous or totalitarian state. (Keynes, 1936, p. 380)

Keynes's contribution to thinking about the role of public spending and fiscal policy in general was taken up by those who followed him. His early budgetary proposals were met with alarm in many quarters, as he seemed to be suggesting running fiscal deficits deliberately in periods of high unemployment. But even Keynes's supporters balked at the idea of running fiscal deficits in the long term. The most common interpretation of what seemed to be proposed was that a government should balance its books, not every year, but over the course of the business cycle.

The creation of the Welfare State, which can reasonably be dated as the end of the Second World War, demanded significant increases in both taxation and in public expenditure. This apparent necessity to increase state spending as a proportion of gross domestic product was merged with Keynes's idea of demand management. Not only were increases in public spending to result in increased welfare (as services were made available to the less well off) but also a high and stable level of public expenditure would insulate the total level of aggregate demand from the wilder forms of economic fluctuations experienced in the past. Thus rising economic welfare and successful demand management and stabilisation were thought to go hand in hand. Moreover the problem of balancing the budget, which had concerned many in the late 1930s, was apparently effectively disposed of by the American economist Evsey Domar in a seminal paper published in 1946. Domar's point was simple enough; it was not the absolute public sector deficit that really mattered. It was the ratio of the debt to the gross domestic product, what he called the debt ratio. As a matter of arithmetic, Domar showed that for any given debt ratio we seek to fix, there is a unique ratio of public sector deficit to gross domestic product which will allow the government to continue to borrow without raising the debt ratio. As we shall see later, this does not in fact dispose of the problem, as we have to decide on what debt ratio to fix. However, for the purpose of justifying persistent fiscal deficits what Domar had to say seemed to be enough. The concept of a balanced budget was consigned to the wastepaper basket as an orthodox anachronism.

The coming of the Welfare State in Britain in the 1940s resulted in a major change in the role of the state as both a taxer and a spender. At the same time a major wave of nationalisation after 1945 created a new industrial public sector, and so extended the role of the state as manager. The reasons for this were several. The Labour Party of 1945 reflected in principle the socialist belief in public ownership of assets. (Indeed, the idea remained a central principle of the Party's platform until 1997 when the famous Clause 4 was finally abandoned.) A second argument at the microeconomic level was that the industries which were nationalised at that time were essentially natural monopolies (or at least monopolistic to a high degree) and, therefore, should be controlled directly by the state. Competition in areas such as railways was regarded as duplication and wasteful. However, successful integration could only be safely undertaken by the state. Finally, yet again the macroeconomy was prayed in aid, as it had been in the case of the Welfare State. The industries which were nationalised represented what were thought to be 'the commanding heights' of the economy. State control over what could be regarded as the basic industries (with the exception of steel that came later) should again provide a stable basis of planned investment which would help to maintain the level of demand, stimulate overall planning, and lead the private sector forward. Rational order was the doctrine of the day.

That nationalisation was not extended further was due initially to the failure of the Labour Party to retain office beyond 1951 and to be excluded from it for another thirteen years. Leaving aside the steel industry, which assumed symbolic prominence, by the time Labour was back in office the leadership of the party had to some extent bought the idea promoted by Anthony Crosland and others that economic growth would provide a sufficient social dividend without further nationalisation to enable the party to continue to fulfil its desire to promote increased welfare and a more equitable distribution of income.

However, ideas of extending further direct controls, of some kind, over private industry persisted into the 1970s, ironically to some extent backed by a corporate view that totally rational organisations, which contained self interest, were possible. One group led by Tony Benn sought to establish what were described as 'planning agreements' with the top twenty-five private companies drawing them into the net of more detailed state control. In addition, this was to be supplemented by the extension of trade union power into the boardrooms of such companies, to increase employee participation in decision making. Such ideas, while not disappearing for some time (viz. the Labour Party election manifesto of 1983), were for all practical purposes swept aside by the advent of the Conservative Party under the leadership of Margaret Thatcher. After June of 1979 matters were never the same.

A significant implication of the ideas described that led up to the Thatcher years was that at a microeconomic level economic growth and the macroeconomic behaviour of the economy were largely immune from the consequences of fiscal policy, government spending and taxation. One way of putting this is to say that the post-Keynesian intellectual tradition, that was so much in keeping with the broad-brush effects of rising public expenditure after 1945, virtually completely neglected its supply side implications. Issues such as the allocation of human effort, the framework of incentives, and the impact of taxation on risk/reward relationships were overshadowed by the belief that demand management was the key to full employment and ever increasing prosperity. In an intellectual sense the major contribution of the Thatcher years was to re-focus attention on the supply behaviour of the economy, and to emphasise the importance of market behaviour in allocating resources, rather than the direction of the state. This led in due course to confrontations between those who advocated a wider role for markets in allocating resources in both the private and the public sectors. It also led to ideas that there was in some sense a trade off between market efficiency on the one hand and social welfare on the other. A belief in the importance of free markets was inconsistent with the idea of a 'caring society'. This is basically untrue. But before addressing these and other issues that we have raised, some discussion of the role and nature of free markets is in order.

THE ROLE OF MARKETS

From Adam Smith, followed by Karl Marx, there has been persistent debate and discussion about how society should be organised to promote the greatest economic and social welfare. As we saw earlier, Adam Smith was supposed to have advocated a 'laissez faire' approach to the relationship between the state and the private sector of the economy. This is not true. But as pointed out by Keynes, the Darwinian theory of natural selection, espoused in the middle of the nineteenth century, was consistent with the view that in the market place the survival of the fittest should ensure optimal economic performance.

In his 1990 presidential address to the British Association for the Advancement of Science, Frank Hahn interpreted the 'invisible hand' as applying to a 'market economy' in which the setting of prices, and more generally the allocation of economic resources, was delegated to private economic agents who made the decisions about the production and consumption of goods and services. His definition of the market economy was as follows:

> By a market economy I shall mean an economy where economic decisions such as what and where to consume are 'predominantly' taken by private agents. This of course means that in considering any particular economy, we may wish to argue about the scope of 'predominantly'. But nothing turns on the answer. Someone may consider central intervention weak enough so that the economy qualifies as a market economy, while someone else might regard it as sufficiently extensive to want to call it 'mixed' or even planned. Nothing of substance lies behind such disagreements. (Hahn, 1992, pp. 1–2)

By the end of the nineteenth century, the working of 'the invisible hand' in the mainstream of economic analysis was being described by a model of the economic world that reflected the outcome of what economists described as 'perfect competition'. In such a world no perceptible influence on output and prices would be exercised by individual producers and consumers. Indeed it was a world that could more graphically be described as one of atomistic competition. In such a world the profits of producers and the utility or welfare of consumers were maximised as each followed their individual self-interest. There were assumed to be diminishing returns from the application of individual inputs of the factors of production, so that in the steady state of general equilibrium of the economic system all economies of scale would be fully realised. In equilibrium the prices of goods and services would be equal to the marginal cost of producing them. The apparently rudimentary observations of Adam Smith were presented in a rigorous analytical framework.

However, while the market may be remarkable in promoting the interests of individuals when they are common, it may be less capable of dealing with situations where they are in conflict. Moreover, even those who espoused the virtues of the working of free markets recognised traditionally that a number of issues arise that may limit its general application.

Given the nature of the competitive framework, under the assumptions made, the outcome with regard to production and consumption was optimal, in the sense that no one could be made better off without someone else being worse off. The economy, to use the jargon, was at a point on its efficiency frontier. However, this raises two problems. The first is that judgements about welfare arising from this state of affairs cannot be made without making judgements about the distribution of income. On the face of it, problems arising from income inequality might be dealt with by appropriate redistribution policies (taxes and subsidies) after the event. However, it is a well known fact that taxes are distortionary so that it is necessary to trade off equity against efficiency. The second problem is that in the analysis discussed, the equilibrium to which the economy tends is not independent of the initial distribution of resources in the hands of economic agents. This evaluation of the market process depend on both the initial and the resultant distribution of economic resources.

Liberal economists have recognised two further problems that arise in this version of the 'invisible hand' story. The first is what is known as the problem of 'missing markets'. As described by Frank Hahn the process of market behaviour 'co-ordinates' the transactions of private agents, producing order and eventually equilibrium, where equilibrium means that there is no possibility of further trading to improve anyone's position. But the world is not static, and we also need to be able to achieve order across time. In certain areas of economic activity we have forward markets, but for reasons of cost and of moral hazard many such markets are almost certainly 'incomplete'. Thus Hahn concludes:

> For these and other reasons we should expect there to be fewer markets than are required for market economies to carry out their co-ordination task. (Hahn, 1992, p. 5)

The second problem identified by liberal economists is that markets may 'fail'. The essential feature of a market economy is that the allocation of resources depends on the behaviour of prices. The arguments for and against the market based rather than the command economy depend on the markets' ability to communicate an 'appropriate' set of economic signals. Market failure occurs when inappropriate signals are transmitted that result in a socially inefficient use of resources or socially inadequate provision of goods and services. Market failure occurs when despite the efficient operation of self interested, economic agents, and given all reasonable information relating to the decision in hand, they systematically reach a conclusion that is not in the social interest. Traditional examples of this relate to problems of pollution, lack of education and training, and cases of basic research. Agents may have no incentive to prevent pollution. Education and research may be under-provided because of a lack of ability to appropriate adequately the benefits from it (staff leave and people steal your ideas). Externalities, information asymmetry and problems of revenue capture are all familiar reasons for possible market failure that lead to equally familiar policy solutions, taxation, subsidy and/or regulation in order to try to achieve some equality between social and private costs and benefits.

These issues all arise even in a perfectly competitive world. But such a model is clearly in general very unrepresentative of the complex industrial world in which we live. In the world as it is we find a wide variety of imperfectly competitive markets in which firms typically influence the prices they charge, and more generally are able to exercise a greater degree of managerial discretion than in the perfectly competitive world. In the case of a natural monopoly, for example, where the firm is congruent with the industry, traditional economics tells us that it will maximise profits and choose a price for its output which is above the perfectly competitive price (where price is equal to marginal cost). In this case, while the monopoly may be producing efficiently (i.e. its output is produced at minimum cost) it may be said to charge a price that is too high, from a social point of view, thus creating inefficiency.

Economists are quite schizophrenic when it comes to utilising the perfectly competitive model. On the one hand it is supposed to represent the ideal that describes the market economy and in this context is easily shot down for the reasons already discussed. It is used to articulate the inadequacies of a free market economy. However, in the next breath the same economist uses it as a paradigm to make welfare judgements of the type illustrated with regard to the alleged welfare losses that arise from pure monopoly. It is also often used in appraising the welfare consequences of other economic developments such as privatisation where, as we shall see later, there is said to be a confusion between competition on the one hand and ownership on the other.

To this point the focus has been on the idea that the 'invisible hand' reflects a process of allocating *existing* resources in order to achieve a desirable collective result. The emphasis on the word *existing* reflects the fact that the analysis is essentially *static* (despite the passing reference to the incompleteness of temporal markets). It is worth pointing out that the competitive model, as such, is essentially neutral as between different forms of ownership of resources. Indeed, prior to and after the Second World War, there was much discussion as to what the analysis implied for market economies versus planned economies. Socialist economists of the 1930s took the view that it would be under socialism rather than capitalism that an efficient (not simply equitable) allocation of resources would be achieved. Managers in the socialist state would be made to follow rules of pricing and behaviour consistent with the requirements of the perfectly competitive model. The neutrality of the model with respect to the nature of economic organisation was tersely summed up by Ian Little over forty years ago:

> In my opinion static welfare theory could only convince someone who was blind to realities and very susceptible to emotive language of the benefits of socialisation. Equally it could only convince someone who was similarly blind and open to suggestion of the benefits of laissez-faire. (Little, 1950, p. 266)

For most advocates of the importance of free markets in the growth and prosperity of the economy, the perfectly competitive model we have discussed has little or no relevance. Its inadequacies are not relevant to the evaluation of market processes, or in many cases to welfare judgements about market structure. The case for free markets does not lie in their ability to determine an optimal allocation of existing resources in a static context. It is in the dynamic development of the economic system that they find their proper place. The issues have been well described by Stephen Littlechild:

> Mainstream economic theory defines the efficiency of an economy in terms of its allocation of available resources taking as given, production technologies and tastes. This definition is too narrow. Resources, technologies, and tastes cannot be assumed to be fixed and known. A central part of the economic problem is to ascertain what they are and indeed to create new resources, technology and tastes. An economy is therefore not to be judged by whether the conditions for perfect competition and Pareto-optimality exist at a particularly time ... Whether prices are equal to marginal costs is less important than whether these costs are continually being reduced, and those products replaced by better ones. It is in this more general and *dynamic* sense that the market system is more effective at serving customers than any alternative type of economy. (Littlechild, 1986, p. 84)

This alternative perception of the nature and role of markets is also illustrated by Norman Barry:

Economic activity consists of continually exploring price differences that exist in a necessarily imperfect world. It is this of course that constitutes profit, a phenomenon that is absent from an equilibrium world. Yet if there were no possibility of profit there would be nothing to drive the system toward equilibrium. In Hayek's instructive phrase, the market is a 'discovery procedure' rather than an 'allocative device' by which means are somehow mechanically directed to the production of given ends. (Barry, 1985, p. 139)

This approach rests on an appreciation of the role of individuals and what Littlechild describes as 'entrepreneurship'. Economic agents are in a chronic state of ignorance, which is resolved substantially by trial and error. The market is the place where these trials are conducted and a process of natural, economic selection takes place. Of ten new products, nine fail the market test. How can we say in advance which will succeed? In a command economy, one will be chosen. The odds on success are poor.

Such a perspective suggests we need a different approach to the issue of competition. The function of management in the free market is to seek to create monopoly, in the form of competitive advantage, in the face of the encroaching tides of competition. The nature and role of profit must be seen in its dynamic context, rather than that of static equilibrium. A practical consequence of this is that the existence of monopoly may not be seen as necessarily representing economic inefficiency in the sense discussed but as a necessary part of the process of change and improvement.

These constitute positive arguments for the importance of free markets. As has been discussed, there are clearly cases of market failure and equity where it is proper for the state to assume responsibility. However, while there is 'market failure' there is also 'government failure'. The ability of governments to manage is limited by both information and experience. Ministers come and go like the flowers in summer. Their appearance on the stage is temporary by comparison with managers in other spheres and they tend to rely (if sensible) on public servants whose degree of continuity is palpably greater. By intervening in the market place in situations not justified by the *prima facie* existence of market failure, governments are claiming authority and a knowledge base that is denied to the market. As in the case of the justification of free markets, judgement in such matters is an issue not of ideology but of competence. It is this that needs to be borne in mind in determining what needs to be reserved for the state rather than left to the market place.

THE PRINCIPLES OF PUBLIC EXPENDITURE AND FISCAL POLICY

The rise in the power and influence of the state as measured by the ratio of public expenditure to gross domestic product has been a key feature of the major industrial countries in the twentieth century. Setting levels of public expenditure is part of the total process of governing a country's fiscal policy. This in turn determines spending, taxation and the extent of public borrowing to meet the state's objectives. In the broadest sense, fiscal policy relates to four, distinct, but interrelated objectives:

- the efficient allocation of economic resources;
- the desired redistribution of income and wealth;
- the stabilisation of output and employment;
- the stabilisation of prices (or, more generally, the inflation rate).

We have already discussed at some length in Chapter 4 and elsewhere the role of fiscal policy in relation to unemployment and monetary stability. The process of setting the levels and nature of public expenditure has clearly macroeconomic implications, as well as the microeconomic consequences discussed below. We deal first with some of the macroeconomic implications of public expenditure, before examining the microeconomic issues that relate to resource allocation and the distribution of income and wealth.

In financing public spending, governments raise taxes, borrow money and print money (i.e. create inflation). To the extent that governments fail to finance spending by raising taxes, the spillover effects may have serious consequences for the macroeconomy. Borrowing may drive up interest rates, so inhibiting private spending, leading to what in the jargon is described as 'crowding out'. Borrowing from the banking system is part of the process of increasing the growth of the supply of money relative to the rate of growth of output, so leading to more rapid inflation. All public spending at the margin is paid for in tax, it is simply a matter ultimately of what form the tax takes – the money out of your pocket, an interest rate tax on private industry, or an inflation tax as the result of the creation of money. These issues are all part of the process of fiscal and nominal demand management and the problems that are raised are not, in themselves, related to issues, discussed below, such as what the overall level of public expenditure should be. They are relevant to the financing of such expenditure and its impact on the macroeconomy. Taxation may have significant effects on the supply side of the economy, affecting incentives, risk taking, and the allocation of and motivation of human resources in particular. Borrowing may impact on the rate of private investment through the effect on interest rates, so affecting the overall rate of economic growth. The creation of inflation will have the deleterious consequences discussed in the last chapter.

Thus at the macroeconomic level we can judge whether government expenditure is excessive in relation to the impact of its financing on interest rates, inflation rates, and subsequently, in open economies, to its effect on exchange rates. In itself, financial instability as generated by governments' choices of how to finance a given level of public spending does not imply that the chosen level of public spending is inappropriate. The key issue here is to what extent does the political market give promises to the electorate of better things to come and thereby outstrips the economic market, that enables real resources to be committed. In oversimplified terms, the problems at a macroeconomic level arise when the political markets set targets that the voters are not directly prepared to pay for. The gap is then financed by excessive borrowing, inflation or some combination of the two.

The financing of public expenditure has implications for the level of the National Debt. As described earlier, concerns over deficit financing as perceived in the pre-Second World War period were to some degree alleviated by the idea that running deficits was not a problem, provided that the consequence was not a continuous rise in the ratio of debt to the gross domestic product. As seen in Table 5.3, debt ratios in the major industrial countries have in general risen significantly over the last fifteen years. The extent to which this constitutes a major problem is not clear, for the simple reason that we cannot precisely determine the economic consequences of considerable variation in such ratios. Whether a ratio of 50 per cent is of major significance compared to a ratio of 70 per cent, for example, is impossible to ascertain. As suggested earlier it may plausibly be the case that, in the OECD countries generally, real interest rates have responded to the generally high experience of public sector deficits, but the evidence remains inconclusive. At the macroeconomic level, the principal issue that relates to public expenditure and the appropriation of economic resources by the state relates, in the short run, to the implications of the way it is financed. In the longer run, the method of financing and the degree and nature of resource use have potentially serious consequences for the supply side of the economy and subsequent effects on the rate of economic growth and prosperity.

At the microeconomic level the first crucial distinction is between the government's direct use of economic resources, the employment of people and the creation of capital assets in the production and supply of goods and services, and the transfer of economic purchasing power by way of tax and subsidy. We distinguish between direct resource use and deployment and what we call transfers.

People's attitudes toward public expenditure covering both the direct use of resources and transfers are determined by many considerations. If there were consensus about social and economic objectives, the resolution of disagreements about the share of resources going to the public sector and the desirable extent of transfers would be easier. In this context it is important to try to distinguish between practical and positive judgements about the consequences of public expenditure decisions for the behaviour of the economy, and value or normative judgements as to what is intrinsically desirable. Those in favour of extensive state involvement in industry in principle on social grounds are clearly disposed toward a high share of public expenditure as a proportion of gross domestic product, compared to those who have an innate predisposition toward reducing the power and influence of the state as such. Ultimately decisions about public spending and the use of economic resources by the state cannot escape the making of important value judgements, more particularly in situations that involve the redistribution of income and wealth.

To begin with let us consider the direct use of economic resources by the state. There should be little dispute, in principle, about the role of the state in providing what are described as 'public goods'. Note that public goods are not synonymous with 'goods produced by the public sector'. Public goods are in the limit defined as goods that are non-excludable in consumption, such as clean air, law and order and defence. The list is not exhaustive. The practical problem as opposed to the issue in principle is how to determine the volume of public goods that should be supplied. The problem is particularly acute since there is no market process that enables us to measure the desire for more policemen on the beat relative to the willingness of the public to pay taxes to support them. Real preferences for public goods are hard to come by. But at least there should in these cases be little dispute about the proper role of government in principle.

The debate, in practice, starts at the point where governments engage in the direct use of economic resources using labour and capital, where there is an argument that such activities should be carried out in the private sector. At this level the issue would appear to be one of relative economic efficiency, rather than an issue of principle. In many areas of government this may indeed be so. To use a contentious example, it is not clear why in the modern world of sophisticated communications and networks, governments should retain monopoly powers over the control of postal services. In most countries it has already been recognised that the development of telecommunications is more efficiently carried out in the private rather than the public sector.

The most difficult contradictions arise where the direct use and deployment of resources are interrelated with issues of income and wealth distribution, and universal commitments to service provision. The classic examples here are, of course, the provision of services by the state for health and education. In these areas of service provision, the issues of principle lead to the belief in the conferment of rights upon the members of the community in the form of health care and the provision of a common standard of education for children. In this context, issues of economic efficiency and consumer choice become mixed with issues of rights and principles. At this point the confrontation between state provision and private provision becomes most acute, and the belief in universal provision becomes most tested. Here also, as will be discussed in the next section, the question of 'affordability' becomes increasingly relevant. Since the demand for health care and the demand for education are likely to be highly income elastic, a new dimension is added to the question as to whether certain services should be supplied by the private sector or the state. The question is whether in the longer term the state mechanism is capable of supplying the increase in output demanded, given the financial constraints that the state may find imposed upon it.

Taking all these factors into account, it is not difficult to assemble a check list of the considerations that should be taken into account when trying to determine the optimal rate of public expenditure on any objective basis. Indeed, to the extent that value judgements are critical to the process, in strict terms no objective basis is possible. But for practical purposes this is not good enough since decisions have to be made. Allocative efficiency, equality and redistribution, public choice and taxable capacity are all clearly relevant but the weights to be given to each will by no means be universally agreed.

A starting point, at least, is to consider some upper limit on public spending by determining what is 'affordable', bearing in mind that what is affordable is not necessarily desirable. At an overall level it can be argued that public expenditure has become excessive at the point where either the burden of taxation is believed to impact significantly on long term economic performance, or the financing of such spending by other means is destabilising to the economy in the short run as a result of its impact on interest rates and inflation, and hence also on employment. It is arguable that in this sense public spending in the 1970s could be deemed excessive and destabilising. Such a concept does not, in itself, determine any particular expenditure ratio, since it will depend on the willingness of the population to pay taxes and the behaviour of financial markets. For this reason rules of thumb have been proposed that would seem to prevent matters getting out of hand such as the maintenance of a given debt ratio. Given the rate of growth of the economy and a target rate of inflation, this would give a determinate answer to what the borrowing requirement should be as a percentage of gross domestic product, and would determine how much needed to be raised in taxes for a given level of public spending. An alternative is the so-called Golden Rule that suggests that public consumption should be paid for out of taxation, while borrowing should be confined to the financing of public investment in the provision of services and infrastructure. However, essentially these are rules for financing public spending, and still maintaining some form of financial stability. There still remain the precise levels of expenditure and taxation to be determined. It is at this point that judgements of 'taxable' capacity need to be exercised.

The difficulty of reaching firm conclusions about levels of public expenditure is that one makes generalisations, such as increasing public expenditure will always be a good thing. On the other side of the coin, that tax cuts will always be beneficial. Neither of these propositions is true. Equally, there is no theoretical case for arguing that a balanced budget will always be an optimal fiscal strategy for governments. It is certainly plausible to argue that it is reasonably sound finance for governments not to borrow for the purposes of consumption. But there is no general case for prohibiting public use of private savings in the creation of capital assets required to support essential services and infrastructure in the economy. Indeed such a rule may be essential in preventing what has happened in the past, namely the pre-emption of public investment by public consumption.

As pointed out earlier, this discussion has focused on the idea of a given level of public spending being 'affordable'. However, it is equally important to consider what activities of the state are necessary, and here we have problems once we go beyond the definition of public goods and services. This raises the question whether some of the activities carried out by the state are better carried out in the private sector. This, as has been frequently pointed out, need not necessarily lead to a reduction in public spending. That will only be the case if such activities are carried out more efficiently. This leads us to the central question of privatisation, to which we now turn.

PRIVATISATION AND REGULATION

Since the Second World War the state has vastly extended its role, not only as taxer and spender but also as manager. As discussed earlier in this chapter, the major expansion of the state in Britain, in its role as manager, came with the burst of nationalisation that occurred after the Second World War. At the time the principle of public ownership was an important one for the Labour Party. Contemporaries argued at the same time that public ownership of the major utilities dealt with problems that arose from the perception of such industries as monopolies. At the same time public control of the major utilities was seen to be a step in the direction of a greater ability to direct the 'commanding heights of the economy'.

Leaving on one side the steel industry, a further clutch of productive activities was added to public ownership in the 1970s, most notably the British Motor Corporation and its satellite businesses. The arguments for taking companies into public ownership at this stage depended critically on the desire to sustain businesses that were going bust and to ensure the maintenance of jobs. Unlike the utilities that had been nationalised nearly a quarter of a century before, these later nationalisations were enterprises which operated in essentially competitive markets, as did some of the public sector firms already under state control, most notably what became British Airways.

As a matter of historical fact, the extent and scope of de-nationalisation (or privatisation) that followed the election of a Conservative government led by Margaret Thatcher in 1979 was hardly believable, even at the outset. The return of a number of former private enterprises to the private sector was not, in itself, particularly remarkable, although it clearly required government commitment to a new industrial perspective to see it through. What was remarkable was the speed with which state-owned enterprises were privatised. For example, in the 1970s the American Nobel Prize winner, Milton Friedman, suggested privatising the United Kingdom coal industry as a remedy for many of the problems that governments faced in dealing with it. Such an idea was generally laughed out of court. The privatisation (and subsequent great success) of British Airways set a new standard for the injection of a public corporation into the private sector. But it was the proposal to privatise British Telecom that started a process which was to set an example throughout the world. To some extent, after BT, the rest followed. But history will recognise the serendipity of the process. After BT anything was possible.

The general arguments for the privatisation of public corporations are familiar. At the outset of the Thatcher administration there was clear dissatisfaction with the way in which the public industries were managed, and the interrelationships between public sector employees, their immediate managers and their political and public service masters. The concept of the public corporation as a vehicle for the state ownership and management of major assets made a late appearance on the scene, when Labour realised the extent of its victory at the 1945 election. The principle of public ownership had to be put into practice. The upshot was a long history of some confusion about the nature of responsibilities and the relationships between the parties concerned as listed above. This was punctuated by periodic reviews of how accountability should be determined and on what criteria capital resources should be made available by the Treasury to finance developments in public sector industry. By the late 1970s, industrial relations had deteriorated materially, with the most significant problems occurring in the public utility sector from the early 1970s onwards. The situation at this time was well summed up by Cento Veljanovski:

> In large measure the crisis in the nationalised industries was a failure of 'regulation'. The defects of the control system were highlighted in a damning study by the National Development Office (NEDO, 1976). The NEDO study painted a picture of *ad hocering* confusion and blatant political manipulation. The regulatory framework was described as 'unsatisfactory and in need of radical change'. Among the deficiencies were lack of trust and mutual understanding between government and management, confusion about roles, and the absence of an effective system for measuring performance and managerial competence. (Veljanovski, 1991, p. 2)

Eventually for the Conservative government of Margaret Thatcher, privatisation was seen as a way to resolve the difficulties of state management of public sector corporations.

Hand in hand with these concerns went the belief that public sector corporations were inherently inefficient and lacked any motivation to control costs and to serve consumers. Such a belief supported the contention of Adam Smith in *The Wealth of Nations*:

> In every great monarchy of Europe, the sale of crown lands would produce a large sum of money, which if applied to the payment of public debt would deliver from mortgage much greater revenues than any which those lands have ever afforded the crown. (Adam Smith, 1776, p. 348)

The proposition here has been much misunderstood. The late Lord Stockton (Harold Macmillan) in a famous phrase described the proceeds of privatisation as one of 'selling the family silver'. In recent discussions of the privatisation of telecommunications in Australia, the government was accused of selling 'the nation's heritage'. The basic argument supported by Adam Smith is not concerned with financing anything. The sale of government assets, with the proceeds used as Smith suggests to reduce the public debt, has no *direct* effect on the financing of public sector deficits at all. The government's net worth is left unchanged. As recognised earlier, a similar conclusion with regard to public spending applies to the privatisation of public services by contracting them out to the private sector. From the point of view of the country as a whole, benefit only arises if the assets sold become more productive and, in the case of public services, are more efficiently produced.

Leaving aside the misplaced sentiments of 'selling the family silver', or 'disposing of national assets', it has been argued that the process of privatisation makes the country no better off than it was before, it has simply substituted forms of private monopoly for public monopoly. If a monopoly is to exist it is better that it is directly controlled by the state 'in the public interest'.

An initial problem with this argument is that it has been precisely the problem of trying to determine the 'public interest' with which governments and public corporations have been trying to deal. But the more substantive issue has been whether Adam Smith was broadly right, namely that the assets managed in the private sector perform more efficiently than they did in the past. In human terms there are two fundamental dimensions to this. The first is the behaviour of managers when freed from political accountability. The second is the joint performance of management and labour as reflected in industrial relations and productivity. Despite assertions about quality of service, there is little doubt that from the point of view of reducing costs and improving resource productivity, generally speaking the process of privatisation in Britain has been a spectacular success. Capital productivity has been significantly raised.

The second argument is that the process of privatisation has confused ownership with competition. In order to improve efficiency, in the United Kingdom electricity industry for example, it was argued that it was not necessary to change the ownership of the industry but to develop comparative standards between its component parts (such as the regional electricity companies). To some degree the issue here again turns on the impact of such alternatives on the behaviour of management and labour. Moreover, that would still leave in place the accountability of individual operating units to the state.

This leads to the third general criticism of privatising utilities, namely that accountability to the state has been replaced by a form of accountability to shareholders and capital markets that is palpably weak. The argument when

BT was privatised was that no government would ever let BT go bankrupt, whereas Unilever, to take an example, would not have any such effective guarantee of survival. The irony of this form of criticism is that, given the general success of the privatised utilities, the new standard line of criticism is not that they pay too little consideration to shareholders and capital markets, but they pay too much! This has been linked to the accusation that in the majority of cases the corporations were floated too cheaply. To some extent, with hindsight, this may be true, but virtually no one anticipated the scope for cost reduction and profitable improvement when such corporations were injected into the private sector. It is from their success rather than their failure that criticism now comes. In valuing their assets bankers had to rely heavily on the managers who had been running the show before.

While the role of government as manager has significantly declined with privatisation, this has been offset by a new growth industry, that of regulation. The process of deregulation has been of widespread significance in the so-called Anglo-Saxon world, with the deregulation of airlines, financial services and labour markets. Here we are concerned with the nature and growth of regulation in the context of the government's privatisation programme. Five privatised industries in Britain – British Telecom, British Airports Authorities, British Gas, water and electricity – can be thought of as regulated utilities. With some differences between them the process of regulation involves the granting of a licence and the appointment of a Director General to ensure that the conditions of the licence are fulfilled. As described by Beesley and Littlechild:

> The statutory duties of the regulators include protecting the interests of producers (licensees), of consumers of various kinds, and of employees and third parties (e.g. environmental concerns). The wording varies, but, for present purposes, three main objectives may be identified in the respective privatisation Acts:
>
> 1) to ensure that all reasonable demands are met, and that licensees are able to finance the provision of these services;
> 2) to protect the interests of consumers with respect to prices and quality of service; and
> 3) to enable or to promote competition in the industry. (Beesley and Littlechild, 1991, p. 30)

Why was it that, following privatisation, regulation assumed such importance? The first reason is to be found in the implication of the perfectly competitive model of free markets that was discussed earlier in this chapter. Economists in one breath use the model as a straw man in the process of criticising what a free market system is about, while in the next breath they use it as a paradigm to evaluate the welfare implications of monopoly. As one of the main criticisms of privatisation was that it simply turned public into private monopolies, the consequences of the unregulated behaviour of the newly privatised industries were analysed in the context of the traditional model of the implications of market structure for economic welfare. Whatever the improvement in economic performance that might arise from the cost side of privatised utilities, on the demand side the argument was that serious inefficiencies would arise from 'excessively high prices', reductions in the quality of service and unacceptable behaviour in preventing and eliminating competition.

As argued earlier in this chapter, the traditional welfare model as a guide for interpreting and understanding market behaviour has little to commend it. Moreover, as a matter of fact, the general implications that the privatised utilities can closely approximate as 'natural monopolies' is simply not true. A large majority of the two dozen or so enterprises that have been privatised since 1979 were in broadly competitive markets. It is indeed the case that at the time of their privatisation, in their core activities, British Telecom, the British Airports Authority and British Gas had market shares approaching 100 per cent of their core activities. This was not inevitable from an economic point of view. What monopoly powers they had were certainly not 'natural'. (It has been argued that special cases, particularly water, differ significantly in economic terms from the industries cited.)

Without a doubt the most effective regulation of price behaviour and efficient resource allocation is competition. In the light of the earlier discussion about the role of markets, it is on the nature of competition and in particular the conditions of entry for others that the importance of regulation turns. It is the dynamic response to opportunities, changing circumstances, and new technologies that is critical to an evaluation of the performance of the public utilities that now operate in the private sector. As listed above, the promotion of competition is a key part of the regulator's task. Unfortunately as Beesley and Littlechild point out:

> Substantial recent literature on potential competition and contestable markets analyses the relationship between the conditions of entry and price. At least one textbook on regulation (Spulber, 1989) is more concerned with entry and competition than with static welfare analysis of pricing for a protected monopoly ... In practice, however, these models are of limited use for the task of promoting competition. Although they analyse the effects of any entry conditions, they do not help to identify what the entry conditions actually are in any political situation, nor what the entry conditions would be as the result of any particular regulatory change. (Beesley and Littlechild, 1991, p. 50)

As originally perceived, the approach to regulation in the United Kingdom was intended to be relatively simple and informal. As far as pricing was concerned, control was to be exercised by the use of a formula that said the average price should be determined by the formula Retail Price Index – X, where X was a number to be determined for each industry. This was in apparent contrast to the regulatory approach in the United States which focused on the rate of return on capital. Such a formula was to be agreed between the industry and its regulator and to ensure that appropriate investments were undertaken to conform with the conditions of the licence. In the event of disagreement between the regulator and the industry, the matter could be referred to the Monopolies and Mergers Commission for a final decision. Such an approach seemed to be in keeping with a degree of informality much favoured in Britain, again in contrast to a strong legally based system in the United States. In practice, the approach has been accompanied with much confusion about the scope and role of regulators, who have been encouraged to open up issues that were clearly not intended at the outset. Moreover, the existing framework clearly does not impose any high degree of uniformity on the way in which the regulators see their jobs. The general tenor of these developments has taken the actual interference of regulators beyond relatively well defined ideas (in principle, if not in practice), beyond a focus on pricing and the promotion of competition. Increasingly, there is pressure on regulators to pronounce on issues that fall way outside of their economic responsibilities (such as the salaries of senior executives or the dividend policies of the enterprises for which they work).

The dangers in all this are clear to see, with problems of the accountability of regulators and concerns about the importance of idiosyncratic regulator behaviour, rather than attempts to act on agreed principles. Any significant move back to public ownership in Britain is clearly quite unlikely. But apart from the complexities and financial implications of such a reversal of trend, those who sought to use public utilities for other than strictly economic ends no longer need to contemplate such a Herculean task. Simply to capture the regulatory process will be enough. That constitutes the most serious threat to the benefits that the privatisation process has already delivered.

PUBLIC EXPENDITURE IN THE UNITED KINGDOM

As argued earlier in this chapter, the establishment of an optimal level of public spending or ratio to gross domestic product involves a number of considerations that relate not only to matters of fact, but also to value judgements. In the early years following the Second World War it seemed to many that equity and efficiency could be made to march hand in hand. Increased government spending could be justified in terms of increased equity and at the same time the increase was interpreted as favourable from a macroeconomic point of view. A high level of public spending was seen as an important factor in the stabilisation of demand. As can be seen from Table 2.2, by the early 1970s the ratio of public expenditure to the gross domestic product had risen to over 40 per cent.

At this point the United Kingdom economy, as elsewhere, was subject to a series of economic shocks: the collapse of the Bretton Woods Agreement, with knock on effects for the stability of exchange rates, the rise in world oil prices, and the consequences of the policy induced economic boom that peaked in 1973. The rise in oil prices presented policy makers with a number of problems, in particular critical decisions with regard to monetary and fiscal policy. The inflationary shock raised the question as to how accommodating monetary policy should be. While with regard to fiscal policy the key issue was the extent to which public expenditure would bear its share of the real burden imposed by the rise in the oil price.

In contrast to the United States and Japan, Europe in general chose to attempt to protect the public sector and most of the adjustment fell on the private sector. Moreover, given the inflexibility of European labour markets, the main burden was imposed on corporate profitability. Real unit labour costs in Europe actually rose after the first oil price shock.

As far as the United Kingdom is concerned, the results of this for public expenditure and the public sector borrowing requirement can be seen in Table 2.2 in Chapter 2. In the financial year 1975–76 public spending rose to nearly 50 per cent of gross domestic product, and the public sector borrowing requirement peaked at 9.5 per cent of gross domestic product. The current account of the balance of payments moved into severe deficit, the pound sterling plunged and the Chancellor of the Exchequer (Denis Healey) made his dramatic return from London airport, when en route to New York, to oversee plans to be rescued by the International Monetary Fund. The facilities granted by the Fund to the United Kingdom came at the price of major reductions in public spending and promises of fiscal rectitude in the future. The share of public spending fell sharply from nearly 50 per cent to 43 per cent in the space of two years.

The respite was short lived. The Conservative government elected in 1979 began with the view that high levels of public expenditure had been a major weakness of the British economy and needed to be substantially reduced. However, it was caught in the draught of the second oil price shock on which were imposed major commitments to raise public sector pay (the so-called Clegg awards) that had been entered into during the election campaign. These commitments, added to the cyclical pressures on public spending as the recession took hold and unemployment rose, resulted in a sharp rise in the public expenditure ratio, back to over 47 per cent and a public sector borrowing requirement of over 5 per cent.

Geoffrey Howe's Budget of 1981 marked a significant turning point in the economic history of Britain since the Second World War. In complete opposition to the economic consensus of the post-war period, fiscal policy was tightened rather than relaxed, in a period of rising unemployment, as part of a programme of reducing public spending, the inflation rate and interest rates. The public expenditure ratio fell from 47 per cent to a low of just under 38 per cent in 1988–89. A substantial part of this decline must be attributed to the faster growth of the economy which was to some degree reversed by the recession of the 1990s. However, work carried out by the Treasury indicates that of the fall in the public expenditure ratio to 1988–89, some 5 percentage points could be attributed to changes in spending policies.

These developments have been succinctly summarised by Andrew Tyrie:

> There were sharp cuts in spending on industry and associated regional programmes, housing and interest on the national debt. The lion's share of the government's stake in industry was privatised and subsidies were removed, despite vigorous objections from vested interests. Most subsidies to private enterprise were also ended. In housing likewise, an explicit policy of severe restriction of local authority new construction was imposed and the existing housing stock was partly privatised under the right-to-buy scheme. Construction of new social housing was also semi-privatised with approximately half of housing associations' money being privately raised. The commitment to reduce public sector borrowing, contributed to reductions in debt. At the height of the cyclical upswing, a budget surplus enabled the debt to GDP ratio to be reduced. (Tyrie, 1996, p. 21)

However, the recession of the early 1990s, together with the rising cost of health care, added over 4 per cent to the public expenditure ratio by 1994–95, only partially offset by the decline in the share of defence. The difficulty of controlling public spending, or more specifically, the difficulty of a permanent shift to a lower gear is said to be illustrated by the fact that by 1995–96 the public expenditure ratio was back to the same level (roughly 42 per cent) that prevailed in the first fiscal year of the Conservative government 1979–80. However, as can be seen from Table 5.3, compared to its peer group, the fiscal policies pursued by the United Kingdom after 1979 enabled it significantly to reduce its sovereign debt ratio. Even after the climb back after 1991, by the mid-1990s the debt ratio was more or less the same as in the early 1980s. The same could not be said of the other members of the G7 countries, or the other comparators recorded in Table 5.3.

The ultimate judgement on public expenditure in the United Kingdom is left over to Chapter 7. Here, however, we may usefully note some important points with regard to the future of public expenditure and some important comparisons with others, particularly in the framework of Europe and the European Union.

The history of public expenditure in Britain, as briefly described, is interpreted by many as illustrating the difficulty of reducing the ratio significantly below a number such as 40 per cent. Equally, for many, such a reduction is not only difficult, it is also undesirable, given the social contribution that public spending is believed to make. As shown in Table 5.4, the three key areas of public spending on which attention is usually focused, and which take up over a half of all public expenditure, are education, health (including personal social services) and social security.

For the foreseeable future, social pressures and a belief in the importance of the development of human capital as a key factor in economic performance mean that demands for an increased supply of health and education services will continue to be strong. This demand will rise proportionally faster than real incomes. As already pointed out, privatising services in these sectors does not, of itself, reduce public spending. The potential reductions in expenditure come from increased efficiency, which is a matter of scepticism in some quarters (e.g. Flemming and Oppenheimer, 1996). The only sure way to save money is to cease to supply a service, leaving the private sector to create it and develop its own channels for delivery.

The largest increase in the public sector share of gross domestic product over the last sixteen years has been in social security payments. Clearly steady growth and job creation can make a significant contribution to reducing social security costs. But demographic and other pressures will keep the spotlight on the long term provision of pensions, while the demographics will also affect the demand for health care that will be demanded by an ageing population.

As has been argued, a particular saving to the public purse has been the government's decision taken in the early 1980s to relate public pension increases to prices rather than earnings. Pressure to change that decision will no doubt continue.

Thus the pressures both from the community, and one suspects from vested interests, will continue to be strong in the foreseeable future. While it is probably the case that the experience of the 1970s resulted in a more realistic attitude to what governments might achieve by taxing and spending, or perhaps a greater awareness of what damage may be inflicted by public finances out of control, there is little evidence that pressures on the public purse will abate.

However, in all these respects, the United Kingdom starts from a much better position than its European counterparts. Leaving aside the United States, Japan and Switzerland (see Table 5.5) Britain has one of the lowest ratios of public expenditure to gross domestic product of the OECD countries. It has the lowest ratio of debt to gross domestic product of all OECD countries with the exception of Switzerland.

The principal reason for this lies in the different welfare systems of Continental Europe, the scale of benefits under various headings, and in particular the obligations of states for future pension payments that are unfunded and on a pay as you go basis. As far as the demographics go, it turns out that Britain is actually much better placed than its European peer group. Other countries such as Germany, in particular, face a more rapidly ageing population. The scale of the differences can be seen in Table 5.5, which also includes public consumption and what are defined in OECD statistics as 'social security transfers' as a percentage of gross domestic product. As can be seen from Table 5.5, while public consumption in Britain, relative to gross domestic product, is relatively high, its ratio of social security transfers to gross domestic product is significantly below the average for the European Union. For the United Kingdom the ratio is 15.4 per cent compared with a European Union average of 20.4 per cent (the EU (15)). Countries with ratios well over 20 per cent include Belgium, Denmark, France, Sweden and the Netherlands – which tops the list with a ratio of 25.1 per cent. Going forward, there are serious questions as to whether such positions among the European Union member states are affordable, given that demands in the pension area in particular are likely to increase in the light of the demographics.

Whatever the differences of opinion with regard to the desirable public expenditure ratio, there is little doubt that the experience of the 1970s generated a significant shift in attitudes toward fiscal control. At the time of writing, such attitudes in Europe have been affected by what are seen as the fiscal requirements for the successful completion of monetary union, which will be discussed in the next chapter. Whatever the upshot of monetary union, the countries of Europe, including the United Kingdom, face difficult choices and a need to focus on the priorities for government expenditure as the world moves into the twenty-first century.

Table 5.4
UK public expenditure since 1979

Year	% of GDP					Total social security[a] (£ bn)	£ billion of which benefits accruing:			
	GGE(X)	Education	Health and personal social services	Defence	Total social security[a]		Elderly	Unemp-loyed	Sick and disabled	Family[b]
1978–79	42.25	5.4	5.4	4.5	10.0	17.0				
1979–80	42.50	5.1	5.4	4.6	9.8	20.1				
1980–81	44.75	5.5	6.1	4.9	10.4	24.3				
1981–82	45.50	5.4	6.2	5.0	11.5	29.6				
1982–83	45.50	5.4	6.1	5.2	12.0	33.1				
1983–84	44.75	5.2	6.0	5.2	12.1	36.9	17.0	5.5	4.5	7.0
1984–85	45.25	5.0	6.0	5.3	12.3	40.0	18.0	6.0	5.0	7.5
1985–86	43.25	4.7	5.8	5.1	12.1	43.5	20.0	7.0	6.0	8.0
1986–87	42.25	4.8	5.8	4.8	10.5	46.8	22.0	7.0	7.0	8.5
1987–88	40.25	4.8	5.7	4.4	11.5	48.9	23.0	7.0	8.0	9.0
1988–89	38.00	4.6	5.7	4.0	10.5	50.2	24.0	5.0	8.5	10.0
1989–90	38.25	4.8	5.7	3.9	10.3	53.3	26.0	4.5	10.0	10.0
1990–91	39.00	4.8	5.9	3.9	10.7	59.5	29.0	5.0	11.0	11.0
1991–92	41.00	5.1	6.4	3.9	12.1	70.6	32.0	8.0	13.5	13.5
1992–93	43.50	5.3	6.8	3.8	13.2	80.0	34.5	9.0	16.0	15.5
1993–94	43.60	5.3	6.8	3.6	13.7	87.6	37.0	10.0	19.0	16.5
1994–95	42.75	5.2	6.9	3.3	13.4	90.6	38.0	9.0	20.5	18.0

[a] including cost of administration
[b] including widows and orphans

Source: Public Expenditure, Statistical Supplement to the Financial Statement and Budget Report, 1994–95 and 1995–96, HM Treasury, February 1995 and 1996

Table 5.5
Public expenditure ratios in 1995

	Public Expenditure Ratio	Consumption Ratio	Social Security Transfers
USA	34.3	15.8	13.1
Japan	28.5	9.8	13.4
Germany	46.6	19.5	18.6
France	50.9	19.3	23.2
Italy	49.5	16.3	18.9
UK	42.3*	21.3	15.4*
Canada	45.8	19.6	14.7
Australia	35.5	17.3	11.4
Austria	48.8	20.2	22.0
Belgium	53.3	14.8	24.3
Denmark	59.7	25.5	21.5
Ireland	39.2*	14.7	14.6*
Netherlands	52.1	14.3	25.1
Spain	41.5	16.6	17.3
Sweden	64.0	25.8	23.4
Switzerland	36.7	15.0	17.6
EU(15)	49.2	18.7	20.4
OECD	38.9	15.9	15.7

* 1994

Source: OECD Historical Statistics, 1960–95, Paris, 1997

CHAPTER 6

BRITAIN IN THE WORLD

INTRODUCTION

At the end of the Second World War, Britain played a major role together with the United States in establishing the post-war economic framework. John Maynard Keynes and Harry Dexter White were the chief architects of the Bretton Woods Agreement that served the Western world well, until its demise a quarter of a century later. Despite the continuous re-writing of history that takes place from time to time, it was the Anglo-Saxons who liberated Western Europe from Nazi domination, and it was the Soviet Union that 'liberated' the East ... although 'liberation' in the East had quite a different meaning.

A quarter of a century later Britain had presided over the virtual dissolution of what had been the largest Empire ever accumulated. The Empire on which the sun never set was still a powerful reality for millions of people pre-war, and for many a still powerful reality for many years after it. But empires ceased to be fashionable or for some acceptable. While the transatlantic relationship between the United States and Britain and the personal chemistry that existed between Roosevelt and Churchill were critical to the waging of the war, even Roosevelt, following American tradition, was suspicious of British aspirations for its Empire in the design of the peace. (For an excellent discussion of these issues see Renwick, 1996.)

Against this post-war background, Churchill's warnings of the threat from the Soviet Union were largely ignored, partly on the grounds that they were based on concern for British possessions in the Far East. In Western Europe the political move to the left both in Britain and elsewhere, for different reasons, signalled sympathy with, if not agreement with, the aims of Communist states. The United States finally woke up to the threat that Churchill foresaw and for practical, if not altruistic, reasons became concerned about economic weakness in Europe, and worried that such weakness might result in the further spread of Communism particularly to France and Italy. The result was the development of the Marshall Plan in 1948 to provide aid for the restoration of the European continent that had suffered the immediate ravages of war. Few, in today's world, appreciate the significance of American action in those times; a *volte face* when contrasted with American isolationism of the 1920s, following the First World War.

Not only did America provide much of the means for European economic recovery, it also played a significant role in pressing for political and institutional developments that would bind the Europeans together. Such developments may be viewed as simply reflecting American self-interest in creating a bulwark against the tide from Eastern Europe, rather than a genuine concern to encourage peaceful cohabitation among the Europeans. Perhaps this view explains the lack of gratitude that currently prevails in Europe toward the United States rather than simply the passing of time and the re-writing of history. The Americans, of course, were divided amongst themselves on this issue. Eisenhower as President sustained in large measure the special transatlantic relationship and while his patience was sorely tried by the British debacle of Suez, the relationship between the United States and Britain was shored up by the personal association between Eisenhower and Macmillan, established during the Second World War. Throughout the period up to and including the creation of the European Economic Community and the signing of the Treaty of Rome, the Europeanists in the State Department pressed continually for some kind of European unity in which Britain was of no particular importance compared to any other European country.

In the light of current developments, the signing of the Treaty of Rome must rank as one of the most important events of the post-war period. Britain's involvement with Europe is the subject of the major part of the remainder of this chapter, but here it is worth raising two questions. The first is: Why did not Britain join with the others? The second is: Was, as many argue with passion, the failure to do so a great opportunity missed?

To understand why Britain did not join one has to understand the ethos of the time. Two factors appear to have dominated the British decision not to participate: the belief in the special relationship with the United States, which some felt would be irreparably damaged by joining, and the consequences for Britain's relationship with its Empire. As for the first, to those with hindsight this was nothing short of self-delusion. That conclusion depends in part on current views about the so-called special relationship which are examined in the next section. Prime Minister Macmillan's specific reason for a lack of enthusiasm for joining Europe derived from his concern for the impact such a step would have on the Empire. On the face of it, Britain already belonged to a significant international community and at the time it was not thought to be easy to relate the Empire to a new style European Community, with what appeared to be a parochial focus on Continental European affairs. At the time, British exports to Continental Europe accounted for only 35 per cent of the total compared to 60 per cent in 1996. The Empire still appeared to be economically important to Britain and it is only with hindsight that the growth of British trade with Europe could have been predicted confidently.

The question as to whether not joining the Community in 1957 was a great missed opportunity raises two issues which must be considered. The first is to what extent could Britain have claimed leadership of a new community, or at least been a major influence on the institutional development and ethos of an economically, if not politically, united Community? The second relates to the economic implications for Britain of not having joined at that time. This issue was reflected in the early 1970s view prior to entry into the Community that staying outside it had prevented Britain from sharing in the benefits of a highly successful economic club. Unfortunately, it was just at the time that Britain joined in 1973 that the performance of the club ran into difficulties which have persisted ever since.

As far as the first issue is concerned, distance, as always, lends enchantment. The memories of disaffected and frustrated civil servants and politicians lend credence to the idea that by not signing the Treaty of Rome, Britain lost the leadership of Europe. Only the transference of a lost arrogance from Empire to a new Europe could have convinced anyone of that possibility. The raw politics of it all was that the encumbrance of Empire and the still (at least) partial existence of the special relationship between Britain and the United States meant there was no way in which France, as represented and symbolised by President de Gaulle, would have permitted the United Kingdom to have assumed any kind of leadership role in Europe. The hostility of France to both Britain and the United States was paramount. Only old men with poor memories and vivid imaginations could believe it otherwise. Indeed, the issue of Britain's role in Europe today (discussed further below) still reeks of this arrogance. There still remains the idea that Britain in Europe can play a major role in influencing the institutional and economic shape of the European Union. It is not that the opportunity was lost, or that paradise can be regained. It never was possible and the illusion cannot be recreated today.

From an economic point of view, there is simply no evidence that Britain's economic performance between the signing of the Treaty of Rome and her formal accession to the European Community was in any significant way affected. As already explained at length in earlier chapters, the relative decline of Britain in economic terms between 1950 and 1973 was virtually inevitable. There was no way in which the catch-up could have been prevented. Moreover, it may be noted that the growth of trade between Britain and the then members of the European Community was proportionately faster than the rate of growth of trade between the then signed up members of the Community. In trade terms, the integration of the United Kingdom with the members of the Community proceeded as rapidly before the entry of the United Kingdom as it did after.

From both the point of view of the ability to lead the future of the European Community as created by the Treaty of Rome, and Britain's economic performance, the failure to join the original conception cannot be seen as a great missed opportunity. The decision that Britain took at the time made sense.

THE ATLANTIC ALLIANCE

A key factor that inhibited both the United Kingdom's desire to join the new European Community, and de Gaulle's desire to keep Britain out, was the so-called special relationship with the United States. Before examining Britain's relationship within the European Union, which has completely dominated discussion of Britain's relationship with the outside world in recent years, it is important to review the history and current characteristics of this special relationship.

As allies in two European world wars, and with strong cultural and institutional similarities, and not least a common language, it is plausible to believe that there always has been and will be in the future a special relationship between the United Kingdom and North America. That said, such a presumption needs to be treated with much caution.

The first issue is that, like in all relationships, personalities and the events of the time are key determining factors. America entered the First World War unwillingly, and its involvement with Europe was brief. No major personal relationships developed between the United States and the British governments. The refusal of the American Congress to ratify the Peace of Versailles was entirely consistent with the American view of the British as imperialists and more widely a serious unwillingness to involve itself in the economics and politics of the Old World. Between the wars there was no special relationship in a political sense between Britain and the United States. Even after the outbreak of the Second World War in Europe, at the popular level there was no great support for Britain – some sympathy perhaps but not much more. Public opinion was led to some degree by Roosevelt, but despite his burgeoning relationship with Churchill (after he became Prime Minister) even Roosevelt could hardly have carried America into a European war in support of Britain. It was left to Japan to strike the blow that finally galvanised the United States into war on a global scale with the attack on Pearl Harbor in 1941.

The history of the relationship between Britain and the United States from that time on has been substantively determined by three factors. First, the cultural and institutional affinities already referred to. Secondly, the interplay of various political and economic factors with the personalities of the respective governments. Thirdly, the more technocratic view, particularly at the administrative level of government of the United States, with regard to the development of economic and political relations between the Europeans.

As emphasised by Robin Renwick, after the Second World War:

> At the heart of the 'special relationship' lay this privileged collaboration, dating from the war, that the British enjoyed on defence, nuclear and intelligence issues. (Renwick, 1996, p. 389)

From the point of view of officials in the State Department, as epitomised by George Ball, there were strong reasons for allowing this relationship to wither on the vine. The fact that it did not wither must, in large measure, be attributable to the Executive. Despite the political defeat of Churchill in 1945, it would appear that the somewhat ascetic association between Truman and Attlee sustained the relationship throughout the early post-war years. Eisenhower supported nuclear collaboration with Britain that had been withdrawn as a result of the MacMahon Act in the United States. And despite the serious impact of the Suez episode, on attitudes in the State Department and those of John Foster Dulles in particular, Macmillan's relationship with Eisenhower and his firm belief in the importance of the relationship between Britain and America was a determining factor in the lack of British involvement in the developments in Europe that led up to the Treaty of Rome.

The story of the relationship between Britain and the United States since the middle 1960s has seen considerable fluctuations depending on the personalities and the events of the time. The advent of Heath as Prime Minister in 1970 ushered in a period of inactivity in Anglo-American relations. Heath and Nixon gave nothing to each other. But more importantly, Heath was the first, and to date the only, British Prime Minister since the Second World War who clearly on the British side had little time for any special relationship between Britain and the United States, and whose principal focus was on the relationship with Continental Europe. Callaghan at the end of the 1970s restored that relationship with President Carter. Margaret Thatcher famously emphasised it with her relationship in the 1980s with Ronald Reagan. Historically, attitudes to the United States have been materially influenced by attitudes to Europe, equally the other way round. The implications of all this have a profound significance for foreign policy issues relating to the European Union that are discussed later in this chapter and to Britain's relations with Europe, a final judgement on which is left over to Chapter 7.

The story told has been succinctly summarised by Renwick:

As this account will have made clear, that there has been an extraordinarily close relationship between Britain and the United States since the desperate summer of 1940 is beyond dispute. The relationship was frequently marked by fierce disagreements, often with good cause, as over Suez, and real clashes of national interest. But to a remarkable extent these were regarded as family quarrels and despite the tensions that marked successive prime ministers ... – particularly those of Eden, Wilson and Heath – the underlying strength of the relationship always seemed to assert itself. On the US side, such political opposites as Presidents Carter and Nixon attached value to it. Eisenhower was deeply imbued with it, though remarkably unsentimental about it. It was a reality also to Presidents Reagan and Bush, despite the latter's recognition that Germany had not only much greater economic power but also, and increasingly, greater political importance. (Renwick, 1996, p. 392)

In his memoirs, the former Foreign Secretary, David Owen recorded that:

Every few years an incident occurs which demonstrates that the Anglo-American relationship is still very important ... Those of us who have operated the relationship will have their own memories of why it matters ... The Anglo-American relationship depends on personal relationships at every level, but particularly between US Presidents and Secretaries of State and their British counterparts. Down-play or denigrate this relationship and it will be Europe, not just Britain that will suffer. The invasion of Kuwait, the seizure of the Falklands, the bombing of Libya are but three recent examples in a long list of post-war incidents where it was tested and not found wanting. (Owen, 1992, p. 798)

It is clear that over time the relationship between Britain and the United States has been changing in the light of events. Britain's involvement in the European Union is manifestly part of that story. The ending of the Cold War and the opportunity for the United States to appraise its relationships with its allies are another. The pull of the Pacific for North America in both an economic and a political sense is another key factor. At this stage as far as the current discussion is concerned, the issue is simply that a future appraisal of Britain's position in the world must take into account a dimension beyond what has become an obsessive concern with Britain's relationship with Europe with which most of the rest of this chapter is concerned. A final overall assessment must remain until Chapter 7.

THE TREATY OF ROME AND AFTER

The European Community was brought into being by the Treaty of Rome in 1957. The reasons for Britain's non-participation have already been discussed. The economic performance of its members in the years before 1973 largely reflected the inevitable catch-up of sophisticated industrial economies following the devastation and disruption that embraced the Second World War and its aftermath. There was no 'miracle' over this period, although for political rather than economic reasons the economic performance of post-war West Germany might be likened to Lazarus rising from the dead. It remains remarkable that the attitude of many Britons to Germany, who repeatedly criticise Britain's economic performance in percentage growth rate terms, do not recognise that after the catch-up period of the 1950s and afterwards, the five year growth rate of Germany declined consistently thereafter.

Up to 1973, the overall economic performance of the members of the European Economic Community seemed remarkable although, as we have recorded, most of it was simply inevitable catch-up. The demise of Bretton Woods and the deep shock of rising oil prices brought the so-called European miracle to a close. And as recorded earlier it was at that point that the United Kingdom, led by Edward Heath, was admitted to the Community. President de Gaulle was dead, and the door was opened.

The economic performance of the Community from 1973 onwards was in marked contrast to the apparent triumphal progress of the 1950s and 1960s, as can be seen in Table 1.1, in Chapter 1. Community members failed miserably to adapt to the new economic environment that was created by the collapse of the Bretton Woods Agreement on the one hand and the rise in oil prices on the other. In this respect, the United Kingdom for once was a market leader! Across the Community the power of organised labour, and the contractual relations between governments and employees (indexation of wages, for example, in Belgium and Italy), all contributed to the rise in real labour costs in the Community, a major reduction of corporate profitability, and a reduction in the rate of Community investment. Government deficits grew, and unemployment began the long march upwards that has left the Community as a whole in the position it is in today.

The economic performance of Europe following the second oil price shock in 1978 was even worse. While inflation did not reach the heights achieved in the previous cycle, unemployment continued to rise and overall growth performance fell below what was achieved even in the disrupted 1970s. In the Community itself, eurosclerosis and weak leadership at the European Commission stirred up general frustration. The impotence of the Commission and the lack of leadership from the Council of Ministers spilled over into the European Parliament, whose influence was, and remains, remarkably little in the context of how the institutions of the European Community (as it then was) functioned.

THE SINGLE MARKET CONCEPT

In 1983, the former member of the French Commissariat du Plan, Michel Albert, and the present author were commissioned by the European Parliament, then under the Presidency of Pieter Dankert, to conduct a study of the European economy (Albert and Ball, 1984). Europe was bathed in gloom. Phrases abounded such as the 'cost of non-Europe' (attributable to Michel Albert) and 'European sclerosis'. The report that resulted was introduced as follows:

> The central theme of this paper is that the main obstacle to the economic growth of the European countries is what we must call 'non-Europe', an expression that is intended to convey the low level of cooperation and the weakness of common policies. This is less to denounce the sterility of the institutions or the defects in their construction than to underline how public opinion is too little aware of the role that it must play from now on. Lacking popular legitimacy, it is this non-Europe that is ossifying and declining on the slippery slope of non-growth. (Albert and Ball, 1984, pp. x–xi)

It should be understood that this theme of the report was seen at the time as couched in strictly economic terms. The central question was how could the European economy be made to function more effectively with regard to economic growth and employment? It was agreed between the authors that there was a need for more labour market flexibility, a restructuring of public finances (which had got out of hand in the 1970s) and control over the rate of inflation. But, by and large, these issues were discussed within the framework of the existing political institutions in the Community: no examination of, or suggestions with regard to, such institutions were undertaken or made.

The report considered largely macroeconomic issues. But in terms of the longer run development of the Community (as it then was) the report focused on the cost of non-Europe as exemplified by a failure to integrate European markets. The 'Common Market' was neither common nor a market. As the report explicitly stated:

> It is clear that, in regard to its industrial position the Community has failed, and continues to fail, to produce a common market. National interests continue to predominate in industrial matters. The need for increased standardization in the Community is paramount if it is to mean anything to its Member States in the immediate future. The need for a common public procurement market is part of the story. But little is likely to happen without a major change of will and an increased commitment among the Member States. (Albert and Ball, 1984, p. 70)

In the event, the theme of market integration as expressed in the report manifested itself in the Single Market programme. The idea was not limited to the integration of trade, but also encompassed the integration of financial markets in general. The report commented:

> As we have seen, Europe should have given priority to boosting its investments. Because the slowdown in growth and the resulting scarcity of savings made it difficult to finance them, it became essential and urgent to create a genuine *common capital market* [author's italics]. (Albert and Ball, 1984, pp. 21–22)

The Single Market programme, supported by the Single European Act (permitting majority voting on a number of issues) and the White Paper of 1985, began a decade ago. It aimed to ensure the approval of relevant directives by the Council of Ministers to enable the Single Market programme to be completed by 1992, and implemented in the appropriate laws of the member states.

In 1989, the Centre for Business Strategy at the London Business School published a collection of essays on the Single Market programme. In introducing the subject, John Kay commented:

> There is a sense in which the real significance of 1992 lies in the hype rather than the programme itself. The marketing campaign has enjoyed a success far beyond its promoters' dreams in alerting business to the potential of European markets, and the opportunities for European ventures and in restoring self-confidence in the European ideal. Objective reality may not have changed, but the manner in which it is perceived has. In this way the spirit of 1992 may have taken on a wider significance greater than the detail of the programme. And the spirit is at once wider and narrower than the programme itself. Wider because it is already apparent that the opportunities will be seized which were not taken before, not because there were official obstacles to them, but because business horizons were too material in outlook. Narrower because in specific areas, such as public procurement or financial market liberalisation, it is the sincerity with which governments pursue the ideals of 1992 that matters, rather than the content of the directives themselves. (Kay, 1989, p. 1)

This is of course to go too far. The content and nature of the directives issued as part of the process of the implementation of the Single Market matter very much. As argued also by Kay, together with Michael Posner:

> 1992 is a staging post on the route to European economic integration. For Britain, the real issues are not national sovereignty versus supranationalisation, but the choice between a liberal, market oriented path to integration and a planned centralised one. (Kay and Posner, 1989, p. 55)

Associating a 'Bismarckian' approach to integration as 'centralised' and a

'Jeffersonian' approach as 'evolutionary' Kay and Posner pose the key question:

> Is the best route to integration one which tears down barriers to trade and leaves the evolution of political and economic structures to follow; or is the development of the political and economic structures a pre-requisite to the advance of integration? A true 'Bismarckian' approach is tight, centralised, and occurs early in the process: the true 'Jeffersonian' approach is loose, local and the ultimate Union-wide solution comes, if at all, later in the day. (Kay and Posner, 1989, p. 55)

Developments in the modern theory of international trade were discussed earlier in Chapter 3. To summarise, the classical theory of trade emphasised the importance of comparative advantage in promoting trade in an economic world of more or less perfect competition under conditions of constant and diminishing returns to scale. Gains from trade resulted primarily from inter-industry shifts that followed from the exploitation of specialisation and relative efficiency. Modern theory recognises the importance of economies of scale in explaining both business performance and behaviour, and the creation of trade. Here the distinction is between *static* (once and for all) and *dynamic* (evolving over time) effects from scale changes. At the same time, modern trade theory also emphasises the importance of imperfect competition. Where competition is limited, economic integration and the dismantling of trade barriers will in theory increase it. Interactive economic integration can affect in principle both productivity and allocative efficiency of the overall economic system. Thus, apart from the classical possibility of gains accruing as a result of integration from the effective exploitation of comparative advantage, more important gains may be had from the exploitation of economies of scale, increased competition, and so greater scope for choice on the part of the consumer.

The theory points to ways in which trade integration should benefit the members of the Community (now the Union). But practical assessment is difficult. The reasons are implicit in the following early prognostications of the European Commission itself with regard to the quantitative and qualitative effects of trade integration on the Community membership:

> In general it can be expected that for the Community internal market programme the direct effects of the market opening measures (e.g. the resource costs of opening certain market barriers) may be less big than the indirect effects on efficiency and costs as a result of *entrenched competition* [author's italics] and dynamic effects may be relatively large compared to the short term static effects. It is however the dynamic effects, important behavioural effects which do not admit of any narrow economic calculus that are the most difficult to measure. It is for this reason that some with reason choose to characterise 1992 not as an event but as a state

of mind, the upshot of which is not a matter of arithmetic but of creativeness. (Emerson et al, 1988, p. 37)

A year previously the Community, in its Annual Report for 1987, asserted that:

> The reduction in costs which will result from the completion of the internal market, economies of scale, increased competition and the broadening of the economic basis for research and development will lead to an easing of the burden of public budgets, productivity gains, and an improvement in competitiveness on external markets and a boost to intra-community trade. The internal market will create fresh opportunities for investment by opening up new horizons for entrepreneurs. (The European Economy, 1987, p. 14)

As will be seen in this section and later in this chapter, a decade later there is little hard evidence to support any of these claims. 1992 is now long gone. It passed without trumpets or celebration. The process of integration continues – slowly. It was always difficult, if not impossible, as we have seen, to be precise about the future benefits of the Single Market programme. As already indicated there is little if any *prima facie* evidence of the benefits from integration as a result of increased competitiveness and economies of scale. The latter is hardly surprising since, for static scale economies, little was to be expected other than in the area of government procurement. Dynamic economies of scale depend on changing patterns of business behaviour, rather than simple directives. Competition and greater diversity of choice always seemed *prima facie* to offer the best hope for the creation of benefit and trade (see Geroski, 1989)

It is too early to make any definitive assessment of what has been achieved to date in the integration of goods, services and financial markets. Restrictions on the movement of capital have been largely lifted. Only Britain, Ireland and Denmark still insist on frontier checks for Union visitors. Cross-frontier mergers and acquisitions more than doubled in the five years prior to 1992.

Nevertheless, for many, progress has been slow. The deregulation of air travel, a key factor in an integrated transport regime, has been fudged. Subsidies are still propping up inefficient, publicly owned airlines. There have been delays in opening up financial services, although here the 'passport' concept has been a great help. The establishment of a free market in basic telephone services has been held over to 1998 – and even then protection will continue for some of the suppliers in the smaller countries. More generally, there has been little opening up of public procurement markets (a development cynically received by the United States, whose suspicions of fortress Europe in this context still remain). Non-national share is less than

THE BRITISH ECONOMY AT THE CROSSROADS

5 per cent of the value of government procurement contracts across the Union. More pervasively, not simply in air travel, but in banking, steel, ships, cars, energy and other transport, subsidies are shamelessly applied where governments consider it to be in their national interest. The sincerity of governments leaves much to be desired. Of the 282 measures needed to translate the vision of the Single Market into a reality (reduced from the original 300), some 222 required legislation on the part of the member states (at March 1997). Roughly half still remain to be processed. While the United Kingdom and Denmark top the league of good performers in this respect, Greece, France and Spain have been much slower. There have been significant delays with respect to public procurement, company law, intellectual and industrial property, and insurance.

Attention has also been focused on trade between member states and the trade of the Union with the world outside it. Liberalisation might be expected to show itself in an increase in trade between the members, while increased economic efficiency across the Union in general might be expected to affect its share of non-Union trade.

As shown in Table 6.1, intra-trade in the Union grew significantly between the late 1950s and the late 1960s. As already recorded, trade between the United Kingdom and the then Community grew even faster than trade between the then members of the Community, despite the fact that the United Kingdom was not even a member. But for fifteen years between 1970 and 1985 it remained more or less on a plateau. However, in the middle 1980s it grew significantly from just over 50 per cent to about 60 per cent, whereafter it has remained more or less at this level. The reason for this is not immediately clear. One thing is certain: the timing of the change can hardly reflect the impact of the Single Market programme. Between 1988 and the present day, the proportion has hardly changed. Moreover, looking back to the developments of the 1960s, the rise in the share of intra-trade over the period cannot be ascribed to liberalisation brought about by the establishment and development of the Community as it then was (consider the performance of the United Kingdom just referred to). A well established model of international trade (the so-called 'gravity model') would have predicted that trade between the geographically contiguous countries, such as members of the Community, would be expected to show trade patterns of the kind we observe in the European context. The bottom line of all this is that it is not possible to conclude anything significant from a study of intra-trading within the Union with regard to the impact of the Single Market programme. (For further discussion of the behaviour of intra-trade in the Union see Chui and Whitley, 1995.)

Table 6.1
European Union intra-trade and share of world trade

European Union % share of Union exports									
1958	1970	1973	1976	1979	1982	1985	1988	1991	1994
37.2	51.8	51.5	51.4	52.7	51.2	54.6	61.0	60.5	61.3

European Union and United States % shares of world exports*				
	1970	1980	1990	1992
European Union	17.2	17.9	15.7	15.5
United States	12.5	12.0	14.0	14.1

* after excluding European Union intra-trade

Source: European Economy Annual Report 1995; Handbook of International Trade and Development Statistics, UNCTAD, 1994

As regards the trade relationship of the Union with the world outside the Union, it can be seen in Table 6.1 that, after stripping out the intra-trade, the position of the Union with regard to world trade is similar to that of the United States. There has been no significant trend in the share of Union exports to the OECD (including intra-trade) since the middle of the 1960s. There is no evidence that any developments resulting from the Single Market programme have had any discernible effect on the trade relationships between the members of the European Union and the outside world.

THE TREATY OF MAASTRICHT

The Treaty on European Union was signed in the Dutch town of Maastricht in December 1991. After some delays, and in some cases political referenda, the Treaty came into force in November 1993.

The Treaty marked the shift in nomenclature from the European Community to the European Union. This was intended to capture the fact that the Union was to be based on the so-called 'three pillars' which included the Community as it was but now gave formal recognition to the development of a common foreign and security policy, which included defence. In addition the Union formally incorporates the European judiciary on the one hand, and establishes cooperation on issues such as crime, terrorism and immigration. The Treaty was to all intents and purposes a revision of the Treaty of Rome. It can be argued that in many respects it went far beyond the philosophy for the Community that had underlain the Single Market programme. However, it is equally fair to point out that in many respects it reflected the broader objectives of the founding fathers who established the Treaty of Rome. Moreover it focused attention on a number of issues, particularly with regard to social and labour relations, that had been assuming greater importance in the Community under the leadership of Jacques Delors to whom, together with François Mitterrand and Helmut Kohl, the Treaty must be principally attributed.

William Nicol has given an overall judgement on the Treaty, which emphasises the newness of the foreign policy dimension:

> What did Maastricht do? It defined what is to be meant by European Union for a period of years to come. It greatly increased the powers of the European Parliament which now has to show whether it can fulfil the responsibilities it has demanded. It created the structures for a common foreign policy, which is what other countries have wanted. As Mr Kissinger used to say – we'd like to talk to Europe and we'd like them to give us a telephone number. It addressed a defence policy but did not define it. It decided with one opt-out to converge economically on the basis of rigorous criteria and thereby fit itself for a single currency with Her Regency Queen Beatrix the first to volunteer to see her head removed from the notes in use in the Netherlands. (Nicol, 1995, p. 44)

For many the Treaty appeared to catapult the old Community into a new trajectory, resulting in closer and closer links between member states, and ultimately ending up in some form of federal political union. This description is by no means universally accepted; indeed many supporters of the Treaty and its ideas would say that it implies no such thing. There is no doubt, however, as to the direction that Helmut Kohl is coming from. The two most contentious parts of the Treaty relate to the provisions laid down for monetary union between the member states and the establishment of the Social Chapter, and many believe that neither development presages any significant steps toward the idea of a federal Europe. Nevertheless, there are strong forces moving in that direction even if it does not follow neatly and logically from the Treaty itself. They are exemplified by the French economist, Michel Albert:

> ... the Single Market, unless it leads rapidly to true political union, will turn Europe into a sort of American sub-system, with a lot less state and a lot more market, an outcome that would delight Margaret Thatcher and distress Jacques Delors. (Albert, 1993, p. 249)

The debate has polarised around the two issues of monetary union and the Social Chapter, although it will be argued later there are other important matters to be taken into consideration. The Treaty on European Union envisaged the implementation of monetary union in stages. The transitional provisions came into effect in January 1994, which constituted Stage 2 of the process. In December 1995 the European Council meeting in Maastricht agreed that the final stage of monetary union (EMU), Stage 3, would begin on 1 January 1999 for those member states that met the necessary conditions for entry (discussed below).

As already recorded, the Maastricht Treaty covers both political and economic change. On the economic and monetary side it provides the legal basis to establish the institutions needed for further progress toward EMU, and as we have seen, proposed that this should happen in three stages. Provisions to discourage excessive government fiscal deficits and sovereign debt ratios are prescribed. There are criteria for economic convergence, which are the basis for deciding whether a country can be on the starting line in January 1999. The Treaty provides for the creation of a European System of Central Banks (ESCB) headed by a European Central Bank (ECB), which will define and implement a common monetary policy for those countries which participate in EMU.

In areas other than monetary policy, the Treaty extends the central powers of the Union. It increases interventionist powers in such areas as social policy, industrial policy, technological policy, consumer protection, the environment, health and education. To put flesh on the bones of the old Community Social Chapter, which had already been part of the Single Market programme, and which evolved into the social protocol of the Treaty, the Union (basically the European Commission for this purpose) is to set common minimum standards in, among others, health and safety requirements at the work place, working conditions, and gender equality. Pension rights would be determined by the Union. All these matters can be resolved by majority vote. There is no veto. The Union may also subsequently enforce those parts of collective bargaining agreements within the Union states which deal with working conditions. Supporters of these developments play down their ultimate consequences, but for the principal architect of the Treaty the vision is clear, expressed five years before the Treaty was signed:

> Ten years hence, 80 per cent of our economic legislation, and perhaps even our fiscal and social legislation as well, will be of Community origin. (Jacques Delors, Debate in the European Parliament, July 1988)

Unlikely, but the sentiment is clear enough.

MONETARY UNION

From the present perspective there are two issues that relate to monetary union. The first is whether in general it is a desirable development for the European Union as a whole. The thesis of the current section is that it is not. The second is, if monetary union between what might be described as the 'core' countries of the Union goes ahead, should Britain join, or would it be disadvantaged by staying out?

The arguments of the European Commission for monetary union are contained in the paper 'One Market, One Money' produced in 1990 (European Economy, 1990). A lengthy technical discussion of the requirements for union is contained in the CEPR Report, 1991, in its series on Monitoring European Integration. More recently in the United Kingdom, we have seen the publication of extensive surveys of the issues by Christopher Taylor (1995) and David Currie (1997).

In analysing the desirability and consequences of monetary union in the European Union there are three interrelated pieces of analysis: the economic arguments for monetary union, the practical consequences for such a union going forward, and the relationship of monetary union to European integration.

First, the economic case for monetary union would probably seem to the person in the street as obvious. The slogan of 'One Market, One Money' could be seen as common sense. After all, if the full benefits of market integration are to be achieved, should not Europe be like the United States and have a single currency? To quote *The Economist*:

> Advocates of a single currency can reel off the advantages. For business EMU would eliminate the cost (reckoned to be $30 billion a year) of foreign exchange transactions and exchange rate hedging. For individual Eurocitizens, it would rid them of currency-exchange robbery (go round the Union changing money at each border and you will end up with half the amount you started with). For governments it would help stabilise the international currency markets. For the Union's single market, inaugurated at the end of 1992 to allow the free movement of people, capital goods and services it would mean added efficiency and an end within the monetary union to 'competitive' devaluation. (*The Economist*, 9 December, 1995, p. 20).

Unfortunately, matters are much more complicated. The economic arguments for monetary union can be divided roughly speaking into two. The first is concerned with the impact of union on costs and the allocation of resources. These effects are directly related to the benefits to be gained from the Single Market. The second relates to the implications of union for monetary policy, particularly the impact on inflation and interest rates.

The theory that relates to monetary union and resource allocation is called the 'theory of optimal currency areas'. The seminal theoretical paper is that provided by the Nobel Prize winner, Robert Mundell (Mundell, 1961). In simplified terms, an optimal currency area is one within which economic shocks are likely to be symmetrical, or at least not strongly asymmetrical. This means that the nature of economic disturbances does not require demand management responses that are specific to a particular region within the currency area. A classic but recent example of an asymmetric shock in the European context is the shock caused by the reunification of Germany. It was this that emasculated the Exchange Rate Mechanism of the European Monetary System. Countries like the United Kingdom and Italy could not (would not! and possibly should not) carry the burden of German real interest rates.

Given shocks to the system, a crucial issue is how flexibly can resources be reallocated in response to such a shock? In a single currency area this requires wage and price flexibility and the relatively free movement of labour and capital. In the absence of a sufficient degree of flexibility, resolving problems between states involves major transfers of resources between countries. This is why on both counts the analogy with the United States is quite misleading. The disparities between the member states of the European Union (that would be made more acute with its extension) are that much greater than between the states of America. In addition, the mobility of factors of production is dramatically less, particularly in the case of labour. (The effect of language as a barrier within Europe is persistently underestimated.) Finally, regional variability in the United States is supported by large transfers undertaken by the Federal Government. This is not the case in Europe (at least not yet!) and as we shall see the proposed criteria for fiscal policies within the Union will make it that much more difficult to adapt to shocks after the safety valve of the exchange rate has been turned off. As observed by Taylor:

> It seems out of the question that fiscal policy (i.e. stabilisation) could cope with the structural problems which EMU will expose in weaker EC economies. Other mechanisms are needed and in most existing monetary unions the central budget makes an important contribution through redistributive taxes and transfer payments. The EU's redistribution mechanism is relatively limited, except in relation to the smallest and poorest countries. At present this is not an acute problem because the exchange rate is still available as an adjustment mechanism for non-core countries as the upsets of the ERM since 1992 show. (Taylor, 1995, p. 70)

(See also the discussion in Feldstein (1997) and Friedman (1997).)

There is no evidence that remotely suggests that the European Union is an optimal currency area. Indeed, quite the contrary. Moreover, a major question mark hangs over the size of the direct or static benefits that monetary union might confer in the form of cost reduction. The direct benefits are not that great, particularly when set against the costs of implementation (which are admittedly one-off). The problem, as with the general issue of measuring gains from trade integration, is the dynamic gains that might occur. Dynamic gains result from changes in behavioural patterns, the magnitude of which is sheer speculation. As the European Commission's own report on monetary union pointed out:

> The larger part of the potential economic gains would not be the automatic result of the institutional changes. The full gains would require the concerted commitment of national governments, employers, and employees, as well as the Community itself to what amounts to a change of economic system. (European Economy, 1990, p. 9)

The overall upshot is that the economic gains from monetary union are highly speculative. A serious case for it has to be made on some political or idealistic basis as a prelude or required condition of major political institutional change in Europe. Trade integration has proceeded apace between the United States and Canada as the result of the Free Trade Agreement, but no one to date has pinned its future success on the need to create a common currency, although in North America cultural and institutional factors are immensely more favourable to such an idea on a working basis than is the case in the Union.

A possible benefit from monetary union over and above the direct effects on trade integration might be better control of inflation for some countries. A more effective monetary policy for member states might emerge from monetary union. The CEPR Report notes:

> Countries that have had long experience of above average inflation expect to enjoy benefits from a stable currency after EMU. In addition to price stability *per se*, such countries may gain from lower interest rates, as financial markets no longer require risk premiums to offset the prospect of recurrent devaluation. Lower interest rates mean lower taxes as the cost of debt service falls. (CEPR Report, 1991, p. 4)

This is manifestly wishful thinking and is entirely speculative on two counts. The first is that in the first round of EMU (and perhaps never) the economies most susceptible to inflation and excessive deficit spending, which would most benefit from a strong dose of monetary discipline, will not be allowed in. Secondly, such outcomes depend critically on the way in which monetary policy is actually conducted and how the European Central Bank actually works (as discussed further below). The illusion that a Euro-currency will simply be another name for the deutschmark is hardly sustainable, and while it may not turn out, as the extreme pessimists believe, to be a 'camembert' currency, it is most likely to reflect some melange of the existing currencies that have been collapsed into it.

The conditions laid down in the Maastricht Treaty for entry into monetary union place requirements on interest rates, inflation rate and exchange rate performance prior to entry, together with the familiar conditions that budget deficits should be no more than 3 per cent of GDP (after cyclical adjustment) and the debt to GDP ratio no more than 60 per cent.

It is arguable, first, that these criteria are not only arbitrary, they are fatally flawed. Indeed, this is recognised by some of EMU's keenest supporters, partly fearing the derailment of the whole project. In addition, a serious question arises with regard to post-EMU credibility. Suggestions for 'fining' countries that do not stick to the criteria after monetary union border on the ridiculous. On these criteria the United Kingdom would have paid out 3 per cent of its GDP in fines since 1991. Are member states seriously intending to expose themselves to this possibility? And if they did and they failed to meet the criteria, what are the sanctions?

The issue of fiscal policy lies at the heart of the technical debate about monetary union. Restrictions on the use of fiscal policy, in the absence of individual state control over monetary policy and exchange rate adjustment, are potentially damaging. Ultimately, damage limitation will surely entail a coordination of fiscal and monetary policy at the European Union level for two reasons. The first, as already suggested, is the need for stronger central transfer mechanisms at Union level as part of the process of adjustment between states. The second is the logical inconsistency of separating monetary and fiscal policy. In some cases this may simply result in instability as argued by the late James Meade and Martin Weale (Meade and Weale, 1991). It is almost inevitable that the push toward the centralisation of monetary policy as a result of monetary union will lead to pressure for the centralisation of fiscal policy.

On this issue, the whistle has clearly been blown by Edouard Balladur, Prime Minister of France between 1993 and 1995, and Minister of Finance in the middle 1980s:

> But the European venture will lose its point if it is reduced to a solely monetary dimension. We have to lay the foundations for a European growth pact. Unless we are to resign ourselves to seeing European growth falter and unemployment grow, we must in my opinion, ensure that the 15 EU member states commit themselves collectively to a target of reducing tax and social security contributions to a level not much higher, over the long term, than those prevailing in American and Japan.

This will in turn require more fiscal harmonisation throughout the Union [author's italics] ... In other words the creation of a common currency does not mean the end of our efforts ... How much more lies ahead! (Balladur, 1997, p. 48)

There are many practical issues that relate to monetary union which go beyond the current discussion. Perhaps the most significant is the nature, role and procedures of the proposed European Central Bank. While for the purpose of this discussion we have treated monetary union as implying a single currency, it need not do so, although it is arguable that any form of arrangement between floating rates and a single currency is unlikely to prove durable. There are in both cases important technical questions with regard to the conduct of monetary policy. To illustrate the point, the Bundesbank in Germany has already gone on record to argue for the retention of compulsory bank 'cash' reserve requirements, which were abandoned in the United Kingdom, as effectively a tax upon banks. This does not matter so much in Germany (and in France) where the development of competitive securities markets has been restricted by one means or another. But it would be a blow to banks in the United Kingdom.

However, leaving on the side these technical questions, a major question relates to the independence of the European Central Bank. There are two issues. The first is that of accountability. The CEPR Report already quoted puts paramount emphasis on the political independence of such an institution. It goes so far as to say *'Price stability requires complete European Central Bank independence.'* (p. xiii).

The first question is the nature of the accountability of the Bank, since independence cannot be synonymous with non-accountability. The suggestion that such accountability should be exercised simply by the Council of Ministers and the European Parliament should hardly be acceptable to the parliaments of the member states. It would certainly be unacceptable in France.

The second question is whether, in the absence of a degree of centralisation in fiscal policy, the Bank will be unable to resist the pressures from individual member states to underwrite financial deficits. On this issue it is clear where the weaker members of the Union are coming from. While no doubt forbidden *ex ante* it is quite unclear how the position is to be sustained *ex post*.

The overall conclusion to the debate on monetary union has been sensibly summarised by Christopher Taylor:

The overall impression from the foregoing review is that the economic case for moving to EMU is not conclusive, despite the Commission's research and

responses to it. The economic issues are highly complex and the exercise unprece-
dented. (Taylor, 1995, p. 68)

As proposed, a two speed Europe, with regard to economic integration,
will not promote the cause of European unity. As a general proposition,
monetary union has little to commend it. An attempt to impose a European
grid of the kind suggested by the proponents of monetary union will not
result in progress toward the integration of the member states as a whole, but
to a fragmentation that will make it difficult to progress to a more collective
European framework. EMU is potentially more feasible in economic terms
for those who have least to gain from it. It has little to do with economics,
but is driven by political considerations in Brussels, Bonn and Paris. Attitudes
to monetary union as stimulated by its principal drivers no longer reflect (if
they ever did) basic economic motivations. At the higher levels, the advocates have other items on their agendas.

IS THE UNION WORKING?

Economic growth, unemployment and public finances are all key and interrelated issues with which the Union is faced. As recorded earlier, Michel
Albert and the present author produced a report in 1984 in the context of
considerable pessimism with regard to the economic performance of what
was then the European Community. Fourteen years later the overall economic situation of the Union is no better than it was then. In some respects,
particularly with regard to unemployment and the public finances, matters
are considerably worse. In the light of this the comments of Michel Albert in
a recent book are somewhat surprising:

> Every newspaper reader knows that the brilliant results chalked up by the Rhine
> economies have lately received a great deal of attention and that the contrast is all
> too vivid when set against the trials and tribulations of the Anglo-Saxon economies
> beset by inflation and debt. (Albert, 1993, p. 138)

It appears that many people in Britain would subscribe to this sentiment,
if not as forcibly but at least sympathetically, in view of the degree of support expressed in many quarters for what we can describe as 'Rhine capitalism', an issue to which we turn in Chapter 7. Here our prime concern is to
focus on the current facts to assess the economic health of the Union.

Some comparisons for the periods of the 1980s and the 1990s are set out
in Table 1.1 (Chapter 1), which examines the European Union, the United
States, Japan and the United Kingdom. It is well understood that such

comparisons are fraught with many kinds of difficulties that relate to differences in economic structure, and timing problems which are affected by stages in the economic cycles which are not coincident across countries. The purpose of the numbers in Table 1.1 in Chapter 1 is to draw some qualitative conclusions rather than precise quantitative ones.

As a starting point it may be noted that the numbers hardly support a claim that the European Union has been a huge success over the periods covered when compared with the United States and Japan. Overall, the United States has grown faster in the 1980s and 1990s than the Union, as indeed has Japan, by a large margin in the 1980s. The United Kingdom grew faster overall than France, Germany, and the average for the EU(15) as a whole, although its comparative performance for the 1990s falls away as a result of the depth of the recession.

The major issue that has preoccupied commentators has, of course, been the slow growth of output per person employed in the United States. As we shall see below, the increase in output in the United States has, unlike the European case, been accompanied by a significant increase in employment, particularly in service industries, and it is possible that the major shift that has occurred between manufacturing and service industries is part of the story. In addition, where the major increase in output is in the service sector, this raises significant problems of measuring productivity and incorporating changes in both product and service quality into the aggregate numbers.

The data, while hardly differentiating the Union from the Anglo-Saxon countries in any significant way, do not in themselves justify the alternative view that in some sense the Union is not working. It is reasonable, given the situation of the early and mid-1980s, that it may be regarded as disappointing that economic growth fell significantly in the 1990s and that the issues raised at the outset of the Single Market, as far as investment and growth are concerned, still remain. As already argued, there is no evidence in the growth data of any visible improvement in performance that might be attributable to the Single Market programme. Despite the disparate performance of overall productivity between the Union and the United States, the overall gap in the *level* of gross domestic product per head of population has not been reduced over the last decade. Whatever its problems and failings, the United States remains the richest country in the world on average by a large margin.

Looking at the growth figures for the European Union should, on the basis of past evidence, provide no basis for great gloom or for self-congratulation. These figures are consistent with the view that other things being equal the Union is capable of steady if unspectacular growth in the foreseeable future. The problem is that other things may not be equal, particularly in view of the poor record of the Union with regard to both job creation and unemployment and the state of its public finances. These issues are at the heart of the Union's longer term economic health and competitiveness in world markets.

The determinants of the rate of unemployment have already been discussed at length in Chapter 4. The behaviour of unemployment is determined by the interaction of the demand and supply for labour, demographic factors and the institutional and fiscal environment in which employment takes place. On the aggregate demand side there are those who believe that unemployment in the Union has been sustained in recent years by an excessive focus of macroeconomic policies on inflation rates rather than employment, and by excessive fiscal tightening as part of the process of preparation for monetary union.

However, there is a widespread belief that unemployment in the Union has been predominantly influenced by supply side factors, which have created major inflexibilities in the way in which labour markets function. (These issues were discussed at length in Chapter 4.)

The future development of service industries is a key factor for employment in Europe. It was argued in Chapter 3 that the share of manufacturing in the total output of the major OECD countries has fallen significantly in the last quarter-century, and will continue in the foreseeable future. The ability to create jobs in the developing knowledge-based industries, with a high service content, is of central importance. In this context at least, Continental Europe faces a severe challenge, in areas in which the United States continues to lead the world. Core countries like Germany will no longer be able to rely on the manufacturing capability of the *Mittelstand*. More is required.

The welfare system, that is part of the problem of unemployment, is also part of the problem besetting the Union's public finances. As can be seen in Table 5.2, the ratio of total public expenditure in the Union as a proportion of gross domestic product has risen from about 30 per cent in 1960 (the EU(9)) to about 50 per cent in 1995. What is not commonly appreciated is that there has been little significant change in this ratio during the last fifteen years. Not surprisingly, the fastest rate of increase in the spending ratio occurred in the 1970s, as the welfare burden rose in the face of the sharp decline in economic growth and the rise in unemployment.

As the new century approaches, many of the Union member states are faced with a new worry, the escalating costs of generous pension provisions made by the state and dealt with on a pay as you go basis. This issue is highlighted by an ageing population and the associated rising costs of health care, all of which will lead to upward pressure on taxation and sovereign borrowing. But as can be seen in Table 5.3, sovereign debt ratios have also risen significantly. At some point, in the absence of any change in the system, taxation and pressure on interest rates must impact on the underlying rate of economic growth. The need for fiscal adjustment is a serious issue in its own right, quite independently of the question of monetary union. The chances that such adjustments will be undertaken by the member states (other than Britain) are minimal.

BRITAIN IN EUROPE

The discussion of Britain's relationship to, and role with, the European Union has degenerated into a polarisation of those who are perceived as Euro-philes and others who are maligned as Euro-sceptics. The central issue should not be cast in terms of whether one is supportive of or opposed to the Union, but what shape the Union should take. Here we summarise key facts and issues that must be taken into account before reaching conclusions.

By and large issues of economic efficiency that have determined much of the history of what is now the Union have been largely set aside to be replaced by political aspirations, particularly those of Germany and France. The principal economic problems of the Union lie in its level of unemployment and the state of its public finances. As argued above, the intellectual case for monetary union is highly debatable. Moreover, other than indirectly pressing for some rehabilitation of the fiscal house, as part of the process of meeting the 'convergence' criteria for monetary union, monetary union as such makes no immediate and obvious contribution to the heart of the problems of member states. In addition, as pointed out, monetary union is more likely to be feasible between those member states who will benefit least from it. Germany is the obvious leading example. And yet monetary union has become the *sine qua non* of commitment to a belief in the Union for its members. The basic economic benefits from which we started have been sidelined in favour of a woolly vision of an integrated Europe, about which rational debate has become more and more difficult.

The actual economic performance of the Union over the last decade and more, following the initiation of the Single Market programme, has shown no significant improvement that enables one to contrast its successful performance with other economies outside the Union. Moreover there has to be a deep concern whether, in the longer term, the institutional and welfare structures of the Continental members of the Union can be sustained. There is a question as to whether, based on such a high proportion of gross domestic product, they are 'affordable', or whether they will lead inevitably to increased taxes and increased borrowing. In Continental Europe there is no significant appetite for reform and change in the light of current circumstances. In the light of all this, Britain has to consider the nature of its ties within the Union, and the views of many who apparently advocate that, although late in the day, it should become more and more like its Continental partners.

The argument that Britain would be seriously disadvantaged by failing to accede to monetary union has no plausibility, unless we assume that the core membership of the Union seeks to impose sanctions and deliberately to disadvantage it. Such developments would serve to illustrate many of the concerns that arise with regard to the attitude of Union membership to the United Kingdom. The role of London as a financial centre would be largely unaffected unless members of the Union which had acceded to monetary union deliberately set out to sabotage it. But neither German nor French is destined to be the international language of finance.

As far as low inflation and monetary stability are concerned, Britain has little or nothing to gain from membership, despite its historical record, if we are to believe the stances taken up by the Conservative governments of the recent past, and the current position of the Labour government. In this context the decision of the British government in 1997 to hand control of interest rates to a monetary committee chaired by the Governor of the Bank of England assumes great importance. As observed by *The Times*:

> An independent Bank of England is a far superior prop than EMU would be. The interest rate for a single currency will be set with regard to the average performance of its members' economies. As we saw in the ERM, these rates could be wholly inappropriate for an individual country in the system. At least the Bank of England would be looking at the British economy alone, when it sets interest rates. Mr Brown has gone this far: he need go no further. (*The Times*, 7 May 1997)

There are, however, other important issues that Britain must consider that fall outside the narrow sphere of economics. The first of these is foreign policy and security which has been introduced as the second of the three pillars on which the Union rests following the Maastricht Treaty. Here there have to be grave doubts about the nature of consensus that needs to exist between member states. There is little doubt that French foreign policy will continue to be made in relation to what are seen to be French national interests. Apart from the fact that so far practical attempts at formulating and implementing Union foreign policy, as in Bosnia, have been abortive, the fact remains that the Union as a whole is unlikely to exert any major influence on world events even if some consensus could be reached. The United States must remain at the centre of the creation of security in the West. The idea of setting up the Union as an equal partner in world affairs is an illusion. The key security issue of the next century will clearly be China, and the major action will be in the Far East, and continue in the Middle East, where *collectively* the Europeans have little to contribute while individually some members have historical links of major significance. Added to this is the complication of the overt hostility of some member states to the United States (and to the Anglo-Saxons in general) which demands great pause for thought for Britain as to how it relates to the proposed foreign policy making process within the Union.

Where the Union clearly has, potentially, an important role to play is in Central and Eastern Europe. The relationship between the Union and Europe to the East remains a key factor in the future of the security of Western Europe. The extension of the Union to the East and to the South is a key issue on the agenda of the Union. How the Union responds will be an important determinant of its ability to perform effectively on an international stage.

The second is the question of national sovereignty. Much of the discussion of national sovereignty has been far too narrowly prescribed. For some economists, it reflects simply a question of whether one has or has not power and influence over one's exchange rate. National sovereignty can then be debated in terms of the advantages or disadvantages of fixed versus floating exchange rates. But there are two more fundamental issues that relate to national sovereignty. The first is the degree of centralisation versus decentralisation of powers of decision-making in the Union. The second is the implication of the existence of institutional and cultural diversity. In oversimplified terms, there is the question of whether institutional frameworks are to be, to use an earlier expression, Bismarckian or whether, within the Union, a thousand flowers may bloom and diversity will be encouraged. As matters stand, it appears that a thousand flowers may indeed bloom provided that they are all the same type and colour and bloom in sequence! This has nothing to do with narrow economic issues or the nature of exchange rate regimes. But it has a great deal to do with how people of different member states wish to be governed. Democracy in France has a very different face from democracy in Germany or the United Kingdom.

Finally, there is the question of the openness and transparency of the Union, and the extent to which its formal institutions constitute an adequate democratic framework. Concern on this matter has been summed up by Vernon Bogdanor:

The main problem facing the Union, ... is not an imbalance between its institutions, but popular alienation from its objectives. If that alienation is not overcome, there could be a complete breakdown in the relationship between the Union and the people of Europe whom the institutions are intended to serve. The fundamental problem that the Union now has to confront is that it seems to be losing democratic legitimacy. (Bogdanor, 1995, p. 57)

While, as Bogdanor points out, the individual country parliamentary approval of the Maastricht Treaty was overwhelmingly great, the consciousness and understanding of the issues among the people are less certain. At the very least, referenda are needed as part of the direct participation of the people of the Union in their future. In mature democracies there must be trust in the people, since without it there is no democracy at all.

CHAPTER 7

BRITAIN AT THE CROSSROADS

INTRODUCTION

The so-called Anglo-Saxon countries have an innate capacity for self-deprecation. Whether it is the United States, the United Kingdom, Canada or Australia there is a persistent perception of decline or a belief that, from an economic point of view, matters are a long way from what they should be. North American commentators have been obsessed with the economic performance of Japan, and latterly with the rise in the countries of South East Asia and the implications for international competitiveness. While the share of the United States gross domestic product in world output still exceeds a fifth, this is indeed a significant shift from the days following the Second World War when it accounted for over a third. On any statistical basis America remains by far the world's richest country. In Europe, the British obsession of the 1990s and before has been Germany, as a model of industrial relations practice, and of business finance unlike the equity dominated system of the Anglo-Saxon world. To some degree all this may be explained by the apparent loss of influence of Britain in the world as she lost an empire. For the United States, a degree of insecurity reflects the close of the 'American Century'. Despite the positions in which both Britain and the United States find themselves (discussed below) their capacity for self-denigration remains high. This is both unnecessary and dangerous. In both cases it may promote the search for so-called solutions to economic problems that will have significantly negative effects (such as protectionism in the United States). Self-denigration is also dangerous because it creates expectations both of a need for radical change, and worse still, an ability to achieve such change that does not exist.

In assessing economic performance we must take account first of what constitutes 'reasonable expectations'. These may be derived from the past history of the economy itself, and from analysing the performance of its peer group. In effect this requires some sort of benchmarking. In this context it is arguable that it is appropriate (from the United Kingdom point of view) to focus on the performance of other principal members of the European Union. Comparisons with the level of per capita income in the United States are not helpful, since it is still significantly above the average of all the major industrial countries. The economic performance of Japan from the early 1960s was accounted for much of the time by catch up, again relative to all the other industrial countries. For similar reasons direct comparison cannot reasonably be made with the economic performance of countries in South East Asia, where due allowance must be made for the opportunity to piggy-back on the shoulders of those who have gone before. These considerations must be taken into account in the process of establishing 'reasonable expectations'.

Actual performance must also be assessed against the background of the way in which economic policy was conducted over the period under consideration. The question of to what extent policy either added to or subtracted from economic performance is not only relevant for historical judgement, but also in defining appropriate policies that may be followed in the future. In addition economic performance in comparison with the peer group may be affected both by structural problems that arise from cultural and social differences, and what may be described as 'institutional failure' which in part reflects 'how things work'. As is frequently pointed out, the process of catch-up is by no means an automatic one. A wide variety of cultural and institutional factors, mostly imperfectly understood, may separate those who are able to exploit the potential for economic growth from those who are not. The question arises as to what institutional redesign is necessary if an economy is to exploit the potential that, in principle at least, is common to the world at large, in terms of patterns of consumption, standards of living and technology.

In the case of the United Kingdom, it was argued in Chapter 1 that at the outset it is important to sub-divide the period since the end of the Second World War into four separate phases: the so-called golden age (1946–1973), the turbulent years of the later 1970s, the decade of the 1980s and the recession and recovery years of the 1990s. It was argued in Chapter 2 that there are no overarching factors that account for performance in each of these four periods. For the purposes of this chapter, the starting point is the argument set out in Chapter 1, that it was not a 'reasonable expectation' for the United Kingdom to have been able to sustain its economic position, relative to its European peers, in the period 1950–1973. This, despite the nomenclature of the golden age, was the period in which the major part of the relative decline of the United Kingdom took place. What happened subsequently must be judged on other criteria. While the date is somewhat arbitrary, it is fair to say that after 1973 there are no excuses.

To put matters into perspective we reprise some of the earlier data with regard to the rates of growth of gross domestic product per capita as a first proxy for the standard of living. Despite beliefs to the contrary, the performance of the United Kingdom economy over the period 1973–89 was equal to the average for the OECD as a whole, and only marginally below that of Germany. This result was, of course, materially influenced by the experience of 1973–79, which we have described as the years of turbulence. In terms of the growth of per capita gross domestic product, of the countries listed in Table 7.1, only Switzerland grew more slowly. Britain seriously underperformed its European peers and lost ground significantly. As argued earlier, in Chapter 2, this poor performance is almost entirely attributable to the misconduct of economic policy, and the disastrous effect of poor industrial relations. The comparison of this poor performance, both with what occurred before and what came after, can hardly be attributed to fluctuations in the structural problems that Britain is reputed to have had, namely, an inadequate financial system, an uneducated workforce, and an excessive focus on shareholder value, to the detriment of the long term health of the economy.

In the decade of Margaret Thatcher's government, gross domestic product per capita in Britain (as can be seen in Table 7.1) outperformed both the OECD average and the EU(15). Only Japan and Italy (still catching up) produced better results. To describe Britain as an economic basket case in crisis on the basis of these numbers since 1973 is to look deliberately through the wrong end of the telescope. A sensible conclusion is that, while the 1970s were economically disastrous, the 1980s were a period of restoration. It can hardly be described as a miracle, but clearly much happened to improve relative economic performance.

This observation is frequently downgraded by reference to the fact that performance in the 1980s was below that of the golden age. The same observation applies to the peer group as can be seen in Table 1.1 in Chapter 1. Martin Wolf reflects a common point of view:

> The good news is that the United Kingdom is no longer falling further behind other advanced industrial countries. The bad news is that this is more because the performance of the others has deteriorated than because that of the UK has improved. (Wolf, 1996, p. II)

There are three points to make with regard to a judgement of this kind. The first is that the overall performance of the United Kingdom economy in the 1980s was considerably better than that experienced in the 1970s. The second is not to underestimate the significance of this in quantitative terms. Figure 7.1 extrapolates gross domestic product from 1973, using the trend rate calculated between the peak years 1979 and 1989. It demonstrates a continuation of the trend between 1955 and 1973. Had this growth rate been experienced the overall level of gross domestic product at the beginning of 1997 would have been 15 per cent higher in real terms than it actually is today. Finally, the use of the word 'deteriorated' to describe the performance of the peer group implies that the previous performance could have been maintained, a proposition that is distinctly dubious. The growth of the peer group in Europe during the 1950s and 1960s was never reasonably sustainable. It was not simply the impact of the rise in oil prices that caused the underlying growth rate of the group to slow down.

Table 7.1
Gross domestic product per capita, % rates of growth

	1973–89	1973–79	1979–89
Australia	1.7	1.5	1.8
Austria	2.4	3.0	2.0
Belgium	2.0	2.1	1.8
Canada	2.4	2.9	1.8
Denmark	1.7	1.6	1.8
France	1.9	2.2	1.6
Germany	2.0	2.5	1.9
Italy	2.7	3.0	2.3
Japan	2.9	2.4	3.1
Netherlands	1.5	1.9	1.3
Sweden	1.7	1.5	1.8
Switzerland	0.9	–0.1	1.7
United Kingdom	1.8	1.5	2.2
United States	1.6	1.6	1.5
Average	2.0	2.0	1.9
OECD	1.8	1.9	1.7
Euro (15)	2.0	2.1	2.0

Source: OECD Historical Statistics 1960–95, Paris, 1997

The period of the 1990s started badly for the United Kingdom with recession, precipitated yet again by inappropriate stabilisation policies in the late 1980s. However, since 1993, the British economy has grown at an average rate of nearly 3%, compared with 1.5% in Germany and 1.4% in France. The unemployment rate in the United Kingdom has fallen to below 6%, compared to 11% in Germany and 12.5% in France. Inflation in Britain in 1997 fell to the lowest rate since the 1960s. Public expenditure as a proportion of the gross domestic product in Britain in 1997 was running at more than 20% less than the average of the other members of the European Union.

This brings us back to the question of 'reasonable expectations'. At the conclusion of an extensive study of Britain's economic performance since 1870, Nicholas Crafts concludes:

... despite continuing worries about innovation and skills, improved industrial relations, a better quality of investment and trends in productivity growth suggest that there may have been a relative improvement sufficient to prevent further economic decline relative to Europe. A new government may find it difficult to raise the growth rate by much. (Crafts, 1997, p. 62)

Under the title 'Are we entering a new golden age of economic growth?', Andrew Sentance has analysed the potential for the growth of the United Kingdom in the medium term. Putting together an analysis of productivity trends in both the manufacturing and the non-manufacturing sectors, forecasts of labour participation and unemployment rates, Sentance concludes that:

The key conclusion from this analysis is that the UK economy has the potential over the decade ahead to exceed the performance of the last decade. Though productivity growth is not expected to be spectacular, the analysis of recent labour market developments suggests that we should be able to run the economy with a much lower level of unemployment over the medium term. Taking up the slack can provide a boost of between 0.3 per cent a year and 0.5 per cent a year to growth. If in addition more optimistic projections of productivity growth turn out to be correct, the UK economy has the prospect of a new 'golden age' of growth, matching the average performance of the 1950s and 1960s. (Sentance, 1995, p. 21)

Now that might be a miracle. What could happen to prevent it?

Figure 7.1
Extrapolation of trend rate of growth of UK GDP

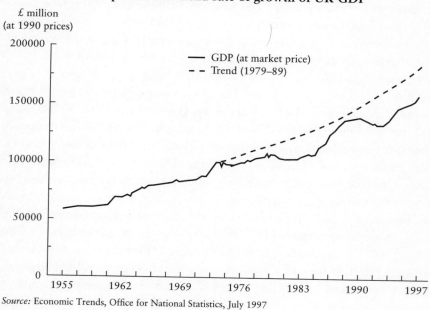

£ million
(at 1990 prices)

GDP (at market price)
- - Trend (1979–89)

Source: Economic Trends, Office for National Statistics, July 1997

The thesis of the remainder of this chapter is that such an outcome is unlikely if Britain sets its face against the major developments of the last eighteen years and rejects the philosophy of the liberalisation of markets, the deregulation of the economy, the importance of the economic consequences of privatisation, and the lessons bitterly learned under both Conservative and Labour governments over the last quarter of a century with regard to the conduct of macroeconomic policy and the control of public expenditure. It will also not happen if Britain ties itself in too tightly into a European economic and social model that is currently past its sell-by date. In the following sections we deal with these issues.

PUBLIC FINANCE AND THE CONDUCT OF POLICY

A central issue for the British economy going forward is the way in which macroeconomic policy will be conducted.

In over-simplified terms, economic policy can be sub-divided into macroeconomic policy, industrial policies and trade policies. This leaves on one side other aspects of public policy such as income distribution and environmental policies which for some transcend the focus on economic policies alone. The principal argument developed so far is that it is the failure of macroeconomic policy which occupies central stage in accounting for any underperformance of the British economy since 1970. Concern with the underlying growth rate of the economy began as long ago as 1960, after it had been wrongly assumed that the problem of cyclical fluctuations and unemployment had been solved. Appropriate demand management, interpreted as the intellectual and practical legacy of John Maynard Keynes, was seen as giving us the power to deal with each of these related issues. The new focus on economic policy began with the creation of the National Economic Development Office in 1961, and was followed up in Harold Wilson's government in 1964 by the creation of the Department of Economic Affairs. These institutional developments reflected the general proposition that 'demand management was not enough' and began to consider the importance of supply side considerations in addition to the management of demand.

These developments under both Conservative and Labour governments of the period between 1960 and 1979 reflected the growth in the belief in what might broadly be described as 'corporatism'. Both Harold Wilson and Edward Heath in their time began to see themselves as exercising responsibility for forms of industrial policy which depicted the government as playing the role of managing director of the United Kingdom Limited. The

Conservative government after 1970 continued a policy of taking private enterprises into public ownership in order to preserve employment. The role of markets was largely ignored by both sides of the political spectrum. This was all in line with what might be described as the 'economic consensus' to which both political parties adhered if not explicitly certainly implicitly. Government was seen to have direct responsibility for both the demand and the supply sides of the economy.

As recorded above, and discussed earlier in Chapter 4, the turning point in macroeconomic policy was the Budget of 1981. This was the defining Thatcher Experiment. For the first time since the Second World War, fiscal policy was tightened in the face of rising unemployment, in the belief that lower inflation and the resultant lower interest rates were key factors in promoting economic recovery – contrary to the economic consensus of the post-war period that we have just described. The judgement was correct. Economic recovery took place as planned. While this is rightly referred to as the Thatcher Experiment, the contribution of Geoffrey Howe, then Chancellor of the Exchequer, and Treasury thinking at the time cannot be under-estimated.

It was a turning point in another sense as well. It marked the bankruptcy of what had passed for Keynesian thinking as to the way in which demand could be managed to promote full employment. For what it is worth, it is quite doubtful that Keynes would have subscribed to the economic policies with which his name became associated after the war. His major contribution, in an intellectual sense, was the provision of a conceptual framework that has been of great service ever since in understanding the effects of fluctuations in demand and in analysing cyclical problems. Beyond that, his influence (hardly directly sought, since he was dead) on the making of policy was nothing short of disastrous. It was the ghost of Keynes, hardly heard of in Germany and Japan, other than by post-graduate students educated in American and British universities, and certainly not by policy makers, that haunted the conduct of macroeconomic policy in Britain until 1979.

It is now widely recognised that the creation of financial stability in the economy is a *sine qua non* of steady and achievable economic growth. But not widely enough. There still remains a hankering after the old religion that suggests that through demand management there is some easy way to remedy the apparent underemployment of human resources. This, in part, reflects an emotional rejection of something that is defined as 'monetarism' which is seen to reflect a dogmatic commitment to a low inflation rate coupled with some political association between low inflation and sound finance. Monetarism is seen as bankers' economics; the economics of figures of the past such as Montague Norman (Governor of the Bank of England in the 1930s) who Keynes felt he had destroyed intellectually if not otherwise.

But there remains considerable confusion. It is widely accepted that monetary instability is undesirable. To quote Tony Blair, then the leader of the Labour Party Opposition:

> I do not need to remind anyone that in the last 25 years, the UK has been one of the most volatile of all the major economies. Since 1970 the British economy has suffered more recession years than other developed economies, and the average rate of inflation since 1970 has exceeded all major economies, except Italy. Even in the most successful years of the post-War period, governments frequently failed to provide the stable macroeconomic background that companies need. In the immediate post-War period governments sought to fine tune the economy to eliminate short term fluctuations. ... Moreover in trying to reduce cycles in economic activity, government policies accommodated real shocks to the supply side of the economy – wage shocks, or oil shocks for example. The consequence of this was inflation ... In his Labour Party conference speech in 1976, Jim Callaghan sounded the death knell of the post-War Keynesian consensus, when he openly admitted that the UK could no longer expect to borrow and spend its way out of recession. (Blair, 1995, p. 7)

The confusion that remains stems partly from the failure to distinguish clearly between the legitimate aims of stabilisation policy (fiscal and monetary policy) in influencing the behaviour of monetary demand, and the legitimate concerns of government in relation to real economic objectives. To quote Tony Blair again:

> They said that government should look after inflation, while growth and employment should be left to look after themselves. (Blair, 1995, p. 4)

It is difficult to discover who 'they' are. What was certainly asserted by Nigel Lawson (Lawson, 1988) was that inflation should be the prime objective of stabilisation policy, while microeconomic policies such as the deregulation of labour markets should be concerned with real economic growth and employment. Nothing was said to the effect that growth and employment should be left to the economy. Any committed supply sider would always be concerned that supply side policies were the main route through which economic growth and employment might be effected. What was said was that it was not legitimate to set real matters such as growth rates and unemployment as real targets to be achieved primarily or even substantially by the conduct of monetary and fiscal policy. The best that such policies could achieve in the medium term was the growth of nominal demand in line with the growth of real output. In other words, the inflation rate.

The issue remains a fundamental one. No one can seriously disagree with the proposition that government can influence and indeed has a responsibility for managing the behaviour of aggregate nominal demand, by the appropriate use of fiscal and monetary policy. There may be some debate as to whether fiscal policy should be used for such a purpose, rather than set with an eye on the supply side of the economy. Nor should there be any disagreement with the proposition that the conduct of stabilisation policy can have serious and lasting effects on the real behaviour of the economy. For example, effects such as its influence on interest rates and, in the short term, on real exchange rates. The major question on stabilisation policies remains whether such policies can do more in the limit other than to equate monetary demand with expanding real supply, and beyond that to set independent targets for employment and real economic growth is unrealistic and unacceptable. Since this is certainly the case, the suggestion in some quarters, that so-called Keynesian policies of real demand management are due for a comeback, will conflict with the scenario outlined at the end of the last section. Equally mistaken and dangerous is the suggestion that the problem is one of conducting stabilisation policy with too much attention paid to controlling the inflation rate rather than stimulating employment. The issue is not that inflation is in some sense more important than employment – it is simply a question of matching the appropriate policy instruments to the desirable policy objectives. As analysed in Chapter 4, the idea that a little more inflation may be traded off in the medium term for a lower rate of unemployment and a higher rate of economic growth is not supported by the evidence.

One spurious issue raised by some commentators is the idea that, in setting some kind of inflation target for central bankers, other effects such as those on real output will be ignored. As already argued, the central issue for policy makers should be the rate of growth of nominal demand, which reflects both price changes and changes in real output. As argued above, to the extent that the equilibrium rate of long term real economic growth is independent of monetary influences, the focus on the inflation rate simply appears as a residual rather than as being, in itself, a central objective.

The macroeconomic background provides the starting point for an assessment of public expenditure and tax policy. Maintaining financial stability in terms of interest rates, exchange rates and the rate of inflation provides an initial constraint on the setting of public expenditure targets and public sector borrowing. This should not, in itself, be a matter of ideology as to whether public expenditure is either inherently good or inherently bad. It should reflect a proper appreciation of, first, the ability and willingness of financial markets to fund government deficits on 'acceptable' terms, and second, the willingness of the population at large to finance public expenditure out of taxation. There are no precise ways of assessing where either of these limits lies. But in principle they constitute serious practical constraints on the setting of public expenditure targets that are consistent with overall financial stability.

The suggestion that there are no macroeconomic consequences of relatively high rates of public spending relative to gross domestic product (as exemplified by the United Kingdom's European peer group) does not stand up to a moment's consideration. High levels of public spending that appear to be correlated with satisfactory economic performance (Germany again is the classic exemplar) are accounted for by the effect of performance on public spending rather than the other way round. An analogy here could be the mistaken British view of the late 1960s that large, aggregated corporations were needed to be competitive rather than the view that competitiveness tended to make corporations large. The economic success of our European peers, in the early days of the EEC, led them to take a substantial part of that economic success in what might be termed a social dividend, a position they can no longer afford as argued in the last chapter. The poor correlation between public expenditure ratios and economic growth does not tell the story that the advocates of relatively high ratios of public expenditure wish to broadcast. For any individual economy, there are limits to public expenditure beyond which economic growth and employment will be seriously affected. Continental Europe, compared to the United States and Japan, has already reached those limits. If the macroeconomic conditions that are necessary to support the medium term scenario (discussed in the last section) are to be achieved, then the risk of any material increase in the ratio of public spending in the United Kingdom remains a serious one.

This is not to say, as some believe, that a British economy with a public expenditure ratio of 30 per cent rather than 40 per cent could be in some sense a 'better' economy than would otherwise be the case. The fact is that after eighteen years of Conservative rule, the inroads that have been made into public spending by a party committed to public expenditure control have been minimal. The principal reason for this has been the substantial rise in social security expenditure (discussed in Chapter 5), which now accounts for a third of total public spending. The fact that total spending as a proportion of gross domestic product has been kept to less than 40 per cent has been due to genuine reductions in other real public expenditure programmes, coupled with the fact that state pension obligations have been indexed to prices rather than earnings (as is the case in much of the Continent where pension rates are substantially higher). Going forward into the twenty-first century the control of public spending, in line with the macro-economic constraints already addressed, must depend not only on attempts to reduce levels of social security spending, but also on establishing clearer priorities for the public purse.

Leaving aside the question of welfare payments, where a radical approach is clearly necessary, the three key areas of pension provision, health and education will continue to present formidable problems. The discouragement of private health care, as reflected in the recent abolition of tax relief on private health care premiums, coupled with a significant attack on the income of pension funds, will only make it more difficult to achieve a workable balance between private and state provision in the future. The former has been based on ideology and the latter on bad economics that were discussed in Chapter 2. In the present context, the government's action on pension fund income will accelerate the demise of corporate defined benefit schemes, and will significantly raise the risk profile of pension provision for individuals, as in the corporate context investment risk is shifted from the employer to the employee.

In these contexts the principles of standardisation, uniformity and universality cannot be maintained without a serious diminution in the quality of what is supplied. Rationing resources is always a key issue, and that leads, not ideologically but practically, to a major reconsideration of what levels of service should be maintained by the state, and what individuals should be encouraged to provide for themselves. This is where true radicalism lies, not in the repetition of old mantras and perceptions of what the state should be responsible for. In the supply of health services, for example, the inexorable rise in health costs, in part determined by advancing technology, cannot be borne across the board by the state. This is also true of the pensions, welfare and personal care that are needed to deal with the consequences of an ageing population. The principal criticism of eighteen years of Conservative government is not the extent to which it abandoned the old ideas that had underwritten the Welfare State after the Second World War, but that it was insufficiently radical to put serious alternatives in their place. It failed in its own terms, not in terms of previously accepted wisdom. In all these areas it is the future relationship between the private and the public sectors that is crucial, both from the point of view of the macroeconomy that we have discussed, and from the point of view of the efficient allocation of resources to achieve the most significant results in terms of community welfare.

THE BEHAVIOUR OF MARKETS

The denigration of Britain's economic performance in the 1980s has been associated with the myths of raw capitalism, the promotion of greed, and the worship of what some see as an immoral form of individualism. In this context, the significant failure of Margaret Thatcher, who was the inspiration of the economic restoration of the 1980s, was a political one. She failed to explain or sell the framework that she was trying to put in place. The commitment to, and understanding of, the nature of a market economy was always skin deep, and her belief that it was always so obviously right constituted a major handicap in changing public perceptions. She must bear the major responsibility for the view that a market based economy encompassed the negatives with regard to individual and corporate behaviour which we discuss elsewhere. Historians will judge that perhaps one of her major achievements was to make the Labour Party electable. The disappointment in all this is that in the process the myth has been created that just as we were once all Keynesians, we are all committed to the market economy now. Fortunately or unfortunately, depending on your point of view, it is simply not true.

The principles of a free market start from the assumptions of the supremacy of consumer sovereignty and the belief that the assessment of economic organisations and institutions is judged primarily by their outputs rather than their inputs. Economic performance starts from the ability of both public and private institutions to deliver to the customer. The free market also implies the principle of *caveat emptor*, namely that economic freedom entails responsibilities on the behalf of the consumer to make choices and to abide by the consequences of those choices. The effective performance that delivers to the consumer, and so justifies employment and economic activity in the long run, will be reflected in profitability and a satisfactory return to investors. That is a key part of the process of keeping score, rather than simply being an end in itself.

Doubts of the primacy of the importance of a market based economy become manifest in several different ways. Examination of the literature relative to the supply side of the British economy, that begins with the establishment of the National Economic Development Office in the early 1960s, followed up by the creation of the Department of Economic Affairs, shows an almost complete absence of the discussion of 'profitability'! The focus of these bodies was on what needed to happen to 'production' and to 'productivity'. It is also clear that in all the various discussions and reports on the subject that were generated in the two decades before 1980, 'productivity' was seen to represent the economic dimension of 'production'. There was little or no conception of the creation of value in the integration of consumer demand and productive resources. Individuals are producers, consumers and investors in different degrees, and, indirectly investors in a way that is not usually taken into account. It has been argued that a commitment to a market based economy is reflected in ideas that what is needed for Britain as an economy going forward is a new relationship between government, business and employees. Such an attitude almost certainly downgrades the importance of key players in a market economy, the consumers and the investors. Relations between corporations and unions are primarily in the interests of the producers (which is what they are), not in the interests of either the consumer or the investor. While current ideas going forward are not in themselves hostile to business, they are without doubt hostile to the idea of the genuine market economy and the interests of individuals, both directly and indirectly as shareholders.

Serious commitment to a market based economy is also influenced by attitudes to the liberalisation and/or control of markets, in particular – on the supply side of the economy – the labour and capital markets. The importance of the flexibility of labour markets has been touched on several times. But as recorded elsewhere (see Chapter 4) there have to be serious concerns as to whether the adaptability of labour markets in Britain that has been reported by Peter Robinson (Robinson, 1996) will not be undermined by signing the Social Chapter of Maastricht and by a return of disproportionate power to organised labour, under some heading or another. A shift in attitude from the perspective that focuses on the profitable economic performance of corporations will, in the long run, without doubt create on a net basis fewer jobs rather than more. Short term palliatives such as lump sum and one-off benefits to make a dent in youth unemployment will not serve as a substitute for steady and profitable economic growth, no matter how well intentioned and justified in the short run they seem to be.

As far as the capital markets are concerned, the myths about excessive dividends continue to predominate; British industry pays out too much in dividends. What is perceived to be an inadequate rate of investment can be corrected by fiscal discrimination in favour of retained earnings. The implication here, with little justification other than in-built hostility, is that there is a massive market failure in capital markets that needs to be corrected. Short-termism and a lack of employee involvement in financial business decision making are seen to be critical factors in determining Britain's economic performance.

Putting all this together the most depressing feature of it is that it is simply not new. This is Old Conservative and Old Labour. It is old wine in new bottles. It is the same set of wrong ideas that dominated thinking about the supply side of the economy in the 1960s and the 1970s. These are the ideas, in their time, of Edward Heath, of Roy Jenkins, and Jim Callaghan and Denis Healey. They are the ideas of the Wilson Committee on financial institutions and the Bullock Committee on the participation of trade unions in corporate governance. What has withered on the vine is a theoretical commitment to public ownership of major industries and the wilder schemes of government interference in business via planning agreements as advocated by Tony Benn and others in the 1970s. The nonsenses of the Labour Party Manifesto of 1983 have gone. What is left, however, are the remnants of the ideas that underlay the fundamental post-war consensus with the notable exception of the belief that these ideas and attitudes could be supported by Keynesian type policies that would ensure the maintenance of overall demand and full employment. One ray of hope that has emerged is that lessons in this respect have been genuinely learned. There are no magic macroeconomic policies that can deliver this desired result. The late Harold Macmillan might have added his name to all these things. But he too was not serious about the importance of the free market. He would have been in favour of much state paternalism, but (as argued below) despite much emphasis on a new collectivism, paternalism is no longer politically correct. Moreover, benign paternalism may not always be beneficial. At some point it can simply disintegrate into dictatorship.

A serious commitment to a market economy is reflected in attitudes to regulation and privatisation. It is clear that re–nationalisation of the major public utilities is unlikely, if only for the fact that there has been a growing realisation that some social objectives of nationalisation may be achieved by the use of regulatory powers. Liberal economic principles would suggest that regulation of some kind is appropriate when there is palpable market failure. Market failure demands regulatory intervention, including the prevention of the exercise of monopoly power and the correction of asymmetries in market information. The former suggests possible concerns with what were public utilities, the latter supports concerns with consumer protection in financial markets where the sellers may have more information than the buyers. However, there is a clearly emerging danger that regulatory powers will be used for purposes other than the amelioration of market failure, such as distribution objectives and the imposition of social values that have nothing to do with market failure at all. A good illustration of the latter is the demand for regulators to interfere with the setting of executive remuneration in the newly privatised utilities.

Privatisation must be regarded as one of the most significant developments of the period since 1979. Leaving on one side the issues of executive remuneration (in an absolute sense) the media's concern over investment returns in the privatised industries is seriously misplaced. Such concerns represent a classic example of being wise after the event. No one in his or her wildest dreams anticipated how inefficient the publicly owned businesses were nor the potential cost reductions and productivity increases that were possible once they were in private hands. This issue was succinctly summed up by *The Economist*:

> Investors in privatisation shares have done well, but not outrageously so. Taxpayers have gained a lot, as already noted. And consumers have profited as well. Thanks to better productivity and a regulatory framework that, for all its faults, divides the gains of greater efficiency between shareholders and customers, prices charged by the public utilities have risen far less rapidly than prices in general. For one reason or another, privatisation may have been unpopular with voters – but in every other way the policy was an unambiguous success. (*The Economist*, 1996a, p. 9)

As pointed out in Chapter 5, the impact of privatisation cannot be assessed in terms of a narrow economic calculus. In organisational terms it transformed the relationship between government and a large part of industry in a largely satisfactory way. In addition, it was a key factor in changing the industrial relations practices of those industries, once government had withdrawn to a safe distance. It gave the managers in these industries the opportunity to manage, which was a key factor in the productivity increases, reduced consumer prices and rises in efficiency, to which some objections have been made as the result of increased profitability and dividends paid.

The danger is that increased regulation and interference will attempt to put the clock back. The replacement of inefficient public ownership by excessive public regulation will indeed be a seriously retrograde step. It would simply constitute governance by the state but in a different form. It would be a new form of corporatism.

The key markets with which we are concerned are the markets for goods and services and the factors of production, labour and capital. It has already been argued that flexibility in labour markets has been an important factor in reducing unemployment in the United Kingdom below the level of its Continental peers.

The performance of the United Kingdom with regard to job creation and unemployment has been discussed in more detail elsewhere, notably in Chapter 4. It has been argued that both in the United Kingdom and in the rest of the European Union, in contrast to the United States, labour market inflexibilities have a central role to play in accounting for such differences.

However, more recently the United Kingdom labour market has appeared to respond more flexibly than in the past as demand has risen following the recession of the early 1990s.

The reasons for this have been disputed. The basic difference of opinion is between those who argue that increased labour market flexibility can be attributed in large measure to the labour market and trade union law reforms introduced in the United Kingdom in the 1980s as opposed to those who attribute more flexible labour markets simply to the incidence of recessions. Those who favour the latter view also emphasise the shift to part-time working, which hides the fact that the 'real' labour market is still not working any differently from before.

But as Peter Robinson has emphasised:

> The most critical point to register in this debate is that those who believe structural unemployment remains very high need to demonstrate that the pace of structural change has *accelerated* [his italics] ... If structural unemployment is now a more serious problem than it was then (i.e. in the 1950s and 1960s) the argument must be that the pace of change has increased, or alternatively that the pace of adaptation of the labour force has slowed down. Instead the evidence ... suggests that the pace of change in the structure of employment has slowed down and that the labour force has been adapting to the changes that have been taking place. (Robinson, 1996, p. 12)

It is difficult not to recognise the dramatic change in the climate of industrial relations between the 1970s and the 1980s and afterwards. It is equally difficult not to accept a *prima facie* case for arguing that the defeat of the miners' strike in 1983 and the changes in the law relating to trade unions have been significant factors in generating such a change. It is these changes that have contributed to more flexible labour markets in the United Kingdom relative to its peer group. The structure of employment has been shifting away from manufacturing and manual employment and towards the service sector and non-manual employment. This is a phenomenon across the major industrial countries of the world. At present at any rate it would seem that the United Kingdom labour markets are handling this process better than most. In his study for the European Commission Robinson concluded:

> If the right stance and balance of macroeconomic policy is maintained in the second half of the 1990s and there are no further shocks to the economy, we might expect only modest further changes in the employment structure. With the stock of qualifications in the workforce rising strongly, there is every reason to think that structural unemployment caused by mismatch between the characteristics of the working-age population and the employment which is available, is falling. As such

it should be possible for the unemployment to fall, perhaps to 5% or less, without this causing any significant increase in wage inflation. (Robinson, 1996, p. 17)

However, as pointed out above, the advent of such a state of affairs does not depend simply on the conduct of macroeconomic policy. It depends critically on the avoidance of any changes that significantly reintroduce labour market rigidities and inhibit job creation. In this context we must remain vigilant to ensure that new legislation will not reverse the spirit of previous trade union reforms. Other concerns are the impact on the demand for labour of the imposition of a minimum wage and the possible impact on United Kingdom labour markets of participation in the so-called Social Chapter of the Maastricht Treaty. In addition there is a need further to consider the nature of changes in the welfare system to encourage job search and the acquisition of requisite skills for today's world.

On the first of these issues there are reasons to be optimistic that legislation at least will not push industrial relations back to the dark days of the 1970s. When Opposition leader, in the mid 1990s, Tony Blair wrote:

... the focus of Labour's new approach to industrial relations is not re-running the union battles of the past, but investing in people and improving the education system. (Blair, 1997, p. 20)

Such a statement may be believed, but yet reasonable doubt may remain that a more aggressive attitude of organised labour in the future would seek to extend trade union power and influence in the direction of the past. Moreover, as we shall see in a moment, such an outcome could result not as a result of United Kingdom legislation but as a consequence of law enacted by the European Union.

The second issue is that of the minimum wage, which was discussed in Chapter 4. Two weak arguments are advanced for having a minimum wage. First, that Britain is the only country in the European Union not to have one – even the United States has a minimum wage. Second, that a minimum wage should not be feared, as it would be set at a level that should not increase business costs significantly. But if costs do not rise there can be no benefit to those whose wage rises as a result of legislation. The acceptance of a minimum wage by business is predicated on the assumption that firms already pay above the minimum rate and so can effectively ignore it. Unfortunately, this may not even turn out to be true in the relatively lowly paid service sector where new jobs are often created. As argued in Chapter 4, minimum wage legislation is no way to help the poor. It is badly targeted and risks disadvantaging those in work at the lower end of the income scale. The Commission on Public Policy and British Business linked the establishment of a minimum wage to in-work benefits, which they encouraged (see below). This has sense, but it is a quite different reason for advocating a minimum wage than is usually the case. To quote the Commission:

> The government should extend in work benefits for low income workers to combat the unemployment benefit trap, but a minimum wage should be introduced to prevent this being exploited by unscrupulous employers at the taxpayers' expense. The minimum wage should not be set too high since it could destroy jobs in some sectors. (Commission on Public Policy and British Business, 1997, p. 195)

Like the minimum wage proposal, attitudes to the Social Chapter of Maastricht (strictly the 'social policy agreement') are, in part, determined by perceptions about its costs. Again these perceptions are affected by beliefs that 'good firms' already accede to what proposals might be enacted under the Chapter. One might add that for 'good' firms one can often read 'large' firms, since the dangers of the Social Chapter are much greater for small firms rather than large ones, and it is most likely that at the margin small firms are creating more jobs than large ones. Others have gone so far in the other direction as to suggest that signing up for the Social Chapter would actually enhance competitiveness.

At this stage of the game it is important to understand from where the Social Chapter is coming and where it might lead, rather than conducting a precise inventory of what has already been enacted and what is currently proposed. The 'social policy agreement' is a set of *procedures*, the context of which can be extremely wide ranging (as set out in Chapter 6). The agreement is, in part, justified by the idea that it is only through enhanced protection of labour and labour rights, through increasing employees' involvement in corporate decision making, and through reductions in working hours that the higher skills needed in a more competitive world will be forthcoming. Under the Social Chapter the powers of trade unions will be considerably enhanced without any changes in British law. Trade unions will monitor and ensure the enforcement of law in relation to contractual relations, employees' rights in relation to employment and the termination of employment, and employee entitlements such as pensions for part-time employees. Already there are employers' concerns about limiting hours of work, which seem to fit with union ideas of how to reduce unemployment. The net effect of the Social Chapter must be to reduce the flexibility of labour markets, on the one hand, and at the same time to shift the influence over such markets to the Commission (in conjunction with what are termed the 'social partners', which are effectively European-wide bodies reflecting the opinion of companies and unions collectively). It will, as it is intended to do, impose labour market conditions across the Union of a kind that are already causing serious problems in Continental Europe. The social dividend that Europe is currently generating is insufficient to pay the indirect costs (not the direct costs which are usually focused on) of such policies.

The enactment of the kind of policies envisaged under the heading of the Social Chapter will compete with other approaches to putting the unemployed back to work, particularly with the use of work-related benefits. Both United Kingdom political parties, however, appear to be committed on the surface to a priority (unlike the situation in most of the rest of the European Union) to find ways of restructuring the benefit system to encourage work. At present, there is still some way to go in developing an alternative framework that has in the past encouraged dependency rather than the search for, and acquisition of, skills. Punitive expropriations from former public utilities, while appearing worthy in their intention of promoting youth employment, do not constitute a radical change in policies. Moreover, it still remains true that the identification of market failure in labour markets is a prior condition for effective and efficient policy making. Employment subsidies cannot be justified otherwise other than as a peculiar form of income redistribution.

THE MARKET ECONOMY AND THE FUTURE OF CAPITALISM

The collapse of the Berlin Wall in 1988 was a symbolic end of the Cold War between the Soviet Union and the rest of the world that had persisted since the end of the Second World War. However, the implications in terms of the foreign policies of many major countries and their commitments to defence programmes remain enormous. But from the point of view of the issues raised in previous chapters, the ending of the Cold War has implications for the war of ideas.

In one sense, the ending of the Cold War settled very little. Some such as Fukiyama (at the time; the recantation seems to have come later) hailed the event as the end of the struggle between the philosophical tradition exemplified by Karl Marx and the inevitable triumph of something that might be described as liberal capitalism espoused by Hegel. Fukiyama's earlier work was appropriately entitled *The End of History* (Fukiyama, 1992). The idea that such developments would have practical relevance to the economic development of Islam or the emerging, and still hard to read, China is to some degree absurd. What the ending of the Cold War did was for the immediate future to discredit the formal structures of Socialist regimes (with a capital S) and to weaken seriously the concepts of the planned economy. As recently as the early 1960s at the beginning of the Presidency of John Kennedy in the United States, there were serious concerns that the economy of the Soviet Union would overtake the United States in a foreseeable future, a concern that was not fully dispelled until the middle of the 1980s when it became apparent that the economy of the Soviet Union was on the point of implosion.

With that important exception, which destroyed a vision of both economists and political activists that had existed from the 1930s, no template has emerged that is widely accepted across countries as an exemplar of industrial and market organisation. There is no such thing as 'liberal capitalism'. There are, as a matter of fact, different forms of market organisation that have been related to different historical experiences and different cultures – the so-called Anglo-Saxon form of capitalism, the so-called Rhine capitalism that has been prevalent in the European Union, and the different forms of market based economies that have existed in Japan (within a very different business culture) and in the dynamic countries of South East Asia. The focus of discussion in the United Kingdom over the more recent period has been with regard to the relative merits of what have been described as the Anglo-Saxon approach to the development of the free market economy and the Rhine capitalism, which, it is claimed, has been the template for the development of the other northern economies of the European Union. More recently in the United Kingdom context the discussion has focused on the merits and demerits of what has been known as the 'stakeholder society'. There has been a search for, and a yearning after, something which is not the socialism of old, or what was perceived as the free market philosophy of the 1980s in Britain. The concept of the 'stakeholder' has been used to discuss the kind of capitalist framework that it might suggest. It has also been used in various forms to justify much else, which is why the concept is so elusive, since its advocates often function as we shall see with very specific agendas.

The initiation of the discussion of the stakeholder society appears to emerge from a serious dissatisfaction with what was perceived as the free market philosophy of the 1980s. A good exemplar of this position is John Kay. The supporters of the liberalisation of markets in the 1980s and who saw it necessary to retreat from the corporatist ideas of the 1970s are lumped together as an obviously unsavoury collection of characters:

The premises of the new right are austere. Private property is the most important social institution; self-interest the central human motive; insecurity the engine of progress. Government is inherently coercive and corrupt; fairness and justice mean respect for other people's property; trust is established by good attorneys and watertight contracts. If there is a place for nobler sentiments, such as altruism and sincerity, it is in our family lives, not in commerce; the social responsibility of business is to maximise profits. (Kay, 1996, p. 39)

It will no doubt come as a considerable surprise to many of those who have urged the retreat from the Moscow of British corporate ideas of the 1970s to have now been labelled, effectively, as moral outcasts. If this is the basis from which one has to start, such a caricature of those, who as discussed below have supported the concept of maximising shareholder value, are left little scope for rational discussion. It was strongly denied in Chapter 5 that a belief that free markets, as the most effective starting point in appraising the workings of the economy, is inconsistent with a sense of community, concern and social responsibility. Fortunately, there is another starting point from which to approach the subject, namely the idea of the inclusive company as set out in the Royal Society of Arts' *Tomorrow's Company* Inquiry (RSA, 1995) and reviewed by Anthony Cleaver (Cleaver, 1995).

The RSA Report starts with the premise that for a successful company the focus on its relationships with shareholders was not enough. The Report identified five key relationships of importance to the company: its relationships with the community (and *inter alia* with the environment), its customers, its employees, its suppliers and its shareholders. The Report was concerned that in the conduct of business there was evidence that insufficient attention was being paid to these various constituencies. An initial response recorded by Cleaver was that the leaders of firms' reaction was, of course: we do these things already:

At first I thought it must be true, and that we in the Inquiry, were simply behind the times. But then I began to realise that there was a gap between reality and perception or aspiration ... The next time a chairman informed me that his company was already doing all this I said that in that case, I presumed his Board had measurements to determine their progress on all five of the key relationships. I assumed that they inspected these at least once a year and spent some time at their Board meetings, at least annually reviewing progress ... If a company really believes that shareholders, customers, employees, suppliers and the community are all vital to its future success, surely all five will receive proper attention from the Board. (Cleaver, 1995, p. 25)

It is hardly possible to disagree with this conclusion. At a *moment of time* some measure of shareholder value such as return on equity may not reflect the sustainable health of a company. It is equally easy to accept that the profitability of the company and the current return to shareholders may not be ends in themselves. But it is important to note that it leaves in place the idea that the maximisation of corporate efficiency in terms of shareholder value may be an appropriate goal for management to pursue. As we shall see, however, this goes nowhere toward satisfying those who advocate the stakeholder concept. In the last analysis, despite their emphasis on the importance of trust, they wish to see incorporated into law the specific targets and processes that deal with the relationships other than those that already exist between company and shareholders. The legal legitimacy of maximising shareholder value must be undermined. Acting in the shareholders' best interests is not seen as necessarily acting in the best interests of the other interested parties – not simply in the short run but in the long run as well.

There are several routes that have been followed to take this further. The quotation from John Kay (above) asserts that property rights are an important social institution. The trick here is to redefine property rights in a relatively idiosyncratic way. Initially this involves arguing that in a significant sense shareholders do not actually own the companies in which they invest, therefore they have no prior right to be considered ahead of other interested parties in a company's economic performance. The argument as put by Kay and Silbertson suggests that owning a company is quite a different matter from owning a house or owning a toothbrush. They question the statement that a company is owned by its shareholders – indeed in effect they try to show that the statement is meaningless:

> Perhaps a large corporation is not owned by anybody at all, at least in the normal sense of ownership – the one we use when we say 'I own my house' or 'I own my toothbrush'. (Kay and Silberston, 1995, p. 87)

Once this is accepted the door for an idiosyncratic redefinition of property rights in relation to corporate businesses is wide open. They are seen to need redefining as particular forms of social institutions in which specific rights are granted to all the participants. In practice, these participants have many 'rights' arising from labour legislation, environmental laws and the law of contract. But these are deemed to be inadequate in relation to the demands that shareholders are supposed to place on management. Charles Handy has argued that:

> ... the idea of a company as a piece of property is fairly bizarre and that the idea that those who bet on it is just crazy and may be costing our children their livelihood. (Handy, 1995, p. 67)

A second approach is to argue that as profitability of companies is simply a means to an end to benefit society and its constituents, rather than simply for the purpose of remunerating shareholders, it is not of central importance. Again we may quote Charles Handy on measuring performance:

Trying to find one number that is the sum of everything is misguided. There is never any one number that will actually explain success in life and we are foolish to think that it might be there. Money certainly isn't it. Businesses know very well that profit is not the only measure ... Nevertheless the myth that pervades our society is that if you are profitable you are successful. Or if you're in the public sector, then efficiency is what matters. But efficiency is not quite the same as effectiveness. You can have a very efficient hospital if you don't take in sick people or people who are not going to get better like the old ones. So you push them outside. You're efficient but not terribly effective. Looking for the one number has corrupted our society. (Handy, 1996, p. 35)

The issue of one number has already been discussed. There is no problem here. Leaving aside the somewhat curious implied definition of efficiency in the quotation, the statement on a general basis appears to suggest that there may be serious trade-offs for society in the longer run between efficiency and welfare. Can we not aspire to an efficient health service that makes the most effective use of resources? The confusion here, and in many people's minds, is between processes and objectives. It is hard to make sense of the idea that organisations that are basically inefficient, or in the case of companies unprofitable, are likely to be adding benefit and value to the community at large. Asking, for example, the question why does the company exist simply begins a debate about what from the social point of view we expect it to do, not how it should be done.

John Kay has given his definition of the purpose of a company:

Producing goods and services people want. Business is about providing employment, providing value for customers, for developing skills of employees, for developing capabilities of suppliers – as well as earning money for shareholders. (Kay, 1997, p. 133)

Just so, as the RSA Inquiry has emphasised. But none of this in itself refutes the idea that as a matter of process in creating jobs, investing in the business and meeting the legitimate needs of the community, maximising shareholder value as an objective for management may not be of central importance. To return to the question of the rights and wrongs of takeovers, Graham Searjeant has observed:

Recent takeovers show that myopic shareholders can and sometimes do prosper at the expense of the long term interest of companies and their other stakeholders. But that is no reason to protect boards from their shareholders. For you will search in vain for companies whose shareholders languish and yet whose other stake-holders prosper. (Searjeant, 1997a, p. 38)

The third direction of attack on the maximisation of shareholder value is easier to understand. There are two parts to it. The first is the view as expressed by the General Secretary of the Trades Union Congress, John Monks, in an interview with *Management Today*. The magazine headlined the story with the observation that:

> Thirty years on he has launched the TUC on the road to a new unionism and into battle against Britain's overemphasis on shareholder returns. (*Management Today*, 1997, February, p. 43)

Individual people are producers, insofar as they are employed or employ themselves, they are consumers and they are investors. Confusion is frequently created by the apparent belief that they constitute different sets of people. On the issue of share ownership, it is appropriate to quote an ardent supporter of the stakeholder concept, John Plender:

> In the absence of changes to the tax system, share ownership will be confined for the foreseeable future to big institutional investors. And this is where the greatest obstacle to a constructive Anglo-Saxon version of stakeholding lies. By introducing the values of the hunting field into the capital markets and the ideology of shareholder value into the boardroom we have killed off what is left of benign paternalism in the workplace. (Plender, 1997, p. 245)

As an aside, there is a great deal to be said for enlightened paternalism but to suggest that its demise has come about as a result of a focus on shareholder returns is to rewrite history. The decline of paternalism has been due to the fact that it has not been seen as politically correct in an environment in which paradoxically the freedom of individuals in a social sense has been at the top of the agenda of the intellectual and opinion forming classes. But the important issue from the point of view of the current discussion is not that, but the argument that shareholdings are held in the interest of institutions. The beneficial interests of almost all shareholdings in the United Kingdom relate to individual people, in some cases as private shareholders but, in the majority of cases, in terms of their interests as policy holders in insurance companies of one kind or another, and interests in pension funds. There is a danger in shifting concern away from individuals as investors in this sense to the concerns of individuals as producers. Given the long term problems relating to health care, pensions and the savings of ordinary people such shifts have only short term benefits to those in work.

The second line of direct attack on shareholder interests has been discussed earlier in Chapter 2. This is simply that the dividend policies pursued by British companies have been at the expense of investment. It is unnecessary to rehearse here again the arguments of Chapter 2. *Management Today*, in its interview with John Monks already referred to, reports that in his view:

> Too much is being paid out by companies to shareholders, not enough is retained. It is, he concludes, the economic problem of our age, and one which he acknowledges is intimately bound up in bigger issues such as wider share ownership and personal pensions. (*Management Today*, 1997, p. 44)

Alongside the demand for a new capitalism based on some stakeholder concept has come pressure to increase the value of businesses to shareholders rather than to reduce it. Concern about corporate governance and executive remuneration has preoccupied this group as well as the proponents of a stakeholder society. These pressures have arisen particularly in the United States, but now also in the United Kingdom. Interestingly enough, demands for attention to be paid to generating greater shareholder value are also arising in Continental Europe and in Japan. These developments are succinctly dismissed by Kay and Silberston. They outline the so-called principal–agent model of Anglo-Saxon capitalism and conclude that:

> ... the near unanimous view of those who criticise the present structure of corporate governance is that reality should be made to conform to the model. The principal agent structure should be made more effective, through closer shareholder involvement and supervision. All experience suggest that this is not likely to happen and would not improve the functioning of corporations if it did. The alternative approach – of adapting the model to reality rather than reality to the model – deserves equal consideration. After all no one disputes that the German and Japanese models produce many successful companies. (Kay and Silberston, 1995, p. 86)

Indeed so, but as already discussed earlier in this chapter and elsewhere in this book, it is no longer possible to generate a plausible *prima facie* case for so-called Rhine capitalism, or stakeholder capitalism, on a worldwide basis, from considerations of economic performance. The argument becomes even less plausible if one now adds in the economic performance of the successful emerging countries, although as argued earlier these are inherently doubtful comparisons. As *The Economist* has pointed out:

> The changes in German and Japanese performance, together with the switch of emphasis towards shareholder value that many of their firms have made should give pause for thought to Anglo-American advocates of stakeholder capitalism. It would be delicately, if sadly ironic, were Britain and America to shift towards such a model just as it was about to be abandoned by its inventors. (*The Economist*, 1996b, 10 February p. 25)

On this subject at this point the last word is left to Samuel Brittan, as he contemplated a brave but imperfect new world, and thought that in it:

> One of the few things that is certain is that companies that do not maximise the value of equity held by their shareholders are going to be in deep trouble. I cannot think of a time when the stakeholder idea has been of greater potential harm. It was a 'half-baked' idea even in the best of circumstances. (Brittan, 1996, p III)

But the world is driven by half-baked ideas, in large measure because economists, politicians, opinion formers and the promoters of special interests can rarely stomach more fully cooked meals. They are simply too indigestible.

EPILOGUE

To sum up, the United Kingdom has much in its favour going forward. All countries have faults at all times, and are always in need of doing better both economically and socially. But as has been argued in chapters past, the United Kingdom has many good things going for it. It has long since ceased to decline in relative terms. Its public finances are more securely based than most of its Continental peers. Its unemployment rate is the lowest in Europe and now just about on a par with the United States. It has undergone a major and painful restructuring of its manufacturing industry, and has great potential in the growing area of the service economy. It is still a world leader in finance. Its prospects in relation to a sensibly defined peer group, as discussed earlier in this chapter, are good. At no time in the last quarter century has Britain been so well positioned. However, if we ignore the lessons of the past and do not appreciate the developments that have taken place since the 1970s then further progress may be denied.

In the middle of all these concerns lies the question of Europe. The European Union as exemplified by the behaviour of the Commission and the Council of Ministers has degenerated into a fundamentally undemocratic enterprise. The desirable objective of trade integration, as for example between the United States and Canada, has been supplemented by political ambitions of the major member states, particularly France and Germany. As argued in Chapter 6, the common currency is technically seriously flawed, and politically will result in a two-tiered Europe. These concerns were discussed, not particularly with regard to the United Kingdom, but more with regard to what kind of a European Union it should be. The principle of subsidiarity is becoming a farce. The pressure for social and legal conformity increases.

None of this is to downgrade the importance of the economic relationships between Britain and the European Union, and between the Union members themselves. It is an objection to the kind of Europe that Germany and France seek to impose upon the rest of the membership. Chapter 6 also objects to the facile idea that British policy toward the Union, from the inception of the Treaty of Rome, has been a story of missed opportunity and the abdication from a leadership role in Europe. Anyone with any sense of history should understand that this was never possible. Not simply because at the outset President de Gaulle was opposed to it, but also because the initial concept was focused almost exclusively on the relationship between France and Germany. And that is true today. Except that in a wider sense this is now a matter of deep concern. The concern of Europe going forward should no longer focus on Franco-German relations, but on the relationship between the Union and its Eastern neighbours. A two-tiered Europe will make that integration even more difficult to achieve.

The idea of a European foreign policy does not stand up to a moment's historical interpretation or suggest anything real in the light of the behaviour of its member states at the time of the Gulf War, in Bosnia and in attitudes to China, where the next concerns of realpolitik will be played out. The United States still holds the key to world security and in this context, while the special relationship is no longer what it was, there remains an important relationship between Britain, the United States and other members of the so-called Anglo-Saxon world. As far as foreign policy is concerned, the idea of Britain at the heart of Europe is a mirage, for two reasons, one negative and one positive: the negative one is the inbuilt hostility to the Anglo-Saxon world, more particularly to the United States, that exists within the Union; the positive one is that Britain can best contribute not by being at the heart of Europe, but by being at the margin. Britain is the interface between the Old World and the New. If it has nothing to contribute in this respect it has little to contribute at all. Britain must assume this position and continue to argue for a Europe in which individual countries can continue to live with their own cultures and their own way of doing things, rather than accepting social and economic models that are past their sell by date.

The conclusion that all this points to is that there is no need for, and indeed danger in, the idea of a New Beginning. There is a great need to consolidate on the gains and advances that were made during the period described earlier as the restoration. But there are clouds in the sky that give rise for concern that some of the factors that have played key roles in the progress achieved since 1979 will be reversed.

Perhaps the most concerning point is the overall view expressed frequently in the context of the 1997 General Election, that nothing of any positive significance actually occurred over this period. It has been eighteen wasted years during which Britain has slipped further and further down the drain. Much of this book has been devoted to arguing that this is not the case. But if that is the starting point, it is not a beginning based on any realistic audit of where Britain stands today.

With regard to a number of key issues discussed earlier the writing is already on the wall. Britain has signed up for the Social Chapter. There will be a minimum wage. Some change will eventually take place in labour legislation, inspired either domestically or from Brussels. Already Ministers at the highest level and the Confederation of British Industry are softening up the public for British entry into a single currency. The concern expressed in Chapter 2 with regard to restrictions on dividends as a promoter of more investment and faster growth has become a reality, reflecting a shift away from an investor to a producer society. This is a particular exemplar of what are being paraded as new ideas and commitments, described earlier as old wine in new bottles. A wider definition of regulation may reintroduce distortions into the market place that will owe more to politics than to economics.

None of this should imply that all is well in contemporary Britain. There must continue to be real concern about poverty. To deal with poverty is not simply a matter of taxation and public spending. It will not be dealt with by minimum wage levels or signing on for the Social Chapter. It can no longer be defined as a position on a simple linear monetary scale, such as it might have been reasonable to assume in a Britain of the 1920s and the 1930s, when some of us (including the author of this book) were growing up. The issue of welfare and the Welfare State demands a radicalism that is not to be found by examining the past. But the old myths and prejudices discussed in this book are still there. Britain is indeed at the crossroads. It is an open question as to whether it will build on its recent achievements or sink back into an outmoded past that we can see in the rear view mirror as we drive along.

REFERENCES

....

Abramovitz, M. (1986), 'Catching up, forging ahead, and falling behind', *Journal of Economic History*, 46 (2), June, 385–406.

Albert, M. (1993), *Capitalism against Capitalism*, London: Whurr Publishers Ltd.

Albert, M. and R.J. Ball (1984), *Toward European Economic Recovery in the 1980s*, Washington Papers, 109, Vol XII.

Anderton, Bob (1996), 'UK trade performance and the role of product quality, innovation and hysteresis: some preliminary results', *National Institute of Economic and Social Research discussion paper*, No. 102.

Bacon, R.W. and W. Eltis (1977), *Too Few Producers*, London: Macmillan.

Ball, Sir James (1989), 'Economic Policy – Fact and Ambition', *Economic Outlook*, London Business School, October, 25–9.

Balladur, E. (1997), *The Economist*, 1 March, p. 48.

Barry, N. (1985), 'In defence of the Invisible Hand', *Cato Journal*, 5 (1), Spring/Summer, 133–48.

Bean, C. (1991), 'The external constraint in the UK', in *External constraints on macro-economic policy: the European experience*, Cambridge: Cambridge University Press.

Bean, C.R. and N.F.R. Crafts (1995), 'British economic growth since 1945: relative economic decline ... and renaissance?', in N.F.R. Crafts and G. Toniolo (eds), *Economic Growth in Europe since 1945*, Cambridge: Cambridge University Press, 1996, pp. 131–72.

Beesley, M.E. and S.C. Littlechild (1991), 'The Regulation of Privatised Monopolies in the United Kingdom', in C. Veljanovski (ed.), *Regulators and the Market*, Institute of Economic Affairs, September, pp. 29–58.

Blair, Tony (1995), *The Mais Lecture*, City University.

Blair, Tony (1997), *The Times*, 31 March, p. 20.

Bogdanor, V. (1995), 'European Union and the people', *European Business Journal*, 7 (3), 57–62.

Bootle, R. (1996), *The Death of Inflation*, London: Nicholas Brealey.

Brittan, S. (1996), 'Britain: The Rogue Piece in Europe's Jigsaw', *The Financial Times*, 12 June, p. III.

Burke, E. (1792), quoted in Keynes, J.M. (1926) *The End of Laissez-Faire*, London: Leonard and Virginia Woolf.

Caborn, R. (1996), *The Times*, Business Section, 12 January.

Callaghan, J. (1976), Labour Party Conference, September.

CEPR report (1991), 'The making of monetary union', *Monitoring European Integration*, No. 2.

CEPR (1995), 'Unemployment: Choices for Europe', *Monitoring European Integration*, 5.

Chui, Michael and John Whitley (1995), 'What has been happening to European trade', *Economic Outlook*, London Business School, August, 19 (4), 4–9.

Cleaver, A. (1995), 'Tomorrow's Company', *RSA Journal*, December.

Commission on Public Policy and British Business (1997), *Promoting Prosperity*, London: Vintage.

Congdon, T. (1992), *Reflections on Monetarism*, Aldershot: Edward Elgar.

Crafts, N.F.R. (1993), *Can De-Industrialisation Seriously Damage Your Wealth?*, Institute of Economic Affairs, Hobart Paper.

Crafts, N.F.R. (1994), 'The Golden Age of Economic Growth in Western Europe, 1950–1973', *The Economic History Review*, August, Vol. XLVIII, No. 3, 429–47.

Crafts, N.F.R. (1995), 'Endogenous Growth: Lessons for and from Economic History', *Paper prepared for the 7th World Congress of the Econometric Society*, Tokyo, Japan.

Crafts, N.F.R. (1997), *Britain's Relative Economic Decline 1870–1995*, Social Market Foundation.

Currie, David (1997), *The pros and cons of EMU*, The Economic Intelligence Unit.

Davis, E., S. Flanders, and J. Star (1992), 'British Industry in the 1980s', *Business Strategy Review*, 3 (1), Spring, 45–69.

Delors, J. (1988), Debate in the European Parliament, July.

Denison, E.F. (1962), *The Sources of Economic Growth in the United States and the Alternatives Before Us*, New York: Committee for Economic Development.

Dixon, H. (1996), 'Deindustrialisation and Britain's Industrial Performance since 1960', *Economic Journal*, January, 106 (434), 170–1.

Dow, Christopher (1964), *The Management of the British Economy 1945–60*, Cambridge: Cambridge University Press.

Drucker, P.F. (1993), *Post-Capitalist Society*, New York: Harper Business.

The Economist (1995), 9 December, p. 20.

The Economist (1996a), *A Survey of Britain's New Politics*, 17 September.

The Economist (1996b), 10 February, p. 25.

Edwards, J. and K. Fischer (1994), *Banks, Finance and Investment in Germany*, Cambridge: Cambridge University Press.

Eltis, Walter and D. Higham (1995), 'Closing the UK competitiveness gap', *National Institute Economic Review*, Issue 154, November, 71–84.

Emerson, M. *et al* (1988), 'The Economics of 1992', Commission of the European Community, *European Economy* No. 35, March.

European Commission (1993), *Growth, Competitiveness, Employment, The Challenges and Ways Forward into the 21st Century*, White Paper.

The European Economy (1987), Annual Economic Report for 1987–88, No. 34 November, Brussels.

The European Economy (1990), 'One market, one money', No. 44, October, Brussels.

The European Economy (1995), Annual Economic Report, November, Brussels.

Feldstein, Martin (1997), 'The Political Economy of the European Economic and

Monetary Union: Political Sources of an Economic Liability', *Journal of Economic Perspectives* Vol. 2, No. 2, Fall, 23–42.

Flemming, J. and P. Oppenheimer (1996), 'Are Government's Spending and Taxes Too High (or Too Low)?', *National Institute Economic Review*, No. 157, July, 58–76.

Friedman Milton, and Anna Schwartz (1963), *A Monetary History of the United States 1867–1960*, Princeton: Princeton University Press for NBER.

Friedman, Milton (1968), 'The Role of Monetary Policy', *American Economic Review*, Vol. LVIII, No. 1, March, 1–17.

Friedman, Milton (1997), 'Why Europe can't afford the euro', *The Times*, 19 November, p. 22.

Fukiyama, F. (1992), *The End of History and the last Man*, London: Penguin Books.

Geroski, Paul (1989), 'The Choice between Diversity and Scale', in *Myths and Realities*, Centre for Business Strategy, London Business School, pp. 29–46.

Gregg, P and J. Wadsworth, 1995, 'A Short History of Labour Turnover, Job Tenure, and Job Security, 1975–1995', *Oxford Review of Economic Policy*, 11(1), Oxford: Oxford University Press, pp. 73–90.

Hahn, F.H. (1992), 'What Markets Can and Cannot Do', in *The Market: Practice and Policy*, London: Macmillan.

Handy, C.B. (1995), *Beyond Certainty*, London: Hutchinson.

Handy, C.B. (1996), 'What's it all for? Reinventing Capitalism for the Next Century', *RSA Journal*, December, 33–9.

Haskel, J. and J.A. Kay (1991), 'Mrs Thatcher's Industrial Performance: Lessons from the UK', in F.H. Gruen (ed.), *Australian Economy Policy*, ANU, pp. 197–231.

Haskel, J. (1996), 'The decline in unskilled employment in UK manufacturing', *CEPR discussion paper*, No. 1356, February.

Henderson, David (1986), *Innocence and Design*, Oxford: Basil Blackwell.

House of Lords (1985), *Report from the Select Committee on Overseas Trade*, Volume I, HMSO.

Hutton, W. (1995), *The State We're In*, London: Jonathan Cape.

Jay, Peter (1976), *Employment, Inflation and Politics*, IEA Occasional Paper.

Kaldor, Nicholas (1966), *Causes of the Slow Rate of Economic Growth in the United Kingdom*, Oxford: Oxford University Press.

Kaldor, Nicholas (1971), 'Conflicts in National Economic Objectives', *Economic Journal*, 81, March, 1–16.

Kay, J.A. (1989), 'Myths and Realities', in *1992 Myths and Realities*, Centre for Business Strategy, London Business School, 1–29.

Kay, J.A. (1996), 'The good market', *Prospect*, May, 39.

Kay, J.A. (1997), *Fortune Magazine*, 17 February, 133–4.

Kay, J.A. and M.V. Posner (1989), 'Routes to Economic Integration: 1992 in the European Community', *National Institute Economic Review*, August, No. 129, 55–68.

Kay, J.A. and A. Silberston (1995), 'Corporate Governance', *National Institute Economic Review*, No. 153, August, 84–97.

Keynes, J.M. (1936), *The General Theory of Employment, Interest and Money*, London: Macmillan.

Krugman, Paul (1994a), *Peddling Prosperity: Economic Sense and Nonsense in the Age of Diminished Expectations*, New York: W W Norton.

Krugman, Paul (1994b), 'Does Third World Growth hurt First World Prosperity?', *Harvard Business Review*, July/August, 113–21.

Krugman, Paul (1994c), 'Competitiveness: A dangerous obsession', *Foreign Affairs*, March/April, 28–44.

Krugman, Paul (1995), 'Growing world trade: causes and consequences', *Brookings Papers on Economic Activity*, I, 1995, 327–62.

Lawson, N. (1988), *The Mais Lecture*, City University.

Little, I.M.D. (1950), *Welfare Economics*, Oxford: Oxford University Press.

Littlechild, S.C. (1986), *The Fallacy of the Mixed Economy*, Institute of Economic Affairs, Hobart Paper 80 (Second Edition).

Lucas, Robert (1988), 'On the mechanics of economic development', *Journal of Monetary Economics*, **22** (1), July, 3–42.

Management Today (1997), 'John Monks', February, pp. 43–6.

Mankiw, N. Gregory (1995), 'The Growth of Nations', *Brookings Papers on Economic Activity*, Vol. I, 275–310.

Marsh, Paul (1990), *Short-Termism on Trial*, Institute Fund Managers Association.

Meade, J. and M. Weale (1991), *On the stability of monetary and fiscal policy*, Department of Applied Economics, Cambridge.

McKinsey Global Institute (1994), *Employment Performance*.

Mill, J.S. (1929), Principles of Political Economy, Bk III, Ashley Ed. New York.

Mundell, R. (1961), 'A theory of optimum currency areas', *American Economic Review*, June, 657–64.

Nickell, S.J. and B. Bell (1995), 'The Collapse in Demand for the Unskilled and Unemployment across the OECD', *Oxford Review of Economic Policy*, Vol. 2, No. 1, Spring, 40–62.

Nicol, W. (1995), 'European Economic and Monetary Union: the EMU that flew', *Perspectives on European Business*, in W. Nicol, D. Norbura and R. Schoenberg (eds.), London: Whurr Publishers, pp. 36–44.

OECD (1994), *The OECD Jobs Study*, OECD, Paris.

Oulton, N. (1995), 'Supply Side Reform and UK Economic Growth: What Happened to the Miracle?', *National Institute Economic Review*, Issue 154, November, 53–70.

Owen, David (1992), *Time to Declare*, London: Penguin Books.

Plender J. (1997), *A Stake in the Future*, London: Nicholas Brealey.

Renwick, Robert (1996), *Fighting Allies*, New York: Random House.

Report of the Commission on Social Justice (1994), London: Vintage.

Robinson, Peter (1996), 'The myths and realities of structural change in the UK labour market', *Economic Outlook*, London Business School, 21 (1), November, pp. 12–17.

Romer, Paul (1995), Comment on N. Gregory Mankiw, 'The Growth of Nations', *Brookings Papers on Economic Activity*, Vol. I, 1995, 313–20.

Rose, Harold (1996), 'Is the financial system to blame for "low" UK investment?',

Economic Outlook, London Business School, August, 20 (4), 10–17.

Royal Commission on the Taxation of Profits and Income (1955), HMSO.

Royal Society of Arts (1995), *Tomorrow's Company*.

Searjeant, G. (1997a), 'Shareholders are still the best guardians of success', *The Times*, 2 January, p. 38.

Searjeant, G. (1997b), 'Dividend Grab is Economic Nonsense', *The Times*, 26 July, p. 29.

Sentance, A. (1995), 'Are we entering a new golden age of economic growth?', *Economic Outlook*, Blackwell Publishers, 20 (1), November, London Business School, 12–21.

Singh, Arjit (1977), 'UK industry and the world economy: a case of de-industrialisation', *Cambridge Journal of Economics*, 1, 113–36.

Smith, Adam (1776), *The Wealth of Nations*, Chicago: Chicago University Press.

Solow, R.M. (1956), 'A Contribution to the Theory of Economic Growth', *Quarterly Journal of Economics*, 65–94.

Soros, G. (1995), *Soros on Soros: Staying Ahead of the Curve*, New York: John Wiley & Sons, Inc.

Stern, N. (1991), 'The Determinants of Growth', *Economic Journal*, 101 (404), January, 122–33.

Tawney, R.H. (1926), *Religion and the Rise of Capitalism*, London.

Taylor, Christopher (1995), *EMU 2000?*, The Royal Institute of International Affairs.

Thirlwall, A.P. (1992), 'The balance of payments as the wealth of nations', in *The Economics of Wealth Creation*, pp. 134–70, Aldershot: Edward Elgar.

The Times (1997), Editorial, 7 May.

Tyrie, Andrew (1996), *The Prospects for Public Spending*, The Social Market Foundation, November.

Veljanovski, Cento (1991) (ed.), *Regulation and the Market*, Institute of Economic Affairs, IEA Readings 35.

Wolf, M. (1996), 'Britain: The Rogue Piece in Europe's Jigsaw', *The Financial Times*, 12 June, p. II.

Wood, Adrian (1994), *North-South Trade, Employment and Inequality: Changing Fortunes in a Skill-Driven World*, Oxford: Oxford University Press.

Wright, Tony (1997), *Why Vote Labour*, London: Penguin.

INDEX

....

Abramovitz, Moses 16, 43
Adenauer, Konrad 8
Albert, Michel 192, 198, 205
American Century 215
Anderton, Bob 110
Anglo-Saxons 215
    and Anglo-Saxon capitalism xviii, 234, 239
    and deregulation 174
    and equity financing 59
    and the concept of the stakeholder 238
    European attitudes towards 241
Atlantic alliance 185–90, 241
Australia 36, 56, 215
Austria 36, 124

Bacon, Robert and Walter Eltis 45, 46, 80
balanced budget 159, 170
balance of payments
    as constraint on economic growth 7, 80, 87–91
    in the post-war period in Britain 91–7
    origin of disturbances to 89–91
Ball, James xv, 192, 193, 205
Ball, George 189
Balladur, Edouard 203–4
Banks
    effects of monetary union on 204
Barber, Anthony 22, 69, 72
Barry, Norman 164–5
Bean, Charles 16–17, 63, 67, 87
Beatrix, Queen 198
Beesley, Michael 174, 175
Belgium 36, 180, 191
Benn, Tony 160, 228
Berlin Wall
    collapse of 233
Beveridge Report 158
Bismarck 8
Blair, Tony xvii, 222, 231
Bogdanor, Vernon 210–11
Bootle, Roger 149
Bosnia 209, 241
Bretton Woods Agreement xvii, 6, 15–16, 24, 72, 92, 97, 98, 99, 107, 115, 119, 120, 177
    demise of 16, 49, 191
    economic significance of 7
    response to the ending of 19, 49
    structure of 5
British Airways 171

British Airports Authority, 174, 175
British Gas 174, 175
British Motor Corporation 171
British Telecom 171, 174, 175
Brittan, Samuel 240
Brown, Gordon 62, 209
Budget of 1981 29, 108, 178, 221
Bullock Committee 228
Bundesbank 131, 204
Burke, Edmund 156
Bush, George 190

Caborn, Richard 54, 60
Callaghan, James 62, 119, 189, 222, 228
camembert currency 203
Canada 24, 36, 57, 131, 202, 215, 240
capitalism 156
    and the Protestant ethic 157
caring society
    and free markets 161
Carter, Jimmy 189, 190
catch up 10, 36, 39, 98
Centre of Economic Policy Research 125, 127–8, 130, 200, 202, 204
China xvi, 35, 210, 233, 241
Chui, Michael 196
Church 157
Churchill, Winston 185, 188, 189
Clause 4 159
Cleaver, Anthony 235
Clegg Commission 29, 178
Cold War xvi
    consequences of the ending of 233–4
    ending of 190
Commission on Public Policy and British Business
    attitude to the minimum wage 231–2
Commission on Social Justice xvi
Common Agricultural Policy 99
comparative advantage 44
    and classical trade theory 100
    and New Strategic Trade Theory 100
    and the development of the Single Market 194–5
competitiveness
    and trade 97–103
    and winning the 'war' 101–2
Confederation of British Industry 242
Congdon, Tim 149
Conservative government 32, 33, 45, 107, 119, 171–2, 177, 209, 220–1

Conservative Party xvii, xviii, 24, 29, 50, 118
convergence in economic growth 9, 35, 42–3
corporate governance 239
Council of Ministers 191, 193, 199, 204
Crafts, Nicholas 9, 16–17, 43, 44, 63, 67, 218–19
credit controls
  abolition of 22, 31
Crosland, Anthony 160
Currie, David 200

de-industrialisation 81
Dankert, Pieter 192
Darling, Alistair 88
Davis, E 93
debt ratios
  economic consequences of 167
  in the G7 153, 167
de Gaulle, Charles 16, 187, 188, 191
Delors, Jacques 198, 199
Denison, E F 41
Denmark 48, 180, 196
Department of Economic Affairs 220, 226
distribution of income
  and taxes and subsidies 153
  growth in income inequality 123
Dixon, Huw 35
Domar, Evsey 159
Dow, Christopher 68
Drucker, Peter 128

Eastern Europe 186
economies of scale
  and international trade 100
  and the Single Market 194–5
economic growth
  theories of 41–5
economic targets 31, 222
Economist 200, 229, 239
Eden, Anthony 190
education and training 40, 163
  and economic growth 65–7
  and employment 135–6
Edwards, J 59
Eisenhower, Dwight 15, 186, 189, 190
Eltis, Walter 111
Emerging Markets 39
Emerson, Michael 195
employment
  the changing pattern in Britain 139–45
endogenous growth 43–4
Erhardt, Ludwig 8
essentialism 83, 86
European Central Bank
  creation of 199
  operation of 202, 204
European Commission 125, 126, 130, 191, 194, 199, 202, 230

and the Social Chapter 232
European Community (see European Union) 68, 186–8, 191
  after OPEC II 24
  after the Treaty of Rome 190–1
  attitude to the Single Market 195
  economic performance of 190–1, 205–8
  effect of oil price increases on 21
  relationship with Britain 186–8
  response to OPEC I 24
European Monetary Union 199, 202–3
  arguments for and against 200–5
  conditions for entry into 203
  possible impact on unemployment 131
  technical background to 200
  theory of 201
European Parliament 192, 204
European Union xviii, 105, 136–7, 179, 187, 206, 210–11
  and democracy 210–11, 240
  and foreign policy 189–90, 209–10, 241
  and national sovereignty 210
  and Rhine capitalism 234
  and unemployment 124–6
  creation of 197–8
  impact of German reunification on 131, 138, 201
  labour markets in 229
  powers of 199
  public expenditure in 180, 218
  trade in 196–7
exchange control
  abolition in Britain 31
  after Bretton Woods 6
  in Britain after the war 6
exchange rate mechanism of the EMS 209
  effect of German reunification on 201
  entry and exit of the United Kingdom 34
exchange rates
  pegged and floating rates 91–2
exports
  and the performance of manufacturing industry 109–10
export led growth 80
externalities
  and the performance of markets 163

Falklands 190
Federal Reserve 16, 22
  and the Great Depression 27, 118
Feldstein, Martin 201
financial system in Britain 40, 45
  effects on economic growth 59–62
fiscal policy 40
  and crowding out 166
  and full employment 49, 67–8
  objectives of 166
Fischer, K 59
Flanders, S 93

Flemming, John 179
Ford, Henry 128
Foster Dulles, John 189
France 5, 10, 17–18, 24, 36, 39, 69, 185,
    187, 196, 204, 208, 218, 240
  and the impact of the minimum wage 133
  unemployment in 138
free trade 10
  threat to 98–102
Friedman, Milton 27, 118, 120–1, 171, 201
Fukiyama, Francis 233

G7 countries 9, 24, 35, 36, 42, 82, 105, 110,
    115
General Agreement on Tariffs and Trade as
    an alternative to the World Trade
    Organization 6
General Election in Britain
  of 1997 xvii, xviii, 242
General Theory 158
Germany 7, 10, 14, 15, 16, 17, 22, 24, 34,
    35, 54, 56, 57, 58, 63, 69, 73, 74, 104,
    118, 119, 180, 191, 204, 208, 209,
    210, 215, 217, 218, 221, 224, 241
  impact of reunification on 28, 34
  post-war recovery in 8
  role of banks in finance 59
  unemployment in 137–8
Geroski Paul 195
globalisation 149
  fear of 99, 101–2
golden age 9, 14, 15, 16, 17, 36, 44, 68, 70,
    71, 72, 74, 216, 219
Golden Rule 170
government failure 165
Great Depression 115, 116, 117, 118
Greece 196
Greenspan, Alan 27
gross public debt
  determination of debt ratios 159
  public expenditure and the National Debt
    167
  ratios in the G7 155
growth accounting 41

Hahn, Frank 161, 162
Handy, Charles 236–7
Haskel, John 52, 128
Hawley-Smoot tariff 97
Healey, Denis 22, 177, 228
health care
  and public expenditure 179, 225
Heath, Edward 22, 121, 189, 190, 191, 220,
    228
Hegel, G.W.F. 233
Henderson, David 83, 86
House of Lords 77, 78, 82, 87, 88
Howe, Geoffrey 178, 221
human capital 40, 52, 74

and public expenditure 179
importance in economic growth 62–3,
    72
Hutton, Will xvi, 53

IBM Corporation 10
imperfect competition 163
  and international trade 100
incomes policies 22–3, 24
India xvi
industrial relations (see also trade unions) 40,
    44
  developments in Britain 62–5
  effects on manufacturing industry 107,
    109
inflation
  and monetary stability 147, 148
  and the inflation tax 156
  costs of 145–6
  ideas about in Britain 146–7
  in the G7 countries 14
  the end of inflation? 149
  trade off between inflation and
    unemployment 147–50, 223
International Monetary Fund
  and aid to Britain 177
  and Third World debt 25–6
  role of 6
investment
  and technology 43
  behaviour in Britain 53–8, 73
  impact of dividend payments on 59–62,
    227, 238–9
  and capital productivity 52–3, 57–8
  role in economic growth 52–3
involuntary unemployment 118
Islam 233
Italy 5, 24, 36, 185, 191, 217
  unemployment in 138

Japan 7, 8, 10, 18, 21, 22, 24, 25, 28, 35,
    54, 56, 58, 59, 62, 63, 69, 70, 71, 86,
    89, 99, 115, 118, 177, 180, 205, 206,
    217, 221, 224, 239
  unemployment in 123–4, 137
Jay, Peter 51
Jenkins, Roy 228
Joseph, Keith 121

Kaldor, Nicholas 78–81, 82
Kay, John 52, 193, 194, 234–5, 236, 237,
    239
Kennedy, John F 16, 119, 120, 234
Keynes, John Maynard 22, 67
  and Bretton Woods 6, 185
  and demand management 159–60
  and individualism 158, 161
  and The General Theory 117–18
  and unemployment xvii, 124–5, 149

influence on economic policies xvii, 15, 49, 220
Keynesianism 15, 16, 22, 25, 30, 117–19
Kissinger, Henry 198
Kohl, Helmut 198
Korean war
 and raw material prices 14, 19
Krugman, Paul 101
Kuwait 190

Labour government 50, 79, 107, 119, 209, 220
labour markets
 and unemployment 127–31
 effects of the Social Chapter on 232–3
 inflexibility of 132
 flexibility in Britain 138–40
Labour Party xvii, 119, 159, 160, 171
laissez-faire 157
 and Keynes 158
Latin America 26
Lawson, Nigel 72, 109, 222
Lend Lease 8
liberal capitalism 233, 234
Libya 190
Little, Ian 164
Littlechild, Stephen 164, 165, 174, 175
Lloyd George, David 158
London
 as a financial centre 209
Lucas, Robert 43

Maastricht, Treaty of 203, 211
 and the creation of the European Union 197–9
 relationship to political and monetary union 198–9
MacMahon Act 189
Macmillan, Harold 172, 186, 189, 228
macroeconomic policy
 and economic growth 67–71
 and employment 129
 and the Keynesian environment 67–8
 effects on economic performance 51
 the conduct of 40, 220–5
Mankiw, Gregory 44
manufacturing industry 40, 46
 effect on future economic performance xvii
 impact on the balance of payments 40, 87–8
 importance of 77–8, 106
 performance in Britain since the war 105–11
 relationship to economic growth 78–82
 relationship to employment 82–7, 126
markets
 and 'entrepreneurship' 165
 and market failure 162–3, 165, 228
 and the invisible hand 161, 162

 as allocators of resources 161–2
Marsh, Paul 60
Marshall Plan 5, 8, 185
Marx, Karl 117, 127, 161, 233
McKinsey 132
Meade, James 135, 203
medium term financial strategy 29, 31
Mill, John Stuart 121
miners' strike 64
minimum wage 231, 242
 a minimum wage for Britain 231–2
 arguments for and against 133–4
 effects in Europe 133
missing markets, 162
Mitterrand, François 198
Monarchy 157
monetarism 119–22
monetary policy 40
 and monetarism 122
monetary stability
 importance of 223
Monks, John 238–9
Monopoly and Mergers Commission 176
Mundell, Robert 201

National Economic Development Office 17, 220
National Economic Plan 17
nationalisation 171
 in Britain after the war 159–60
 relationships between nationalised industries and the state 171–3
Netherlands 15, 17, 118, 180
neutrality of money 122
New Strategic Trade Theory 100
Nicol, William 198
Nixon, Richard 16, 120, 189
Norman, Montague 222
North American Free Trade Agreement 202
North Sea oil 32, 81–2, 109, 110
 and competitiveness 109–10
 benefits and opportunities xviii
 economic effects of 32–3
 effects on exchange rates 29
Norway 124

OECD 132, 216–17
OECD countries 24, 28, 36, 39, 40, 43, 53, 77, 83, 102, 105, 123, 156, 180, 207
OPEC I 18, 19, 22, 24, 25, 49, 50, 51
OPEC II 19, 23, 24, 25, 26, 29, 51
OPEC III 27
Oppenheimer, Peter 179
Oulton, Nicholas 64, 65, 69, 70
Owen, David 190

Pax Americana 98
Peace of Versailles 188
Pearl Harbor

consequences of 188
pensions 46
  and public expenditure 156, 180, 224
  and taxation of dividends 61–2
perfect competition model 161, 163
  and privatisation 163, 174–5
performance assessment 216–19
Plender, John 238
Posner, Michael 193–4
privatisation 227
  achievements of 229
  and the responsibilities of regulators 176, 228
  approaches to 176
  criticisms of 172–3
  reasons for 171
productivity 40, 226
  and investment 52
  effects of industrial relations on 63–5
  in manufacturing industry 107–8, 219
property rights 156
  redefinition of 236
protectionism 8
public expenditure 40
  and the macroeconomic background 167, 223–4
  in Britain 176–82
  measurement of 45–6
  relationship to economic growth 45–51, 71–2
  the determination of 168–70, 223–5
  the future of in Britain 179–80
public goods 153, 168
public sector 46
  employment in 46
public sector borrowing requirement 32, 170

rates of return on investment in Britain xviii, 60
Reagan, Ronald 25, 45, 189, 190
regulation
  the development of in Britain 174–6
Renwick, Robert 185, 189, 190
research and development
  and endogenous growth 43
Rhine capitalism
  as a model for Britain xviii, 234
Ricardo, David 100, 111
Robinson, Peter 140, 142, 227, 230–1
Romer, Paul 43–4
Roosevelt, Franklin 185, 188
Rose, Harold 59
Royal Commission on Taxation 60–1
Royal Society of Arts 235

saving
  rate of 41–2
Schwartz, Anna 27, 118
Searjeant, Graham 61–2, 237–8
Selective Employment Tax 79

Sentance, Andrew 219
service sector
  and the economic future of Europe 207
  relationship to manufacturing 77–8, 83
shareholder value 235–40
short-termism 60, 227
Silberston, Aubrey 236, 239
Singh, Arjit 81, 82, 87, 88, 109
Single European Act 193
Single Market 200, 206
  and the Albert and Ball Report 192–3
  development of 192–7
  the implications of 194–6
Smith, Adam 77, 78, 86, 157, 161, 162, 172, 173
Smithsonian agreement 18
social capability 9
  and economic growth 44–5
Social Chapter, 198, 199, 227, 231, 242
  and labour market flexibility in Britain 139
  creation of 199
  possible consequences of 232–3
socialisation of investment 158
socialism 156
Solow, Robert 41
Soros, George 101
South East Asia 215–16
sovereign debt
  after OPEC I 25–6
Soviet Union 5, 233
Spain 196
stabilisation policy
  conduct of 223
stakeholder society 234–40
Star, J 93
State Department 186
Stern, Nicholas 41
stop-go 49
structural snobbery 86
Suez 186, 190
supply side policies 122
Sweden 48, 124
Switzerland 124, 180

Tawney, R H 157
taxation, 49, 154, 166–7
  and economic growth 47–9
  and incentives 160
  and its impact on interest rates and debt ratios 156
Taylor, Christopher 200, 201, 204–5
technical progress 41–2, 43
technology 9, 216
  and endogenous growth 43
  as a public good 44
  effect on income distribution 128
  impact on employment 127, 137
  impact on manufacturing industry 86–7
Thatcher, Margaret xv, 24, 45, 108, 121, 160, 189, 198, 217

and controls over industry 160
and privatisation 171–2
and the electability of the Labour Party 226
attitude to the exchange rate 30
early years of her administration 28–9
economic performance during her government 217
opposition to economic consensus 30
Thatcher Experiment 30, 221
Thatcherism 154
Third World
effect on industrial countries 102–5, 129
problems of sovereign debt 26
Thirlwall, Tony 87, 88
Times, The 209
letter from 364 economists 30
trade unions
and labour market inflexibility 132
effects on economic growth 63–5
impact on industrial relations in Britain 63
training (*see* education and training)
Treaty of Rome 186, 187, 188, 190–1, 197–8
Tyrie, Andrew 178

unemployment
and labour market inflexibility 130, 132, 229–30
and the future of Europe 207–8
equilibrium rate of 125
impact of technology on 127–8
in Europe 115, 123–31
in the OECD since 1974 116
persistence in Europe 129–31
policies for 131–6
Unilever 174
United Kingdom 9, 24, 28, 32, 33, 35, 39, 42, 43, 46, 49, 51, 65, 68, 71, 73, 104, 105, 109, 110, 111, 119, 171, 176, 196, 210
and its European future 190, 208–11, 240–1
economic performance 1960–1995 34–6, 215–20
fiscal deficits since 1950 50, 68
in Europe 186–7, 208–11
investment and economic growth in 40, 53–8
the debt ratio 153
the financial system and economic growth 59–62

unemployment and the labour market in 136–45
volatility of growth in gross domestic product 69–71
United States xviii, 10, 21, 22, 27, 54, 56, 57, 69, 71, 86, 89, 97, 105, 119, 120, 176, 177, 180, 188, 197, 201, 206, 218, 229
and free trade 5, 6
and Reaganomics 154
and the 'twin deficit problem' 26
and the effects of the Vietnam War 69
and the Great Depression 115–17
and the minimum wage 231
fiscal deficit after 1983 25
position after the war 7
relative decline of 10, 99–100
role in Europe after the War 185–6
unemployment in 123, 124, 126, 129, 130, 131, 137
Uruguay round 98

Veljanovski, Cento 172
Vietnam War 16, 18, 69
Volcker, Paul 22

Wall Street
the crash of 1987 27
the crash of 1929 116–17
Weale, Martin 203
welfare
and aggregate statistics 35
Welfare State 158
and social expenditure 179–82
and the reform of public expenditure 225, 242
development in Britain after the war 158–9
in Europe 130
White, Harry Dexter 6, 185
Whitley, John 196
Wilson Committee 228
Wilson, Harold 15, 17, 22, 79, 190, 220
Wolf, Martin 217
Wood, Adrian 102
world trade
growth of *intra* trade 110–11
growth relative to output 14
World Trade Organization 6, 98
Wright, Tony xvi–xvii

years of turbulence 18–22, 36, 216